Elements of Literature®

Fourth Course

The Holt Reader, Adapted Version

HOLT, RINEHART AND WINSTON

ISBN 978-0-03-099643-6
ISBN 0-03-099643-0
2 3 4 5 018 11 10 09 08

Contents

To the Student

A Book for You

A book is like a garden carried in the pocket.
—Chinese Proverb

The more you put into reading, the more you get out of it. This book is designed to do just that—help you interact with the selections you read by marking them up, asking your own questions, taking notes, recording your own ideas, and responding to the questions of others.

A Book Designed for Your Success

The Holt Reader, Adapted Version goes hand in hand with *Elements of Literature*. It is designed to help you interact with the selections and master important language arts skills.

The Holt Reader, Adapted Version has three types of selections: literature, informational texts, and documents that you may encounter in your various activities. All the selections include the same basic preparation, support, and review materials. Vocabulary previews, skill descriptions, graphic organizers, review questions, and other tools help you understand and enjoy the selections. Moreover, tips and questions in the side margins ensure that you can apply and practice the skills you are learning as you read.

The selections in the book are all from your textbook, *Elements of Literature*. You will find that some of the selections are worded exactly as they were worded in *Elements of Literature*. In this book, those selections have been broken into sections. Each section is followed by a short note titled "In Other Words." That note restates the previous text in different words. Other selections have been rewritten or retold slightly to make them easier to understand; these are called adapted selections. You can tell which ones are adapted because you will see the words "based on" in the Table of Contents or on the first page of the selection.

A Book for Your Own Thoughts and Feelings

Reading is about *you*. It is about connecting your thoughts and feelings to the thoughts and feelings of the writer. Make this book your own. The more you give of yourself to your reading, the more you will get out of it. We encourage you to write in this book. Jot down how you feel about the selection. Write down questions you have about the text. Note details you think need to be cleared up or topics that you would like to investigate further.

A Walk Through the Book

The Holt Reader, Adapted Version is arranged in collections, just like Elements of Literature, the book on which this one is based. Each collection has a theme or basic idea. The stories, poems, articles, or documents within the collection follow that theme. Let's look at how the arrangement of The Holt Reader, Adapted Version helps you enjoy a collection as a whole and the individual selections within the collection.

Before Reading the Collection

Literary and Academic Vocabulary
Literary and academic vocabulary refers to the specialized language that is used to talk about books, tests, and formal writing. Each collection begins with the literary and academic terms that you need to know to master the skills for that collection.

Before Reading the Selection

Preparing to Read
From experience, you know that you understand something better if you have some idea of what's going to happen. So that you can get the most from the reading, this page previews the skills and vocabulary that you will see in the reading.

Literary Focus
For fiction selections—stories, poems, and plays—this feature introduces the literary skill that is the focus for the selection. Examples and graphic elements help explain the literary skill.

Reading Focus
Also in fiction selections, this feature highlights a reading skill you can apply to the story, poem, or play. The feature points out why this skill is important and how it can help you become a better reader.

Informational Text Focus
For informational, or nonfiction, selections, this feature introduces you to the format and characteristics of nonfiction texts. Those texts may be essays, newspaper articles, Web sites, employment regulations, application forms, or other similar documents.

Selection Vocabulary
This feature introduces you to selection vocabulary that may be unfamiliar. Each entry gives the pronunciation and definition of the word as well as a sentence in which the word is used correctly.

Into the Story
This feature provides an introduction about the selection related to the author, setting, historical events, or other topics that may be unfamiliar.

While Reading the Selection

Side-Column Notes
Each selection has notes in the side column that guide your reading. Many notes ask you to underline or circle in the text itself. Others provide lines on which you can write your responses to questions.

Quick Check These notes ask you to pause at certain points so that you can think about basic ideas before proceeding further. Your teacher may use these notes for class discussions.

Here's How This feature shows you how to apply a particular skill to what you are reading. It models how you might think through the text. Each Here's How note addresses the selection's Reading Focus, Literary Focus, Language Coach, or Vocabulary.

Your Turn In these notes, you have a chance to apply vocabulary skills and practice the same reading, literary, and language skills introduced and modeled earlier. You might be asked to underline or circle words in the text or to write responses in your own words.

Literary Analysis These notes take basic comprehension a step further and ask you to think more deeply about what you have just read.

After Reading the Selection

Skills Practice

For some selections, graphic organizers reinforce the skills you have practiced throughout the selection.

Applying Your Skills

This feature helps you review the selection. It provides additional practice with selection vocabulary and literary, reading, and informational text focus skills.

After Reading the Collection

Skills Review

On the first page of the Skills Review, you can practice using the collection's academic vocabulary and selection vocabulary.

Language Coach

The second Skills Review page draws on the Language Coach skills in the *Elements of Literature* Preparing to Read pages. This feature asks you to apply those skills to texts from throughout the collection.

Writing Activity

You may have found that you need more practice writing. These short writing activities challenge you to apply what you have learned to your own ideas and experiences.

Oral Language Activity

Writing Activities alternate with Oral Language Activities. These features are designed to help you express your thoughts clearly aloud. The features are particularly helpful if you are learning English or if you need practice with Standard English.

Plot and Setting

© Images.com/Corbis

Literary and Academic Vocabulary for Collection 1

LITERARY VOCABULARY

plot (PLAHT) *n.:* the series of related events that make up a story.

The plot of the mystery story was so exciting that I could not stop reading.

chronological sequence (KRAH NUH LAH JIH KUHL SEE KWEHNS) *n.:* the order in which events happen.

The police wanted to know the exact chronological sequence of events that happened on the night of the crime.

mood (MOOD) *n.:* the emotional feeling of a story.

The mood of the novel was playful.

predictions (PRIH DIHK SHUHNZ) *n.:* guesses about what will happen in the future.

Good readers make predictions about what will happen next in a story based on what they have already read.

visualize (VIH ZHOO UH LYZ) *v.:* imagine what something looks like.

The story was so well written that I could visualize the setting perfectly based on how the author described it.

ACADEMIC VOCABULARY

aspects (AS PEHKTS) *n.:* parts or features of a subject.

The roller coaster was just one of the many aspects of the amusement park that we enjoyed.

credible (KREHD UH BUHL) *adj.:* believable; trustworthy.

Because John was always honest, he was considered a credible witness.

tension (TEHN SHUHN) *n.:* strained feeling.

The tension in the plot caused me to bite my fingernails while reading.

evaluation (IH VAL YOO AY SHUHN) *n.:* judgment; assessment.

I am hoping to get a good evaluation on my book report.

Contents of the Dead Man's Pocket

By Jack Finney

LITERARY FOCUS: PLOT: TIME AND SEQUENCE

The series of events that make up a story is called the **plot**. The plot of a story usually includes a problem, called a conflict. Different events happen until the problem is solved. Take the fairy tale *Cinderella* as an example. The problem is that Cinderella is treated badly by her family. The story's plot leads to the problem being solved: Cinderella finds a nicer family with the prince.

The order of the events in a story and the time it takes for these events to happen is very important. Another word for the order of events is sequence. **Chronological order** is when events are told in the same sequence as they happened.

READING FOCUS: UNDERSTANDING CAUSE AND EFFECT

A **cause** is the reason something happens. An **effect** is the result of an action. Causes and effects usually happen in chains. For example, imagine that by closing the window you make your room hot. That heat causes you to turn on a fan. The chain continues that way. As you read "Contents of the Dead Man's Pocket," notice how each event is a cause that leads to an effect. Each effect then becomes another cause.

VOCABULARY

Review the following words before reading the following selection.

projection (PRUH JEHK SHUHN) *n.:* something that juts out from a surface.

exhalation (EHKS HUH LAY SHUHN) *n.:* breath; something breathed out.

imperceptibly (IHM PUHR SEHP TUH BLEE) *adv.:* in a barely noticeable way.

rebounded (RIH BOWND IHD) *v.:* bounced back.

irrelevantly (IH REHL UH VUHNT LEE) *adv.:* in an unrelated manner.

SKILLS FOCUS

Literary Skills
Understand structural elements of plot.

Reading Skills
Understand cause and effect.

CONTENTS OF THE DEAD MAN'S POCKET

By Jack Finney

> ### INTO THE SHORT STORY
> In the 1940s and 1950s, computers did not exist. At that time, if you wanted to type something, you had to write it by hand or use a typewriter. So it was not easy to make back-up copies of documents. As this story will show you, losing even a single piece of paper could lead to big problems.

At the little living-room desk Tom Benecke rolled two sheets of flimsy[1] and a heavier top sheet, carbon paper sandwiched between them, into his portable. *Interoffice Memo*, the top sheet was headed, and he typed tomorrow's date just below this; then he glanced at a creased yellow sheet, covered with his own handwriting, beside the typewriter. **A** "Hot in here," he muttered to himself. Then, from the short hallway at his back, he heard the muffled clang of wire coat hangers in the bedroom closet, and at this reminder of what his wife was doing he

10 thought: hot—guilty conscience. **B**

He got up, shoving his hands into the back pockets of his gray wash slacks, stepped to the living-room window beside the desk and stood breathing on the glass, watching the expanding circlet of mist, staring down through the autumn night at Lexington Avenue,[2] eleven stories below. He was a tall, lean, dark-haired young man in a pullover sweater, who looked as though he had played not football, probably, but basketball in college. Now he placed the heels of his hands against the top edge

A HERE'S HOW

Vocabulary

I do not know what a *memo* is. Knowing what a *memo* is will help me understand what Tom is doing. I know he is typing something, and it seems official. I looked up *memo* in my dictionary and learned that it is "a written message, especially in business." I was right that Tom is typing something important.

B HERE'S HOW

Literary Focus

I wonder why Tom feels guilty. I think his guilt may affect the **plot** of the story. I will have to read more to find out.

From "Contents of the Dead Man's Pocket" by Jack Finney. Copyright © 1956 by Crowell-Collier Co.; copyright renewed © 1984 by Jack Finney. Reproduced by permission of **Don Congdon Associates, Inc.**

---

1. **Flimsy** is thin paper used for making carbon copies.
2. **Lexington Avenue** is a main street in New York City.

© The Image Bank/Getty Images

of the lower window frame and shoved upward. But as usual the

20 window didn't budge, and he had to lower his hands and then shoot them hard upward to jolt the window open a few inches. He dusted his hands, muttering. **A**

IN OTHER WORDS Tom Benecke was working at his typewriter. He looked at a yellow piece of paper he had written on. He heard his wife in the hallway and felt guilty. The room became very hot and Tom decided to open a window. At first the window stuck, but finally Tom got it open.

But still he didn't begin his work. He crossed the room to the hallway entrance and, leaning against the doorjamb, hands shoved into his back pockets again, he called, "Clare?" When his wife answered, he said, "Sure you don't mind going alone?" **B**

"No." Her voice was muffled, and he knew her head and shoulders were in the bedroom closet. **C** Then the tap of her high heels sounded on the wood floor, and she appeared at the

30 end of the little hallway, wearing a slip, both hands raised to one ear, clipping on an earring. She smiled at him—a slender, very pretty girl with light brown, almost blond, hair—her prettiness emphasized by the pleasant nature that showed in her face. "It's just that I hate you to miss this movie; you wanted to see it, too."

"Yeah, I know." He ran his fingers through his hair. "Got to get this done, though."

She nodded, accepting this. Then, glancing at the desk across the living room, she said, "You work too much, though, Tom—and too hard."

40 He smiled. "You won't mind, though, will you, when the money comes rolling in and I'm known as the Boy Wizard of Wholesale Groceries?"

"I guess not." She smiled and turned back toward the bedroom.

IN OTHER WORDS Tom's wife, Clare, was getting ready to go to the movies. Tom wanted to go with her, but he had to stay home and work. Tom worked for Wholesale Groceries and he wanted the company to be successful. Clare told Tom that he works too much, but she knew his work was important.

At his desk again, Tom lighted a cigarette; then a few moments later, as Clare appeared, dressed and ready to leave, he set it on the rim of the ashtray. "Just after seven," she said. "I can make the beginning of the first feature."

He walked to the front-door closet to help her on with her
50 coat. He kissed her then and, for an instant, holding her close, smelling the perfume she had used, he was tempted to go with her; it was not actually true that he had to work tonight, though he very much wanted to. This was his own project, unannounced as yet in his office, and it could be postponed. **D** **E** But then they won't see it till Monday, he thought once again, and if I give it to the boss tomorrow he might read it over the weekend . . .

"Have a good time," he said aloud. He gave his wife a little swat and opened the door for her, feeling the air from the building hallway, smelling faintly of floor wax, stream gently past his
60 face. **F**

D **HERE'S HOW**

Language Coach

I know that the **prefix** *–un* means "not." So I know that Tom's *unannounced* project is one that he has not announced, or told, to anyone else.

E **HERE'S HOW**

Vocabulary

I am not sure what the word *postponed* means. From its context I think *postponed* means "put off until later."

F **QUICK CHECK**

Why did Tom tell Clare that his work had to be done tonight? Was that the truth?

_____

_____

_____

_____

A HERE'S HOW

Vocabulary

Resisted means "fought against." I think when the door *resisted*, it just would not close all the way.

B HERE'S HOW

Vocabulary

Current can be an adjective, meaning "belonging to the present." Here, I think it is a noun, meaning "air moving in the same direction."

C YOUR TURN

Reading Focus

Re-read this paragraph. What **causes** the piece of paper to fly out the window?

_____

_____

_____

_____

D HERE'S HOW

Vocabulary

I have not seen the word *heaved* before, but I think it might mean "tried very hard." My teacher defines it as "pulled with a lot of effort," so I was close.

He watched her walk down the hall, flicked a hand in response as she waved, and then he started to close the door, but it resisted for a moment. **A** As the door opening narrowed, the current of warm air from the hallway, channeled through this smaller opening now, suddenly rushed past him with accelerated force. Behind him he heard the slap of the window curtains against the wall and the sound of paper fluttering from his desk, and he had to push to close the door.

70 Turning, he saw a sheet of white paper drifting to the floor in a series of arcs, and another sheet, yellow, moving toward the window, caught in the dying current flowing through the narrow opening. **B** As he watched, the paper struck the bottom edge of the window and hung there for an instant, plastered against the glass and wood. Then as the moving air stilled completely, the curtains swinging back from the wall to hang free again, he saw the yellow sheet drop to the window ledge and slide over out of sight. **C**

IN OTHER WORDS As Clare left for the movies, Tom went over to her to say goodbye. For a moment, he wanted to go with her. But Tom knew he should stay home and work. Actually, he wanted to work. Tom was working on a project but he had not told anyone about it yet. After Clare left, he closed the front door. It caused the air in the apartment to move. The yellow paper on Tom's desk flew out the window.

He ran across the room, grasped the bottom of the window and tugged, staring through the glass. He saw the yellow sheet, dimly now in the darkness outside, lying on the ornamental 80 ledge a yard below the window. Even as he watched, it was moving, scraping slowly along the ledge, pushed by the breeze that pressed steadily against the building wall. He heaved on the window with all his strength, and it shot open with a bang, the window weight rattling in the casing. **D** But the paper was past his reach and, leaning out into the night, he watched it scud[3]

---

3. **Scud** means "glide or move quickly."

steadily along the ledge to the south, half plastered against the building wall. Above the muffled sound of the street traffic far below, he could hear the dry scrape of its movement, like a leaf

90 on the pavement.

The living room of the next apartment to the south projected a yard or more further out toward the street than this one; because of this the Beneckes paid seven and a half dollars less rent than their neighbors. And now the yellow sheet, sliding along the stone ledge, nearly invisible in the night, was stopped by the projecting blank wall of the next apartment. It lay motionless, then, in the corner formed by the two walls—a good five yards away, pressed firmly against the ornate corner ornament of the ledge by the breeze that moved past Tom

100 Benecke's face. **E**

IN OTHER WORDS Tom ran across the room and went to the window. He saw that the yellow piece of paper was outside, stuck on the window ledge below him. The paper was pinned against the building by the blowing wind. Tom opened the window all the way and reached for the paper. He could not reach the paper. Tom looked down and saw the cars on the street far below him. The outer wall of the apartment below stuck out farther than the wall of Tom's apartment. The paper was stuck in the corner of these walls.

He knelt at the window and stared at the yellow paper for a full minute or more, waiting for it to move, to slide off the ledge and fall, hoping he could follow its course to the street, and then hurry down in the elevator and retrieve it. **F** But it didn't move, and then he saw that the paper was caught firmly between a projection of the convoluted corner ornament and the ledge. He thought about the poker from the fireplace, then the broom, then the mop—discarding each thought as it occurred to him. **G** There was nothing in the apartment long enough to reach

110 that paper.

E **YOUR TURN**

Vocabulary

The narrator explains that the next apartment *projected*, or stuck out, toward the street. What word in this paragraph is the adjective form of *projected*?

_____

_____

F **HERE'S HOW**

Vocabulary

I am not sure what *retrieve* means. I know Tom hopes he can go downstairs and get the paper. *Retrieve* must mean "get." I looked retrieve up in my dictionary, and it means "get back" or "pick up." Both of these are close to my definition.

G **YOUR TURN**

Language Coach

Circle the **prefix** in the word *discarding*. Think about other words that begin with *dis–*. Then write a definition for *discarding*.

_____

_____

_____

A **QUICK CHECK**

What had Tom written on the piece of yellow paper?

_____

_____

_____

It was hard for him to understand that he actually had to abandon it—it was ridiculous—and he began to curse. Of all the papers on his desk, why did it have to be this one in particular! On four long Saturday afternoons he had stood in supermarkets, counting the people who passed certain displays, and the results were scribbled on that yellow sheet. From stacks of trade publications, gone over page by page in snatched half hours at work and during evenings at home, he had copied facts, quotations, and figures onto that sheet. **A** And he had carried

120　it with him to the Public Library on Fifth Avenue, where he'd
spent a dozen lunch hours and early evenings adding more.
All were needed to support and lend authority to his idea for a
new grocery-store display method; without them his idea was
a mere opinion. And there they all lay, in his own improvised
shorthand—countless hours of work—out there on the
ledge. **B**

IN OTHER WORDS Tom looked around, but there was
nothing in his apartment that he could use to reach the
paper. Tom began to think about how important that piece
of paper was. He had been working for a long time getting
information. He had written all the information on the yellow
piece of paper. From that research, Tom came up with a new
idea about how to display food at grocery stores. That idea
was on the yellow piece of paper.

For many seconds he believed he was going to abandon
the yellow sheet, that there was nothing else to do. The work
could be duplicated. But it would take two months, and the time
130　to present this idea was *now*, for use in the spring displays. He
struck his fist on the window ledge. Then he shrugged. Even
though his plan was adopted, he told himself, it wouldn't bring
him a raise in pay—not immediately, anyway, or as a direct result.
It won't bring me a promotion either, he argued—not of itself.
But just the same—and he couldn't escape the thought—this
and other independent projects, some already done and others
planned for the future, would gradually mark him out from the
score of other young men in his company. They were the way to
change from a name on the payroll to a name in the minds of
140　the company officials. They were the beginning of the long, long
climb to where he was determined to be—at the very top. And
he knew he was going out there in the darkness, after the yellow
sheet fifteen feet beyond his reach. **C D**

By a kind of instinct, he instantly began making his
intention acceptable to himself by laughing at it. The mental

B **HERE'S HOW**

Literary Focus

I know that this piece of
paper is very important to
Tom. Since I know this, I am
guessing that Tom will want
to get the paper. But the
paper is eleven stories above
the ground. I think that the
rest of the **plot** will focus on
how Tom tries to solve the
problem.

C **LITERARY ANALYSIS**

How would you describe
Tom's personality from the
information presented in this
paragraph?

_____

_____

_____

D **HERE'S HOW**

Reading Focus

I know that Tom has worked
very hard on a plan for
displays at supermarkets.
He hopes that the **effect**
of his hard work will be
recognition at his company.

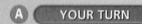

picture of himself sidling along the ledge outside was absurd—it
was actually comical—and he smiled. He imagined himself
describing it; it would make a good story at the office and, it
occurred to him, would add a special interest and importance to
150 his memorandum, which would do it no harm at all. **A**

To simply go out and get his paper was an easy task—he
could be back here with it in less than two minutes—and he
knew he wasn't deceiving himself. The ledge, he saw, measuring
it with his eye, was about as wide as the length of his shoe, and
perfectly flat. And every fifth row of brick in the face of the
building, he remembered—leaning out, he verified this—was
indented half an inch, enough for the tips of his fingers, enough
to maintain balance easily. **B** It occurred to him that if this
ledge and wall were only a yard aboveground—as he knelt at the
160 window staring out, this thought was the final confirmation of
his intention—he could move along the ledge indefinitely.

IN OTHER WORDS Tom thought about leaving the paper
out on the ledge. But he knew that he had to do something
to be noticed by his company. He laughed thinking about how
he was going to get the paper. He could stand on the ledge
that stuck out from the wall and hold on to the bricks for
balance, but it would be very dangerous.

On a sudden impulse, he got to his feet, walked to the front
closet, and took out an old tweed jacket; it would be cold outside.
He put it on and buttoned it as he crossed the room rapidly
toward the open window. In the back of his mind he knew he'd
better hurry and get this over with before he thought too much,
and at the window he didn't allow himself to hesitate.

He swung a leg over the sill, then felt for and found the
ledge a yard below the window with his foot. Gripping the
170 bottom of the window frame very tightly and carefully, he slowly
ducked his head under it, feeling on his face the sudden change
from the warm air of the room to the chill outside. With infinite
care he brought out his other leg, his mind concentrating on

what he was doing. **C** Then he slowly stood erect. Most of the putty, dried out and brittle, had dropped off the bottom edging of the window frame, he found, and the flat wooden edging provided a good gripping surface, a half inch or more deep, for the tips of his fingers. **D**

180 Now, balanced easily and firmly, he stood on the ledge outside in the slight, chill breeze, eleven stories above the street, staring into his own lighted apartment, odd and different-seeming now.

First his right hand, then his left, he carefully shifted his fingertip grip from the puttyless window edging to an indented row of bricks directly to his right. **E** It was hard to take the first shuffling sideways step then—to make himself move—and the fear stirred in his stomach, but he did it, again by not allowing himself time to think. **F** And now—with his chest, stomach, and the left side of his face pressed against the rough cold brick—

190 his lighted apartment was suddenly gone, and it was much darker out here than he had thought.

IN OTHER WORDS Tom made his mind up. He put on a jacket and climbed out the window. Tom stood on the ledge. He was eleven stories above the street. He was afraid, but made himself move along the ledge slowly, holding on to the bricks. It was dark and cold outside of his apartment.

Without pause he continued—right foot, left foot, right foot, left—his shoe soles shuffling and scraping along the rough stone, never lifting from it, fingers sliding along the exposed edging of brick. He moved on the balls of his feet, heels lifted slightly; the ledge was not quite as wide as he'd expected. But leaning slightly inward toward the face of the building and pressed against it, he could feel his balance firm and secure, and moving along the ledge was quite as easy as he had thought it would be. He

200 could hear the buttons of his jacket scraping steadily along the rough bricks and feel them catch momentarily, tugging a little, at each mortared crack. He simply did not permit himself to look

C YOUR TURN

Vocabulary

Infinite means "without limit" or "very great in amount." What is Tom doing with *"infinite* care"?

_____

D HERE'S HOW

Vocabulary

I looked *putty* up in the dictionary, and it is a paste used for sealing glass panes in windows. Now I understand that this paste has dried and fallen off, so Tom can hold on to the bottom of the window frame for balance.

E YOUR TURN

Language Coach

Think about the **prefix** *–in*. Do the first two letters in the word *indented* serve the same purpose as they do in words like *incorrect* or *invalid*? Explain your answer.

_____

_____

F YOUR TURN

Vocabulary

Does *shuffling* mean a) "rearranging a deck of cards," b) "walking by dragging one's feet," or c) "looking through things quickly"?

_____

A YOUR TURN

Vocabulary

Circle the word in this sentence that has the same meaning as *permit*.

B YOUR TURN

Literary Focus

Re-read this paragraph. Do the events happen in **chronological order**?

_____

_____

C LITERARY ANALYSIS

Considering Tom's nature, are you surprised that he is risking his life by climbing out the window? Or does this seem fitting for what you know about Tom? Explain your answer.

_____

_____

D YOUR TURN

Vocabulary

How do you picture Tom "half *squatting*" on the ledge? If necessary, check a dictionary for the definition of *squatting*.

_____

_____

E QUICK CHECK

What happens when Tom grabs the piece of paper?

_____

down, though the compulsion to do so never left him; nor did he allow himself actually to think. **A** Mechanically—right foot, left foot, over and again—he shuffled along crabwise, watching the projecting wall ahead loom steadily closer. . . . **B**

IN OTHER WORDS Tom kept walking slowly and carefully along the ledge. He moved his fingers along the bricks as he was pressed up against the wall. Tom thought it would be better if he did not look down.

Then he reached it, and at the corner—he'd decided how he was going to pick up the paper—he lifted his right foot and placed it carefully on the ledge that ran along the projecting
210 wall at a right angle to the ledge on which his other foot rested. And now, facing the building, he stood in the corner formed by the two walls, one foot on the ledging of each, a hand on the shoulder-high indentation of each wall. His forehead was pressed directly into the corner against the cold bricks, and now he carefully lowered first one hand, then the other, perhaps a foot farther down, to the next indentation in the rows of bricks. **C**

Very slowly, sliding his forehead down the trough of the brick corner and bending his knees, he lowered his body toward the paper lying between his outstretched feet. Again he lowered
220 his fingerholds another foot and bent his knees still more, thigh muscles taut, his forehead sliding and bumping down the brick V. Half squatting now, he dropped his left hand to the next indentation and then slowly reached with his right hand toward the paper between his feet. **D**

He couldn't quite touch it, and his knees now were pressed against the wall; he could bend them no farther. But by ducking his head another inch lower, the top of his head now pressed against the bricks, he lowered his right shoulder and his fingers had the paper by a corner, pulling it loose. At the same instant he
230 saw, between his legs and far below, Lexington Avenue stretched out for miles ahead. **E**

IN OTHER WORDS Tom stood in the corner where the paper was stuck. He bent down carefully to pick it up. He could not reach and had to bend down more. Finally, Tom was able to grab the corner of the paper and pull it loose. As he did so, Tom could see the street far below him.

He saw, in that instant, the Loew's theater sign, blocks ahead past Fiftieth Street; the miles of traffic signals, all green now; the lights of cars and street lamps; countless neon signs; and the moving black dots of people. And a violent, instantaneous explosion of absolute terror roared through him. For a motionless instant he saw himself externally—bent practically double, balanced on this narrow ledge, nearly half his body projecting out above the street far below—and he began to

240　tremble violently, panic flaring through his mind and muscles, and he felt the blood rush from the surface of his skin. **F**

In the fractional moment before horror paralyzed him, as he stared between his legs at that terrible length of street far beneath him, a fragment of his mind raised his body in a spasmodic jerk to an upright position again, but so violently that his head scraped hard against the wall, bouncing off it, and his body swayed outward to the knife-edge of balance, and he very nearly plunged backward and fell. **G** **H** Then he was leaning far into the corner again, squeezing and pushing into it, not only his face

250　but his chest and stomach, his back arching; and his fingertips clung with all the pressure of his pulling arms to the shoulder-high half-inch indentation in the bricks.

He was more than trembling now; his whole body was racked with a violent shuddering beyond control, his eyes squeezed so tightly shut it was painful, though he was past awareness of that. His teeth were exposed in a frozen grimace, the strength draining like water from his knees and calves. It was extremely likely, he knew, that he would faint, slump down along the wall, his face scraping, and then drop backward, a limp

260　weight, out into nothing. And to save his life he concentrated on

Contents of the Dead Man's Pocket　13

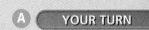

holding on to consciousness, drawing deliberate deep breaths of cold air into his lungs, fighting to keep his senses aware. **A**

IN OTHER WORDS For the first time since he climbed out the window, Tom saw all the way down the street. Suddenly Tom became very afraid. He stood up quickly and lost his balance. He almost fell but held on to the wall. He started shaking because he was so afraid. To make sure he would not pass out and fall, Tom began to deeply breathe in the cold air.

Then he knew that he would not faint, but he could not stop shaking nor open his eyes. He stood where he was, breathing deeply, trying to hold back the terror of the glimpse he had had of what lay below him; and he knew he had made a mistake in not making himself stare down at the street, getting used to it and accepting it, when he had first stepped out onto the ledge.

It was impossible to walk back. **B** He simply could not do
270 it. He couldn't bring himself to make the slightest movement. The strength was gone from his legs; his shivering hands—numb, cold, and desperately rigid—had lost all deftness[4]; his easy ability to move and balance was gone. Within a step or two, if he tried to move, he knew that he would stumble clumsily and fall. **C**

Seconds passed, with the chill faint wind pressing the side of his face, and he could hear the toned-down volume of the street traffic far beneath him. Again and again it slowed and then stopped, almost to silence; then presently, even this high, he would hear the click of the traffic signals and the subdued roar
280 of the cars starting up again. During a lull in the street sounds, he called out. Then he was shouting *Help!* so loudly it rasped his throat. **D** But he felt the steady pressure of the wind, moving between his face and the blank wall, snatch up his cries as he uttered them, and he knew they must sound directionless and distant. And he remembered how habitually, here in New York, he himself heard and ignored shouts in the night. If anyone heard

---

4. **Deftness** means "coordination" or "skillfulness."

him, there was no sign of it, and presently Tom Benecke knew he had to try moving; there was nothing else he could do. **E**

IN OTHER WORDS Tom focused his mind so that he would not faint. He knew he should have looked down at the street the moment he stepped out on the ledge. That way, he would be used to seeing what was below him. As he stood out there on the ledge, Tom could not move. He became very scared and tried to call for help, but nobody could hear him. Tom knew that he had to try to move again because there was no other way out of this situation.

290   Eyes squeezed shut, he watched scenes in his mind like scraps of motion-picture film—he could not stop them. He saw himself stumbling suddenly sideways as he crept along the ledge and saw his upper body arc outward, arms flailing. He saw a dangling shoestring caught between the ledge and the sole of his other shoe, saw a foot start to move, to be stopped with a jerk, and felt his balance leaving him. He saw himself falling with a terrible speed as his body revolved in the air, knees clutched tight to his chest, eyes squeezed shut, moaning softly. **F**

300   Out of utter necessity, knowing that any of these thoughts might be reality in the very next seconds, he was slowly able to shut his mind against every thought but what he now began to do. With fear-soaked slowness, he slid his left foot an inch or two toward his own impossibly distant window. Then he slid the fingers of his shivering left hand a corresponding distance. For a moment he could not bring himself to lift his right foot from one ledge to the other; then he did it, and became aware of the harsh exhalation of air from his throat and realized that he was panting. As his right hand, then, began to slide along the brick edging, he was astonished to feel the yellow paper pressed to the bricks underneath his stiff fingers, and he uttered a terrible, abrupt bark

310   that might have been a laugh or a moan. He opened his mouth

E **YOUR TURN**

Literary Focus

Time moves very slowly in this story. Yet a lot of things seem to happen. Explain why you think the **plot** is still interesting even though very little time is passing.

_____

_____

_____

F **YOUR TURN**

Language Coach

What do you think the **prefix** re– means in the word revolved? List two other words that you know with the same prefix.

_____

_____

_____

and took the paper in his teeth, pulling it out from under his fingers. **A**

IN OTHER WORDS Tom kept picturing himself falling off the ledge. He had to make himself move slowly back to the window. He opened his mouth and held the yellow paper in his teeth.

By a kind of trick—by concentrating his entire mind on first his left foot, then his left hand, then the other foot, then the other hand—he was able to move, almost imperceptibly, trembling steadily, very nearly without thought. But he could feel the terrible strength of the pent-up horror on just the other side of the flimsy barrier he had erected in his mind; and he knew that if it broke through he would lose this thin artificial control of his

320 body. **B**

During one slow step he tried keeping his eyes closed; it made him feel safer, shutting him off a little from the fearful reality of where he was. Then a sudden rush of giddiness swept over him and he had to open his eyes wide, staring sideways at the cold rough brick and angled lines of mortar, his cheek tight against the building. **C** He kept his eyes open then, knowing that if he once let them flick outward, to stare for an instant at the lighted windows across the street, he would be past help.

He didn't know how many dozens of tiny sidling steps he

330 had taken, his chest, belly, and face pressed to the wall; but he knew the slender hold he was keeping on his mind and body was going to break. **D** He had a sudden mental picture of his apartment on just the other side of this wall—warm, cheerful, incredibly spacious. And he saw himself striding through it, lying down on the floor on his back, arms spread wide, reveling[5] in its unbelievable security. The impossible remoteness of this utter safety, the contrast between it and where he now stood, was more

---

5. **Reveling** means "taking delight or great pleasure in something."

---

than he could bear. **E** And the barrier broke then, and the fear of the awful height he stood on coursed through his nerves and

340 muscles.

IN OTHER WORDS Tom moved very slowly along the ledge. He had to control his mind to make himself move. He could see himself making it back inside his warm apartment. But the more he thought about it, the less he thought he would actually reach the window without falling.

A fraction of his mind knew he was going to fall, and he began taking rapid blind steps with no feeling of what he was doing, sidling with a clumsy desperate swiftness, fingers scrabbling along the brick, almost hopelessly resigned to the sudden backward pull and swift motion outward and down. **F** Then his moving left hand slid onto not brick but sheer emptiness, an impossible gap in the face of the wall, and he stumbled.

His right foot smashed into his left anklebone; he staggered

350 sideways, began falling, and the claw of his hand cracked against glass and wood, slid down it, and his fingertips were pressed hard on the puttyless edging of his window. His right hand smacked gropingly beside it as he fell to his knees; and, under the full weight and direct downward pull of his sagging body, the open window dropped shudderingly in its frame till it closed and his wrists struck the sill and were jarred off. **G**

For a single moment he knelt, knee bones against stone on the very edge of the ledge, body swaying and touching nowhere else, fighting for balance. Then he lost it, his shoulders plunging

360 backward, and he flung his arms forward, his hands smashing against the window casing on either side; and—his body moving backward—his fingers clutched the narrow wood stripping of the upper pane.

For an instant he hung suspended between balance and falling, his fingertips pressed onto the quarter-inch wood strips. Then, with utmost delicacy, with a focused concentration of all

E **YOUR TURN**

Vocabulary

What does *remoteness* mean in line 336?

_____

_____

F **QUICK CHECK**

Why do you think Tom is taking "rapid blind steps"?

_____

_____

_____

_____

G **YOUR TURN**

Reading Focus

What **causes** the window to close before Tom can go inside?

_____

_____

_____

_____

_____

his senses, he increased even further the strain on his fingertips hooked to these slim edgings of wood. **A** Elbows slowly bending, he began to draw the full weight of his upper body

370 forward, knowing that the instant his fingers slipped off these quarter-inch strips he'd plunge backward and be falling. Elbows imperceptibly bending, body shaking with the strain, the sweat starting from his forehead in great sudden drops, he pulled, his entire being and thought concentrated in his fingertips. Then suddenly, the strain slackened and ended, his chest touching the windowsill, and he was kneeling on the ledge, his forehead pressed to the glass of the closed window. **B**

IN OTHER WORDS Tom knew he was going to fall. He lost his balance for a moment, but was able to right himself. Tom was able to pull himself up by his fingertips and hang on to the edge of the window.

Dropping his palms to the sill, he stared into his living room—at the red-brown davenport[6] across the room, and a

380 magazine he had left there; at the pictures on the walls and the gray rug; the entrance to the hallway; and at his papers, typewriter, and desk, not two feet from his nose. A movement from his desk caught his eye and he saw that it was a thin curl of blue smoke; his cigarette, the ash long, was still burning in the ashtray where he'd left it—this was past all belief—only a few minutes before. **C**

His head moved, and in faint reflection from the glass before him he saw the yellow paper clenched in his front teeth. Lifting a hand from the sill he took it from his mouth; the

390 moistened corner parted from the paper, and he spat it out.

For a moment, in the light from the living room, he stared wonderingly at the yellow sheet in his hand and then crushed it into the side pocket of his jacket.

---

6. A **davenport** is a sofa or couch.

He couldn't open the window. It had been pulled not completely closed, but its lower edge was below the level of the outside sill; there was no room to get his fingers underneath it. Between the upper sash and the lower was a gap not wide enough—reaching up, he tried—to get his fingers into; he couldn't push it open. The upper window panel, he knew from

400 long experience, was impossible to move, frozen tight with dried paint. **D**

IN OTHER WORDS Tom looked into his living room. Everything was just as he had left it minutes ago. Tom put the yellow paper in his pocket and tried to open the window. He could not open the window.

Very carefully observing his balance, the fingertips of his left hand again hooked to the narrow stripping of the window casing, he drew back his right hand, palm facing the glass, and then struck the glass with the heel of his hand.

His arm rebounded from the pane, his body tottering, and he knew he didn't dare strike a harder blow. **E**

But in the security and relief of his new position, he simply smiled; with only a sheet of glass between him and the room

410 just before him, it was not possible that there wasn't a way past it. Eyes narrowing, he thought for a few moments about what to do. Then his eyes widened, for nothing occurred to him. But still he felt calm; the trembling, he realized, had stopped. At the back of his mind there still lay the thought that once he was again in his home, he could give release to his feelings. He actually *would lie* on the floor, rolling, clenching tufts of the rug in his hands. He would literally run across the room, free to move as he liked, jumping on the floor, testing and reveling in its absolute security, letting the relief flood through him, draining the fear from his

420 mind and body. His yearning for this was astonishingly intense, and somehow he understood that he had better keep this feeling at bay. **F**

D **YOUR TURN**

Literary Focus

Remember how difficult it was for Tom to open the window from inside at the beginning of the story. Why do you think it is important to the **plot** of the story that the window is "impossible to move"?

_____

_____

_____

E **YOUR TURN**

Language Coach

Check the definition of *rebounded* on the Preparing to Read page. Then explain how the **prefix** *re–* fits into that definition.

_____

_____

_____

F **HERE'S HOW**

Reading Focus

Tom seems more hopeful now than he was earlier. Even though he is still stuck on the ledge, having reached the window seemingly **causes** him to feel more optimistic.

© Alan Schein Photography/Corbis

Contents of the Dead Man's Pocket

IN OTHER WORDS Tom hit the window glass but his hand only bounced back. He thought about what to do next. He did not know how to get back inside his apartment. He thought about how good it would feel to be back inside.

He took a half dollar from his pocket and struck it against the pane, but without any hope that the glass would break and with very little disappointment when it did not. After a few moments of thought he drew his leg up onto the ledge and picked loose the knot of his shoelace. **A** He slipped off the shoe and, holding it across the instep, drew back his arm as far as he dared and struck the leather heel against the glass. The pane

430   rattled, but he knew he'd been a long way from breaking it. **B** His foot was cold and he slipped the shoe back on. He shouted again, experimentally, and then once more, but there was no answer.

The realization suddenly struck him that he might have to wait here till Clare came home, and for a moment the thought was funny. He could see Clare opening the front door, withdrawing her key from the lock, closing the door behind her, and then glancing up to see him crouched on the other side of the window. He could see her rush across the room,

440   face astounded and frightened, and hear himself shouting instructions: "Never mind how I got here! Just open the wind—" She couldn't open it, he remembered, she'd never been able to; she'd always had to call him. She'd have to get the building superintendent or a neighbor, and he pictured himself smiling and answering their questions as he climbed in. **C** "I just wanted to get a breath of fresh air, so—"

He couldn't possibly wait here till Clare came home. It was the second feature she'd wanted to see, and she'd left in time to see the first. She'd be another three hours or— He glanced at his

450   watch; Clare had been gone eight minutes. It wasn't possible, but only eight minutes ago he had kissed his wife goodbye. She wasn't even at the theater yet! **D**

A **QUICK CHECK**

Why is Tom not surprised or even disappointed when the half dollar coin does not break the glass?

_____

_____

_____

B **YOUR TURN**

Reading Focus

What **causes** the window pane to rattle? Is this the **effect** Tom wanted?

_____

_____

_____

C **YOUR TURN**

Vocabulary

A *superintendent* is someone who manages something—in this case, an apartment building. Why would Clare have to get the building *superintendent*?

_____

_____

D **YOUR TURN**

Literary Focus

Tom realizes that only eight minutes have passed since Clare left. Why is it important to the **plot** of the story to notice how much time has passed?

_____

_____

Tom hit the glass with a coin and his shoe, but the glass would not break. Tom thought he would have to wait until Clare got home. Then he realized that it had only been eight minutes since Clare left for the movies. It would still be a few hours until she came home.

It would be four hours before she could possibly be home, and he tried to picture himself kneeling out here, fingertips hooked to these narrow strippings, while first one movie, preceded by a slow listing of credits, began, developed, reached its climax, and then finally ended. There'd be a newsreel next, maybe, and then an animated cartoon, and then interminable scenes from coming pictures. **A** And then, once more, the
460   beginning of a full-length picture—while all the time he hung out here in the night.

He might possibly get to his feet, but he was afraid to try. Already his legs were cramped, his thigh muscles tired; his knees hurt, his feet felt numb, and his hands were stiff. He couldn't possibly stay out here for four hours or anywhere near it. Long before that his legs and arms would give out; he would be forced to try changing his position often—stiffly, clumsily, his coordination and strength gone—and he would fall. Quite realistically, he knew that he would fall; no one could stay out
470   here on this ledge for four hours. **B**

A dozen windows in the apartment building across the street were lighted. Looking over his shoulder, he could see the top of a man's head behind the newspaper he was reading; in another window he saw the blue-gray flicker of a television screen. No more than twenty-odd yards from his back were scores of people, and if just one of them would walk idly to his window and glance out. . . . **C** For some moments he stared over his shoulder at the lighted rectangles, waiting. But no one appeared. The man reading his paper turned a page and then
480   continued his reading. A figure passed another of the windows and was immediately gone. **D**

A   **HERE'S HOW**

Vocabulary

I have not seen the word *interminable* before, but it looks related to the word *terminate*, which means "end." I think *interminable* may mean "never ending." I checked my dictionary and I was right.

B   **YOUR TURN**

Reading Focus

Tom realizes he cannot wait for Clare to get home. Why? What **causes** Tom to realize that? What **effect** do you think his realization will have on his actions now?

_____

_____

_____

_____

C   **YOUR TURN**

Vocabulary

Does *scores* mean a) "gets a goal in a game," b) "music for a movie," or c) "a lot of something"?

_____

_____

D   **QUICK CHECK**

Do you think anyone in the other apartments will notice Tom?

_____

_____

IN OTHER WORDS Clare would not return home for four hours. Tom knew he could not wait that long. Nobody could stay on that ledge for four hours. Tom knew he would fall. He could see into other apartment buildings, but nobody noticed him.

In the inside pocket of his jacket he found a little sheaf of papers, and he pulled one out and looked at it in the light from the living room. It was an old letter, an advertisement of some sort; his name and address, in purple ink, were on a label pasted to the envelope. **E** Gripping one end of the envelope in his teeth, he twisted it into a tight curl. From his shirt pocket he brought out a book of matches. He didn't dare let go the casing with both hands but, with the twist of paper in his teeth, he

490 opened the matchbook with his free hand; then he bent one of the matches in two without tearing it from the folder, its red-tipped end now touching the striking surface. With his thumb, he rubbed the red tip across the striking area.

He did it again, then again, and still again, pressing harder each time, and the match suddenly flared, burning his thumb. But he kept it alight, cupping the matchbook in his hand and shielding it with his body. He held the flame to the paper in his mouth till it caught. Then he snuffed out the match flame with his thumb and forefinger, careless of the burn, and replaced the

500 book in his pocket. Taking the paper twist in his hand, he held it flame down, watching the flame crawl up the paper, till it flared bright. Then he held it behind him over the street, moving it from side to side, watching it over his shoulder, the flame flickering and guttering in the wind. **F**

IN OTHER WORDS Tom pulled a piece of paper and matches out of his pocket. He lit the match and burned the paper. Tom waved the flame from side to side, hoping someone would see him.

There were three letters in his pocket and he lighted each of them, holding each till the flame touched his hand and then

E **HERE'S HOW**

Vocabulary

I have not seen the word *sheaf* before. Tom takes the "*sheaf* of papers" out of his pocket, so I think a *sheaf* might be a bundle of objects, like paper. I checked my dictionary, and I was right.

F **YOUR TURN**

Reading Focus

What **effect** does Tom hope to achieve by burning the papers?

_____

_____

_____

Copyright © by Holt, Rinehart and Winston. All rights reserved.

A **LITERARY ANALYSIS**

How do you think Tom feels when the man reading the newspaper walks away, seemingly without noticing him?

_____

_____

_____

_____

B **YOUR TURN**

Vocabulary

Eternal means "lasting forever." What does Tom think the "*eternal* mystery" would be if he fell?

_____

_____

_____

C **HERE'S HOW**

Vocabulary

I do not know what *incomprehensible* means. I know that no one would understand Tom's death or the yellow piece of paper he carried. This makes me guess that *incomprehensible* means "unable to be understood." I checked my dictionary, and I was right.

---

dropping it to the street below. At one point, watching over his shoulder while the last of the letters burned, he saw the man across the street put down his paper and stand—even seeming, to Tom, to glance toward his window. But when he moved, it was only to walk across the room and disappear from sight. **A**

There were a dozen coins in Tom Benecke's pocket and he dropped them, three or four at a time. But if they struck anyone, or if anyone noticed their falling, no one connected them with their source, and no one glanced upward.

His arms had begun to tremble from the steady strain of clinging to this narrow perch, and he did not know what to do now and was terribly frightened. Clinging to the window stripping with one hand, he again searched his pockets. But now—he had left his wallet on his dresser when he'd changed clothes—there was nothing left but the yellow sheet. It occurred to him irrelevantly that his death on the sidewalk below would be an eternal mystery; the window closed—why, how, and from where could he have fallen? **B** No one would be able to identify his body for a time, either—the thought was somehow unbearable and increased his fear. All they'd find in his pockets would be the yellow sheet. *Contents of the dead man's pockets*, he thought, *one sheet of paper bearing penciled notations—incomprehensible.* **C**

IN OTHER WORDS Tom kept trying to get someone's attention. He burned three letters that were in his pocket. He dropped coins on the street. But nobody saw him. He did not know what to do and was very afraid. If Tom fell, no one would know who he was or how he had fallen. Tom had left his wallet inside, so no one would be able to identify him. They would just see the piece of yellow paper that he was carrying when he fell.

He understood fully that he might actually be going to die; his arms, maintaining his balance on the ledge, were trembling steadily now. And it occurred to him then with all the force of a revelation that, if he fell, all he was ever going to have out of life he would

510

520

530

then, abruptly, have had. Nothing, then, could ever be changed; and nothing more—no least experience or pleasure—could ever be added to his life. He wished, then, that he had not allowed his wife to go off by herself tonight—and on similar nights. He thought of all the evenings he had spent away from her, working; and he regretted them. He thought wonderingly of his fierce ambition and of the direction his life had taken; he thought of the hours he'd

540 spent by himself, filling the yellow sheet that had brought him out here. *Contents of the dead man's pockets,* he thought with sudden fierce anger, *a wasted life.* **D** **E**

He was simply not going to cling here till he slipped and fell; he told himself that now. There was one last thing he could try; he had been aware of it for some moments, refusing to think about it, but now he faced it. Kneeling here on the ledge, the fingertips of one hand pressed to the narrow strip of wood, he could, he knew, draw his other hand back a yard perhaps, fist clenched tight, doing it very slowly till he sensed the outer limit

550 of balance, then, as hard as he was able from the distance, he could drive his fist forward against the glass. **F** If it broke, his fist smashing through, he was safe; he might cut himself badly, and probably would, but with his arm inside the room, he would be secure. But if the glass did not break, the rebound, flinging his arm back, would topple him off the ledge. He was certain of that. **G**

IN OTHER WORDS Tom thought about his life ending. He wished he had spent more time with his wife instead of working. Tom did not want to fall. He did not want to die. Tom knew then there was one last thing he could try. He could try to break the glass with his fist.

He tested his plan. The fingers of his left hand clawlike on the little stripping, he drew back his other fist until his body began teetering backward. But he had no leverage now—he could

560 feel that there would be no force to his swing—and he moved his fist slowly forward till he rocked forward on his knees again

D **QUICK CHECK**

What are some regrets that Tom has, now that he thinks he is going to die?

_____

_____

E **YOUR TURN**

Reading Focus

In this paragraph, Tom thinks about his life and his possible death. How did his past **cause** him to be trapped on the ledge?

_____

_____

_____

F **HERE'S HOW**

Vocabulary

I can guess what *clenched* means by thinking about Tom's actions. Tom is making a fist that is "*clenched* tight," so *clenched* must mean "pulled into a tight ball."

G **YOUR TURN**

Vocabulary

Re-read the last two sentences of this paragraph. Use context clues to write a definition for *topple.*

_____

_____

and could sense that his swing would carry its greatest force. Glancing down, however, measuring the distance from his fist to the glass, he saw that it was less than two feet.

It occurred to him that he could raise his arm over his head, to bring it down against the glass. But, experimentally in slow motion, he knew it would be an awkward blow without the force of a driving punch, and not nearly enough to break the glass.

Facing the window, he had to drive a blow from the
570 shoulder, he knew now, at a distance of less than two feet; and he did not know whether it would break through the heavy glass. It might; he could picture it happening, he could feel it in the nerves of his arm. And it might not; he could feel that too—feel his fist striking this glass and being instantaneously flung back by the unbreaking pane, feel the fingers of his other hand breaking loose, nails scraping along the casing as he fell. **B**

He waited, arm drawn back, fist balled, but in no hurry to strike; this pause, he knew, might be an extension of his life. And to live even a few seconds longer, he felt, even out here on this
580 ledge in the night, was infinitely better than to die a moment earlier than he had to. His arm grew tired, and he brought it down and rested it.

IN OTHER WORDS Tom knew he would have to swing hard in order to break the glass. But he did not have a lot of space to pull back and punch with enough force to break the glass. If the glass did not break, the force of the punch would send Tom backwards and he would fall to his death.

Then he knew that it was time to make the attempt. He could not kneel here hesitating indefinitely till he lost all courage to act, waiting till he slipped off the ledge. Again he drew back his arm, knowing this time that he would not bring it down till he struck. His elbow protruding over Lexington Avenue far below, the fingers of his other hand pressed down

 HERE'S HOW

Vocabulary

I do not know the word *leverage*, but I know a *lever* is a tool that gives its user more strength. *Leverage* must also involve the amount of strength or force one has.

B **YOUR TURN**

Reading Focus

What **effect** does Tom fear may result from striking the glass?

_____

_____

_____

_____

590 bloodlessly tight against the narrow stripping, he waited, feeling the sick tenseness and terrible excitement building. It grew and swelled toward the moment of action, his nerves tautening. He thought of Clare—just a wordless, yearning thought—and then drew his arm back just a bit more, fist so tight his fingers pained him, and knowing he was going to do it. Then with full power, with every last scrap of strength he could bring to bear, he shot his arm forward toward the glass, and he said "Clare!" **C**

He heard the sound, felt the blow, felt himself falling forward, and his hand closed on the living-room curtains, the

600 shards and fragments of glass showering onto the floor. And then, kneeling there on the ledge, an arm thrust into the room up to the shoulder, he began picking away the protruding slivers and great wedges of glass from the window frame, tossing them in onto the rug. And, as he grasped the edges of the empty window frame and climbed into his home, he was grinning in triumph. **D**

He did not lie down on the floor or run through the apartment, as he had promised himself; even in the first few moments it seemed to him natural and normal that he should be

610 where he was. He simply turned to his desk, pulled the crumpled yellow sheet from his pocket, and laid it down where it had been, smoothing it out; then he absently laid a pencil across it to weight it down. He shook his head wonderingly, and turned to walk toward the closet.

There he got out his topcoat and hat and, without waiting to put them on, opened the front door and stepped out, to go find his wife. He turned to pull the door closed and warm air from the hall rushed through the narrow opening again. As he saw the yellow paper, the pencil flying, scooped off the desk and,

620 unimpeded by the glassless window, sail out into the night and out of his life, Tom Benecke burst into laughter and then closed the door behind him. **E** **F**

C LITERARY ANALYSIS

Why do you think Tom calls out Clare's name? How might his calling her name connect to his feelings about her?

_____

_____

_____

D HERE'S HOW

Literary Focus

By getting back inside, Tom has solved the problem he faced during most of the story's **plot**. I will keep reading to see how the experience impacts him.

E YOUR TURN

Vocabulary

Unimpeded means "not blocked." Underline the phrase that tells you what happens to the _unimpeded_ paper.

F HERE'S HOW

Literary Focus

The **plot** of this story takes place over a short amount of time. Even so, Tom goes through a great change. Tom laughs at the end of the story. I guess he really changed out on the ledge. He called out Clare's name when he tried to break the window. And now he is going to find Clare at the movie theater. I think Tom realized that love is more important than work.

IN OTHER WORDS Tom tried to get ready to break the glass. When he finally was set to punch, he yelled his wife's name as he hit the glass. The window broke. Tom climbed through the broken glass and into his apartment. He put the yellow paper back down on his desk. Tom went to the closet and got his jacket and hat. He walked out of the apartment to go find his wife. As he closed the front door, the yellow paper blew out the window again. Tom laughed and closed the apartment door behind him.

Applying Your Skills

Contents of the Dead Man's Pocket

LITERARY FOCUS: PLOT: TIME AND SEQUENCE

DIRECTIONS: Number the following events from earliest (1) to latest (5) to indicate the correct **chronological order** of events in the story's **plot**.

_____ Tom leaves the apartment to find Clare at the movie theater.

_____ Tom sets fire to a few scraps of paper.

_____ Clare asks Tom if he wants to join her at the movie; Tom declines.

_____ Tom reaches the corner of the ledge, where the yellow paper is.

_____ Tom drops a few coins onto the street below him.

READING FOCUS: UNDERSTANDING CAUSE AND EFFECT

DIRECTIONS: Complete the following exercise by writing either a **cause** or an **effect** in the chart below.

Cause	Effect
Tom wanted to make himself stand out from the other workers in the company.	1.
2.	Under the downward pull of his body, the window slammed shut.
Tom thought of Clare and called out her name as he tried again to break the glass.	3.

Word Box

projection

exhalation

imperceptibly

rebounded

irrelevantly

VOCABULARY REVIEW

DIRECTIONS: Fill in the blanks with the correct words form the Word Box. Not all words will be used.

1. Inch by inch, Tom moved slowly, almost _____ toward the window.

2. Tom struck the window with the half dollar coin, but not surprisingly, it just _____ back toward him.

The Trip

Based on the story by Laila Lalami

LITERARY FOCUS: SETTING AND MOOD

Setting is the time and place in which a story happens. The setting can bring a story to life. If described well, it can make you feel like you are right there in the story. A scary story, for example, might take place in a haunted mansion at midnight. Maybe the mansion is far away from any other houses.

The setting helps create a story's **mood**. The mood is the overall feeling that you get from a story. Think again of the haunted mansion. If it is described well, you will feel a mood of fear as you read the story.

READING FOCUS: VISUALIZING

When you **visualize** something, you imagine what it looks like. Visualizing a story as you read it can give you a deeper understanding of what you are reading. Luckily, authors often use descriptive words to help you. For example, read the following sentences: "The old stone house was enormous and crumbling. It loomed in the dark, with broken windows that looked like jagged teeth." Notice all of the descriptions the author gave you. Do they help you picture the haunted mansion perfectly in your mind?

VOCABULARY

Practice saying the following words out loud.

dirhams (DIHR HUHMZ) *n.:* unit of money in Morocco; 20,000 dirhams is more than $2,000 American.

hijab (HIH JAHB) *n.:* scarf that many Muslim women wear to cover their hair.

grim (GRIHM) *adj.:* bleak, unhappy.

menacing (MEHN IH SING) *adj.:* posing a threat to.

INTO THE STORY

Morocco is a country in North Africa. It is only a short boat ride from Spain. People like the character Murad in this story sometimes leave Morocco and try to enter Spain illegally. They hope to have a better life there. However, the trip to Spain can be dangerous. Even if they get to Spain, many travelers are sent back to Morocco.

SKILLS FOCUS

Literary Skills
Understand setting and mood.

Reading Skills
Visualize a story's setting and plot events.

THE TRIP

Based on the story by Laila Lalami

© Fernando garcia/Cover/Corbis

Fourteen kilometers. Murad has thought about that many times, trying to decide whether the risk was worth it. Some days he told himself that the distance was nothing, that the crossing would take only thirty minutes if the weather was good. He thought about what he would do once he was on the other side. He imagined the job, the car, the house. Other days he could think only about the dangers and the cost. He wondered how fourteen kilometers could separate not just two countries but two worlds.

10   Tonight the sea appears calm. The captain has ordered all the lights turned off, but with the moon up and the sky clear, Murad can still see. The inflatable motor boat is meant to hold eight people. Thirty huddle in it now, looking anxious. Ⓐ Ⓑ

Murad wears three layers: undershirt, turtleneck, and jacket; below, thermal underwear, jeans, and sneakers. He checks his watch: 3:15 A.M. He wonders how much money Captain Rahal will make. If everyone paid as much as Murad did, the take is almost 600,000 dirhams. That's enough for a small house in a Moroccan beach town. Ⓒ

From "The Trip," adapted from *Hope and Other Dangerous Pursuits* by Laila Lalami. Copyright 2005 © by Laila Lalami. Retold by Holt, Rinehart, and Winston. Reproduced by permission of **Algonquin Books of Chapel Hill, a Division of Workman Publishing.**

Ⓐ **QUICK CHECK**

Where is Murad? What do you think he is doing there?

_____

_____

Ⓑ **HERE'S HOW**

Literary Focus

Lines 1–13 describe the story's **setting**. These lines tell me where the story takes place. I know it is night and that Murad is on a boat. The lines also create a **mood**. I feel nervous when I read these lines. I think the people in the story are nervous, too.

Ⓒ **HERE'S HOW**

Vocabulary

The word *dirhams* appears in line 18. The author also mentions Morocco. I think that a *dirham* is a unit of money in Morocco, the way a dollar is a unit of money in the United States.

He looks at the Spanish coastline, as it grows closer. The waves look black, except for foam that shines white under the moon. Murad can see the town where they're headed. It's worth it, Murad tells himself. Some time on this flimsy boat and then a job. At first he'll work in the fields like everyone else, but he'll also look for something better. He doesn't want to spend the rest of his life picking oranges and tomatoes. He'll find a real job, where he can use his training. He has a degree in English and he speaks Spanish fluently, unlike some of the harraga.[1]

He moves his ankle around. To his left, the girl (he thinks **30** her name is Faten) shifts slightly. She looks eighteen, nineteen maybe. "My leg was asleep," he whispers. Faten nods but doesn't look at him. He doesn't understand why she's wearing a hijab scarf for a trip like this. Does she think she can walk down the street in Tarifa in a headscarf without getting caught? **A**

Across from Murad is Aziz. He's tall and lanky and sits hunched over in the narrow space. This is his second attempt at crossing the Strait of Gibraltar. He told Murad that he'd bargained with Rahal over the price of the trip. He said that he should get a deal since he was a repeat customer. Murad tried to bargain, too, **40** but he still had to borrow almost 20,000 dirhams from one of his uncles. He'll pay his uncle back as soon as he can get a job.

Aziz asks for a sip of water. Murad hands over his bottle. Then he offers the last bit to Faten, but she shakes her head. Murad was told to drink a lot of water, and he has. He feels a sudden urge to urinate but contains it.

Next to Aziz is a middle-aged man with <u>a large scar across his cheek, like Al Pacino in *Scarface*.</u> <u>He wears jeans and a short-sleeved shirt.</u> Murad heard him say that he was a tennis teacher. <u>His arms are muscular, but he seems rough, like he's used</u> **50** <u>to trouble with the law.</u> Murad notices that Scarface has been staring at <u>the little girl sitting next to him. She seems to be about ten years old.</u> Scarface asks her name. "Mouna," she says. He offers her chewing gum, but the girl quickly shakes her head. **B**

---

1. **harraga:** Moroccan slang term for people fleeing for Spain.

Sidebar

A YOUR TURN

Vocabulary
Re-read this paragraph. What do you learn about what a *hijab* is? Why do you think the author decided to use the Arabic word instead of an English translation?

_____

_____

_____

_____

_____

B HERE'S HOW

Reading Focus
This paragraph describes two of the people on the boat. I have underlined the details that help me **visualize** them in my head.

Her mother, Halima, gives Scarface a threatening look. She wraps one arm around her daughter and the other around her two boys. Halima's gaze is direct, not shifty like Faten's. She seems determined, and Murad respects her. But he thinks she's irresponsible for risking her children's lives on this trip.

On Aziz's right is a slender African woman. She said she was

60　Guinean. She cradles her body with her arms and rocks gently. Rahal barks at her to stop. She looks up, tries not to move, and then throws up on Faten's boots. Faten cries out. **C**

"Shut up," Rahal snaps.

The New Guinea woman whispers an apology in French. Faten says that it's okay. Soon the little boat smells like vomit. Halima sits up and exhales loudly. Rahal glares at her. He tells her to hunch down to keep the boat balanced. **D**

"Leave her alone," Murad says.

Halima turns to him and smiles for the first time. He won-

70　ders what her plans are. He thinks about some of the illegals who, instead of going on a boat, try to sneak in on vegetable trucks headed from Morocco to Spain. Last year the Guardia Civil[2] found the bodies of three illegals, who suffocated on a tomato truck. At least that won't happen on a boat. **E**

The boat's motor stops. In the sudden silence, everyone looks at Rahal, holding their breath. He pulls the starter cable a few times, but nothing happens.

"What's wrong?" Faten asks, anxiously.

Rahal doesn't answer.

80　"Try again," Halima says.

Rahal yanks at the cable.

"This trip is cursed," Faten whispers. Everyone hears her.

Rahal bangs the motor with his hand. Faten recites from the Qur'an. "'God, there is no God but Him, the Alive, the Eternal. Neither slumber nor sleep overtaketh Him—'"

"Quiet," Scarface yells. Looking at the captain, he asks, "Is it the spark plug?"

---

2. **Guardia Civil:** Spanish police force with both military and civilian functions.

C　YOUR TURN

Reading Focus

The author is very careful to tell you where on the boat people are sitting. Does this information make it easier or harder for you to **visualize** the characters? Explain.

_____

_____

_____

_____

D　HERE'S HOW

Literary Focus

The author describes sights, sounds, and even smells. These descriptions help set the **mood** and help me imagine what it feels like to be on the boat.

E　YOUR TURN

Literary Focus

This paragraph describes other ways people have tried to get to Spain. These details take the reader off the boat, to a different time and place. Which of the following **moods** do these details create: comfort, suspense, excitement, fear, calmness?

_____

_____

_____

A

YOUR TURN

Literary Focus

In this scene, people speak in short sentences. What **mood** does their speech help create?

_____

_____

B **HERE'S HOW**

Literary Focus

I try to picture the scene when the boat stops. I notice details, like Aziz crawling in the boat. Picturing the scene helps me understand the **mood** better. It is scary!

C **HERE'S HOW**

Vocabulary

I am not sure what *grim* means. When I think about the story, though, the boat does not seem peaceful. I think *grim* means "uneasy" or "unhappy." There could be an uneasy peace between the people on the boat. I will check the dictionary to be sure.

"I don't know. I don't think so," says Rahal.

Faten continues to pray, this time more quietly.

90 Rahal yanks at the cable again.

Aziz calls out, "Wait, let me see." He gets on all fours and climbs over the vomit. He moves slowly to keep the boat stable.

Faten starts crying. Her distress spreads, and Murad can hear someone else sniffling.

"What are you crying for?" Scarface asks, leaning forward to look at her face.

"I'm afraid," she whimpers. **A**

"Leave her be," Halima says, holding her children close.

"Why did she come if she can't handle it?" he yells, pointing

100 at Faten.

Murad snarls. "Who the hell do you think you are?" He's surprised by his anger.

"And who are you?" Scarface says. "Her protector?"

A cargo ship blows its horn, startling everyone. It glides in the distance, its lights blinking.

"Stop it," Rahal yells. "Someone will hear us!" **B**

Aziz studies the motor. He pulls at the hose that connects it to the tank. "There's a gap here," he tells Rahal. "Do you have some tape?"

110 Rahal pulls out a roll of duct tape. Aziz wraps some around the hose. The captain pulls the cable. Finally the motor wheezes and the boat starts moving.

"Praise be to God," Faten says, ignoring Scarface.

The crying stops and a grim peace falls on the boat. **C**

Tarifa, Spain, is about 250 meters away now. It'll only take another few minutes.

The water is still calm, but Murad knows better than to trust the Mediterranean. He's known the sea all his life.

"Everyone out of the boat now!" Rahal shouts. You have to

120 swim the rest of the way."

Aziz immediately rolls out into the water and starts swimming.

Like the other passengers, Murad looks stunned. They expected to be taken all the way to the shore. Swimming the rest of the way will be unbearable, especially for those who are not from Tangier and used to its waters.

Halima raises a hand at Rahal. "You thief! We paid you to take us to the coast."

Rahal says, "You want to get us all arrested? Get out of the boat if you want to get there. I'm turning back."

Someone makes an abrupt movement to reason with Rahal, but the boat loses balance and then it's too late. **D** Murad is in the water. His clothes are soaked. The shock of the cold water makes his heart go still for a moment. He gasps for air and realizes that there's nothing left to do but swim. **E**

Led by crosscurrents, people are slowly scattering around him. Rahal struggles to right his boat but someone is hanging on to the side. He hears screams, sees a few people swimming. Aziz is already far ahead of the others, going west. Murad starts swimming toward the coast, afraid he might be pulled away by the water. From behind, he hears someone call out. Murad turns and holds his hand out to Faten. She grabs it and the next second she is holding both his shoulders. He tries to pull away, but her grip tightens.

"Use one hand to move," he yells.

She doesn't move. Her body is heavy against his. Each time they bob in the water, she holds on tighter. He tries to loosen her

D HERE'S HOW

Language Coach

A **synonym** is a word that has the same or nearly the same meaning as another word. I am not sure what *abrupt* means. My dictionary says it means "sudden and unexpected." Now I know that a synonym for *abrupt* is *sudden*.

E YOUR TURN

Literary Focus

The **mood** and part of the **setting** changes suddenly in lines 119–135. What happens in the story to change the mood and setting?

_____

_____

_____

_____

_____

_____

_____

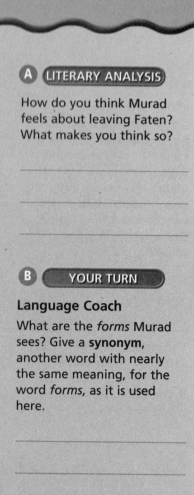

A **LITERARY ANALYSIS**

How do you think Murad feels about leaving Faten? What makes you think so?

_____

_____

_____

B **YOUR TURN**

Language Coach

What are the *forms* Murad sees? Give a **synonym**, another word with nearly the same meaning, for the word *forms*, as it is used here.

_____

_____

C **YOUR TURN**

Reading Focus

List three details you can **visualize**, or picture, on this page. How do these details help you understand what Murad is going through?

_____

_____

_____

_____

_____

_____

grip but she won't let go. He yells out. Still she holds on. They'll never make it if she doesn't loosen her grip. He pushes her away.

150 Free at last, he moves quickly out of her reach.

"Beat the water with your arms," he yells. His fingers and toes have gone numb, and he has to start swimming or he'll freeze. He faces the coast. He tries to focus on the motion of his limbs.

He swims until he feels the sand against his feet. He tries to control his breathing, the beating of his heart in his ears. He lies on the beach, the water licking his shoes. He rests there for a little while, then pushes himself to his knees.

He stands, legs shaking. He turns around and scans the dark

160 waters, looking for Faten. **A** He can see a few forms, struggling, but can't tell who is who. **B** Aziz is nowhere to be seen, but the Guinean woman is getting out of the water a few meters away.

In the distance, a dog barks.

Murad knows he doesn't have much time before the Guardia Civil come after them. He takes a few steps and drops to his knees on the sand. With a trembling hand, he pulls out a plastic bag from his pocket. In it is a mobile phone, with a Spanish SIM card.[3] He calls Rubio, the Spaniard who will drive him north to Catalonia.

170 "Soy Murad. El amigo de Rahal."

"Espéreme por la caña de azucar."

"Bien."[4]

He takes a few steps forward, but he doesn't see the sugar cane. He continues walking anyway. He sees a hotel. He walks toward it and spots the sugar cane. He sits down. He hears another dog bark. He takes his shoes off, curls his cold toes, and rubs them. He puts his shoes back on, lies back, and takes a deep breath. He can't believe his luck. He made it. **C**

It will be all right now. He imagines the office where he'll

180 be working. He can see his fingers moving over his keyboard.

---

3. **SIM Card:** a device used in cellular phones.
4. **"Soy Murad . . . Bien":** "I am Murad, Rahal's friend." "Wait for me by the sugar cane." "Okay."

He pictures himself going home to a modern apartment, his wife greeting him, the TV in the background. **D**

A light shines on him. Murad sits up. He sees the dog, a German shepherd, and the menacing form holding the leash. **E**

The officer from the Guardia Civil wears fatigues and a black beret. His name tag reads Martinez. He sits in the van with Murad and the other illegals, the dog at his feet. It's only fourteen kilometers, Murad thinks. If they hadn't been forced into the water, if he'd swum faster, if he'd gone west instead of east, he would have made it.

When he gets out of the van, Murad notices a wooded area and, beyond it, a road. The guards are busy. Murad takes off, running as fast as he can. Behind him, he hears a whistle and the sound of boots. But he keeps running. When he gets closer to the road, he sees it is a four-lane highway, with cars whizzing by. He pauses. Martinez grabs him by the shirt.

The clock on the wall at the Guardia Civil post says it is 6:00 A.M. Murad sits on a metal chair, handcuffed. There are men and women, all wrapped in blankets like him, huddled close together to stay warm. He doesn't recognize many of them. Scarface sits alone, smoking a cigarette. There is no sign of Aziz. He must have made it. **F**

Lucky Aziz. Murad curses his own luck. If he'd landed just a hundred meters west, away from the houses and the hotel, he might have been able to escape. How will he be able to show his face again in Tangier? He stands up and hobbles to the dusty window. He sees Faten outside, her head bare. She is in a line with some of the other people from the boat. A wave of relief washes over him, and he calls her name. She can't hear him. At last she looks up and sees him. Then she looks away.

A woman in a dark business suit arrives, her high heels clicking on the tiled floor "*Soy sus abogada*,"[5] she says. She tells them they are here illegally and that they must sign the paper that the Guardia Civil are going to give them.

---

5. **"Soy sus abogada":** "I am your lawyer."

D HERE'S HOW

Reading Focus

Murad imagines details of his new life. He imagines his keyboard and TV at his new home. Just as Murad **visualizes** this, so do I. I can tell that Murad's imagination helps keep him going.

E HERE'S HOW

Vocabulary

The word *menacing* appears in this sentence. I think it means "scary," because of how it is used in the sentence. I also have heard the phrase "*menace to society*." I know that means that some person or thing might harm society. *Menacing* must be related to *menace*. I checked my dictionary, and *menacing* means "posing a threat to."

F YOUR TURN

Reading Focus

What can you **visualize** in the room? How do you imagine it feels to be there?

_____

_____

_____

_____

_____

_____

_____

Literary Focus

What is the **mood** now, at the end of the story? How is it like the mood at the beginning of the story? How is it different?

_____

_____

_____

_____

_____

_____

_____

_____

_____

Murad puts in a false name even though it won't matter. He is taken to the holding station. On his way there, he sees a body bag on the ground. He doubles over and the officer lets go of him. Murad stumbles to the side of the building and vomits. It could have been him in that body bag. It could have been Faten. Maybe it was Aziz or Halima. **A**

The guard takes him to a moldy cell with two other prisoners. Murad sits on the floor and looks up through the window at the blue sky. Seagulls flutter and fly away. For a moment he envies their freedom. Tomorrow the police will send him back to Tangier. He will return to the same old apartment, to live off his mother and sister, without any possibility to advance. He thinks of Aziz, who is probably already headed to Catalonia. He wonders—if Aziz can make it, why not him? At least now he knows what to expect. It will be hard to convince his mother. But in the end he knows he will convince her to sell her gold bracelets. It will pay for another trip. And next time, he'll make it. **B**

Applying Your Skills

The Trip

LITERARY FOCUS: SETTING AND MOOD

DIRECTIONS: The **mood** in "The Trip" is complicated. It shifts and changes as the story happens. Sometimes a change in setting also affects the mood. The square below lists different moods within the story. Below each mood, list details from the story that help create that feeling.

Desperate	Hopeful
Nervous	Menacing

READING FOCUS: VISUALIZING

DIRECTIONS: Find a description in the story that really helped you picture the setting. Write a short explanation of what makes the description so good. What in the description helped you **visualize** the time and place so clearly?

_____

_____

_____

VOCABULARY REVIEW

DIRECTIONS: Fill in the blanks with the correct words from the Word Box.

Word Box

dirhams

hijab

grim

menacing

1. James was _____ when the subject of next week's test came up.

2. I used the money calculator to figure out how many _____ are in a dollar.

3. The German shepherd bared its teeth in a _____ way.

4. Faten wore a _____ because she was a devout Muslim.

In the Shadow of Man

Based on an excerpt from the memoir by Jane Goodall

INFORMATIONAL TEXT FOCUS: MAIN IDEA AND SUPPORTING DETAILS

The **main idea** is the most important point a writer wants to express. To figure out what the main idea is, you can look for important statements. You can also look for **supporting details**. For example, the main idea of a political speech might be that health care is too expensive. How does the candidate support that idea? Does he or she give statistics or tell stories about people who have not been able to pay for health care?

Sometimes it is difficult to figure out a writer's main idea. That is why it is important to look for supporting details. You might also try the following tips when looking for a main idea:

1. Read the title of what you are reading. Sometimes the title is very close to the main idea.

2. Skim through opening paragraphs. Writers will often introduce you to their main idea at the very beginning of a piece—or at least hint at it.

3. Consider what is said in the final paragraphs. The writer might summarize the main idea more clearly here than anywhere else.

VOCABULARY

With a partner, practice using these words in complete sentences.

bushpig (BUHSH PIHG) *n.:* a type of pig that lives in Africa, in dense plant life.

rodents (ROH DUHNTS) *n.:* animals with long front teeth for gnawing wood, including mice, rats, squirrels, and guinea pigs.

mammals (MAM UHLZ) *n.:* animals with hair and a spine that feed their young with milk from the mother's breasts.

INTO THE MEMOIR

Jane Goodall is a scientist known for studying chimpanzees in their natural surroundings. Between 1960 and 1975, Goodall observed chimpanzee behavior in the Gombe Stream Game Reserve in Tanzania, Africa. As this selection opens, Goodall has just set up camp in the Mlinda Valley.

SKILLS FOCUS

Informational Text Skills
Identify the main idea in a text; identify and understand supporting details.

IN THE SHADOW OF MAN

Based on an excerpt from the memoir by Jane Goodall

As time passed, the chimpanzees became less afraid. Often when I was out gathering food, I came across chimpanzees. After a time I found that some of them would allow my presence if they were in fairly

© Michael Nichols/National Geographic Society

thick forest. I had to sit still and stay sixty to eighty yards away. And so, I could sometimes make more detailed observations.

10   It was then that I began to recognize different individuals. I gave them names. Some scientists feel that animals should be labeled by numbers. But I am interested in the differences between individuals. A name is more individual than a number. It is also easier to remember. I chose names that seemed to suit the individuals. **A**

The easiest individual to recognize was Mr. McGregor. The top of his head, his neck, and his shoulders were almost entirely bald. He was old—thirty to forty years of age. During the first months I knew him, if I accidentally came too close, McGregor

20   would threaten me by jerking his head and shaking branches. Then he would climb down and vanish. He reminded me of the old gardener in *The Tale of Peter Rabbit*.

Ancient Flo was also easy to recognize. She had ragged ears and two young children: two-year-old Fifi and seven-year-old Figan. Flo often traveled with another old mother, Olly. The fluff of hair on the back of Olly's head reminded me of my aunt, Olwen. Olly, like Flo, had two children. **B**

Then there was William. He must have been Olly's brother. They looked alike. Both had long upper lips that wobbled.

30   William also had several scars running down his face.

A HERE'S HOW

Reading Focus

Jane Goodall names the chimpanzees. I think this makes the animals more like human beings. I think that chimps being like humans might be a **main idea** in this memoir. I will keep reading to see if I am right.

B YOUR TURN

Reading Focus

You have now read four paragraphs about different chimpanzees. Why do you think the author includes these examples and stories? How are these **supporting details**?

_____

_____

_____

From "First Observations" (retitled "In the Shadow of Man") adapted from *In the Shadow of Man* by Jane Goodall. Copyright © 1971 by Hugo and Jane van Lawick-Goodall. All rights reserved. Retold by Holt, Rinehart and Winston. Reproduced by permission of **Houghton Mifflin Company** and electronic format by permission of **Soko Publications c/o G. T. E. Parsons, Esquire.**

Two other chimpanzees I knew by sight were David Graybeard and Goliath. Like David and Goliath in the Bible, these two were often together. Goliath had a splendid body and moved like an athlete. **A** David Graybeard was less afraid of me than the other chimps were. I was always pleased when I saw him in a group. With David to calm the others, I could watch them more closely.

Soon I made two really exciting discoveries. And I had David Graybeard to thank for both. **B**

One day I found a small group of chimps in the upper branches of a tree on the Peak. I saw that one of them was holding a pink-looking object. From time to time, he pulled pieces from it with his teeth. A female and a youngster both reached out toward him. Their hands touched his mouth. Soon the female picked up a piece of the pink thing and put it to her mouth. Then I realized that the chimps were eating meat.

After each bite of meat the male picked some leaves with his lips and chewed them. Often, after chewing he spat out the remains into the female's hands. Once he dropped a small piece of meat. In a flash the youngster swung after it to the ground. As he reached to pick it up, a little bushpig charged toward him. **C** Screaming, the chimp leaped back into the tree. Soon I saw that the chimps were eating a baby pig. For three hours I watched them eat. David occasionally let the female bite pieces from the pig's body. Once he actually tore off a small piece of flesh and placed it in her hand.

Of course I was not sure that David Graybeard had caught the pig for himself. Even so, it was exciting to know that these chimpanzees ate meat. Before, scientists had believed that these apes were mostly vegetarians and fruit eaters that occasionally ate insects or rodents. No one had guessed that they might hunt larger mammals. **D**

Within two weeks, I saw something even more exciting. It was October and the rains had begun. One morning I climbed up to the Peak. There I saw a movement in the grass nearby. It was David Graybeard.

40

50

60

He was squatting beside the red earth mound of a termite nest. He carefully pushed a long grass stem down into a hole in the mound. Then he pulled it out and picked something from the
70 end with his mouth. I couldn't see what he was eating. But it was clear that he was using a grass stem as a tool.

Twice before, observers in West Africa had seen chimpanzees using objects as tools. But I had never dreamed of seeing anything so exciting myself.

E **QUICK CHECK**

What has Goodall seen that makes her so excited?

_____

_____

_____

For an hour David feasted at the termite mound. When he had gone I looked at the mound. I found a swarm of termites sealing the entrances where David had poked his stems. I picked up a stem and pushed it into a hole. I felt the pull of termites as they seized the grass. When I pulled it out some termites
80 clung to it.

More than a week later, David Graybeard and Goliath arrived again. They worked for two hours. They scratched open the entrances to the mound. They bit ends off their tools when they became bent, or used the other end. Sometimes they replaced them with new ones. Both often picked a few stems at once, and put the spares beside them to use later.

Most exciting, a few times they picked small leafy twigs and stripped off the leaves. This was the first recorded example of a wild animal actually changing an object. It showed they were
90 *making* tools, not just *using* them. **F**

F **YOUR TURN**

Reading Focus

Goodall's discovery is the **main idea** of this part of her story. What **supporting details** has she provided on this page? Underline them.

G **HERE'S HOW**

Reading Focus

I suspected that Goodall was leading up to her biggest **main ideas**. All of the examples, stories, and facts she wrote about point to the last two paragraphs. She discovered that chimps eat meat and use and make tools.

Until then, man had been defined as the only tool-making animal. But my observations convinced some scientists to come up with a better definition for man. Or else, as Louis Leakey put it, we should accept the chimpanzee as Man.

I sent telegrams to Louis about both of my new observations—the meat-eating and the toolmaking. He was wildly enthusiastic. In fact, I believe that the news helped him find money to support my work. Shortly after, he told me that the National Geographic Society in the United States had agreed to
100 fund another year's research. **G**

© Karl Ammann/Corbis

In the Shadow of Man **43**

In the Shadow of Man

USE A MAIN IDEA MAP

The **main idea** is the major message or point that a writer wants to get across to the reader. When you read nonfiction, it is always important to identify the main idea. The idea map below can help you do this.

DIRECTIONS: In the outer circles, fill in the **supporting details** that Jane Goodall gives in the selection. These details will lead you to the main idea. Write this main idea in the center circle.

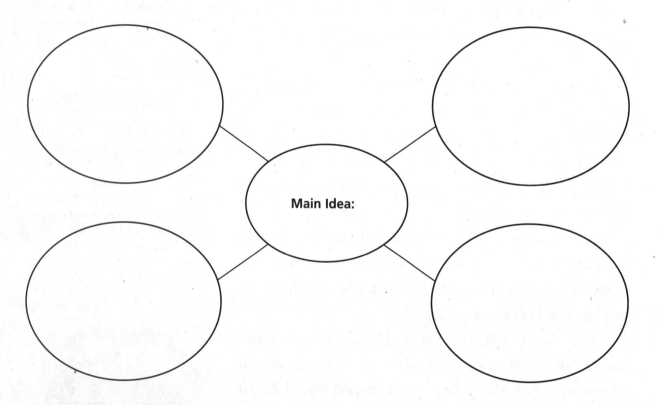

Main Idea:

Applying Your Skills

In the Shadow of Man

INFORMATIONAL TEXT FOCUS: MAIN IDEA AND SUPPORTING DETAILS

Nonfiction selections like "In the Shadow of Man" always include at least one **main idea**. This main idea connects all of the information in the selection. However, sections of a selection can also have separate, smaller main ideas. For example, the main idea of the first paragraph in this selection is that the chimpanzees became less afraid of Goodall.

DIRECTIONS: Re-read each section listed below. For each section, identify the main idea. Then back up your answer with **supporting details** from the section.

Section	The main idea is:	Supporting details that prove this are:
Lines 1–39		
Lines 40–56		
Lines 63–90		

VOCABULARY REVIEW

DIRECTIONS: Find a picture of each type of animal listed below. Then write a short description of each animal.

1. bushpig: _____

_____

2. rodent: _____

_____

3. mammal: _____

_____

Skills Review

Collection 1

VOCABULARY REVIEW

DIRECTIONS: Match each vocabulary word with its definition. Then, write the letter of the correct definition on the blank line.

_____	**1.** irrelevantly	**a.**	scarf worn by Muslim women
_____	**2.** imperceptibly	**b.**	bleak, unhappy
_____	**3.** exhalation	**c.**	animals with hair and a spine
_____	**4.** rebounded	**d.**	bounced back
_____	**5.** menacing	**e.**	posing a threat to
_____	**6.** hijab	**f.**	in an unrelated manner
_____	**7.** grim	**g.**	breath
_____	**8.** mammals	**h.**	something that juts out
_____	**9.** projection	**i.**	in a barely noticeable way

DIRECTIONS: Look at the word and topic pairs below. For each pair, write a sentence about the topic using the word provided.

1. Word: grim; **Topic:** the plot of "The Trip"

_____

_____

_____

_____

2. Word: projection; **Topic:** Tom's situation in "Contents of the Dead Man's Pocket"

_____

_____

_____

_____

Skills Review

Collection 1

LANGUAGE COACH: SYNONYMS

DIRECTIONS: Synonyms are words that have the same or nearly the same definition. Write a synonym for each bold faced word below.

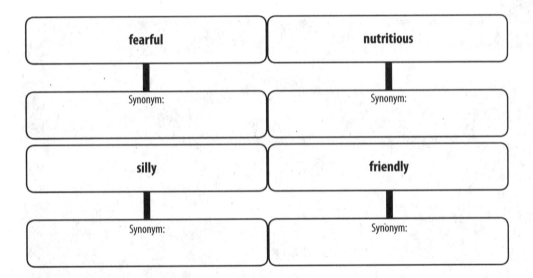

fearful	nutritious
Synonym:	Synonym:
silly	friendly
Synonym:	Synonym:

ORAL LANGUAGE ACTIVITY

DIRECTIONS: With a partner, discuss what you have read about how **causes** and **effects** make up the **plot** of a story. Take turns answering the following questions. Answer in complete sentences. When you have finished your discussion, write your answers on the lines below.

1. What is a story's plot?

_____

2. What does *cause* mean? Give an example.

_____

3. What does *effect* mean? Give an example.

_____

4. Give an example of a cause-and-effect chain that would make a good story.

_____

_____

Collection

2

Character

Cotton Fields, Sunflowers, Blackbirds and Quilting Bees (1997). Acrylic on canvas; painted and pieced border (76.5" × 75.25"). Private Collection. From the Series: *The American Collection, #8* by Faith Ringgold. ©Faith Ringgold, 1997

Literary and Academic Vocabulary for Collection 2

LITERARY VOCABULARY

character traits (KAR IHK TUHR TRAYTS) *n.:* qualities, features, beliefs, and quirks belonging to a character in a story.
One of Tanya's character traits is that she is very shy.

conflict (KAHN FLIHKT) *n.:* the main struggle in a story.
The argument between the mother and daughter was a major conflict in the story.

inferences (IHN FUHR EHN SEHZ) *n.:* intelligent guesses based on current evidence and things you already know.
When an author does not tell you much about a character, you have to make inferences about what he or she is like.

motivation (MOH TUH VAY SHUHN) *n.:* reason for a character to take action.
I wonder what Jack's motivation is for calling me on the phone ten times a day?

ACADEMIC VOCABULARY

acquire (UH KWYR) *v.:* get or gain.
By reading several books, Maury was able to acquire a better understanding of the subject.

attitude (AT UH TOOD) *n.:* a state of mind or feeling about something.
Natalie had a positive attitude toward work.

reveal (RIH VEEL) *v.:* make known; show.
The way a person acts in an emergency may reveal a lot about his or her character.

tradition (TRUH DIHSH UHN) *n.:* handing down of beliefs, opinions, customs, and stories.
The tradition of passing down quilts from mother to daughter resulted in a beautiful family collection.

Everyday Use
For Your Grandmama

By Alice Walker

LITERARY FOCUS: CHARACTER TRAITS

Character traits are the qualities and features that make a person unique. These qualities can include anything from behaviors, to beliefs, to habits. Real people have character traits. So do characters in stories. Think about the fairy-tale character Goldilocks. She tries three types of porridge and chairs. From her behavior, we know that curiosity is one of her character traits. In the following selection, notice how the character traits of the three women make them very different from each other.

READING FOCUS: MAKING INFERENCES ABOUT CHARACTERS

An **inference** is an intelligent guess. You make inferences based on evidence. In a story, evidence includes what characters say or do. By "listening" and "watching" characters, you can infer, or guess, what the characters are like. Suppose that a character adopts stray dogs and helps her elderly neighbors. Even if the author does not tell you directly, you can infer that the character is a caring person. Making inferences while you read helps you know more about the characters than the author tells you.

VOCABULARY

With a partner, practice using these words in complete sentences.

sidle (SY DUHL) *v.:* move in a slow, shy, sideways manner.

furtive (FUR TIHV) *adj.:* secretive; trying not to be seen.

cowering (KOW UHR IHNG) *v.:* used as *adj.:* crouching or hiding in shame or fear.

oppress (UH PREHS) *v.:* hold down unfairly.

INTO THE SHORT STORY

This story is set in the American South in the 1960s. At this time, the civil rights movement was taking place. African Americans struggled to gain equal treatment. In the South, African Americans had been treated like second-class citizens since the time of slavery. Finally, southern African Americans' lives were changing. Their expectations were also changing. You will see how this affects the way the characters in the story behave.

SKILLS FOCUS

Literary Skills
Understand character traits.

Reading Skills
Make inferences about characters.

EVERYDAY USE

For Your Grandmama

By Alice Walker

Quilts on the Line (1990) by Anna Belle Lee Washington/SuperStock

I will wait for her in the yard that Maggie and I made so clean and wavy yesterday afternoon. A yard like this is more comfortable than most people know. It is not just a yard. It is like an extended living room. When the hard clay is swept clean as a floor and the fine sand around the edges lined with tiny, irregular grooves, anyone can come and sit and look up into the elm tree and wait for the breezes that never come inside the house.

Maggie will be nervous until after her sister goes: She will stand hopelessly in corners, homely and ashamed of the burn
10 scars down her arms and legs, eyeing her sister with a mixture of envy and awe. **A** She thinks her sister has held life always in the palm of one hand, that "no" is a word the world never learned to say to her. **B**

"Everyday Use" from *In Love & Trouble: Stories of Black Women* by Alice Walker. Copyright © 1973 by Alice Walker. Reproduced by permission of **Harcourt, Inc.** and electronic format by permission of **Wendy Weil Agency, Inc.**

A (HERE'S HOW)

Language Coach

Because Maggie is ashamed of the way she looks, I think *homely* means "unattractive." **Antonyms** are words that have opposite meanings. I think *attractive* would be a good antonym for *homely*.

B (HERE'S HOW)

Reading Focus

I just read that Maggie will hide in corners when her sister is around. From this evidence, I can **infer** that Maggie is shy. I think Maggie feels she is not as good as her sister.

Vocabulary

I am not sure what the word *embrace* means. I know that the family on TV is happy to see each other. I read on and learned that when the child sees her parents, she "wraps them in her arms." I think the family members are hugging. I looked up *embrace* in my dictionary, and it means "hug," so I was right.

Vocabulary

Circle the word in this sentence that tells you what an *orchid* is.

Literary Focus

This paragraph gives me a good physical description of the narrator, Mama. I learn that the narrator is a large woman with "rough, man-working hands." I think this description gives me a sense of the narrator's **character traits**, as well. The narrator works outside all day and does tasks usually reserved for men. I think a character trait of the narrator is that she has a strong work ethic.

You've no doubt seen those TV shows where the child who has "made it" is confronted, as a surprise, by her own mother and father, tottering in weakly from backstage. (A pleasant surprise, of course: What would they do if parent and child came on the show only to curse out and insult each other?) On TV mother and child embrace and smile into each other's faces. **A**

20 Sometimes the mother and father weep; the child wraps them in her arms and leans across the table to tell how she would not have made it without their help. I have seen these programs.

IN OTHER WORDS I wait for her in the yard Maggie and I cleaned yesterday. Maggie will be nervous when her sister is with us. Maggie will stand in corners by herself, embarrassed at how she looks. Maggie has burn scars down her arms and legs. Maggie will look at her sister with both respect and jealousy. She thinks her sister has had an easy life. There are TV shows where successful children meet their parents again. They hug and cry on TV. I have seen TV shows like these.

Sometimes I dream a dream in which Dee and I are suddenly brought together on a TV program of this sort. Out of a dark and soft-seated limousine I am ushered into a bright room filled with many people. There I meet a smiling, gray, sporty man like Johnny Carson[1] who shakes my hand and tells me what a fine girl I have. Then we are on the stage, and Dee is embracing me with tears in her eyes. She pins on my dress a large orchid,

30 even though she had told me once that she thinks orchids are tacky flowers. **B**

In real life I am a large, big-boned woman with rough, man-working hands. In the winter I wear flannel nightgowns to bed and overalls during the day. I can kill and clean a hog as mercilessly as a man. My fat keeps me hot in zero weather. I can work outside all day, breaking ice to get water for washing; I can eat pork liver cooked over the open fire minutes after it

---

1. **Johnny Carson** was the former host of *The Tonight Show* who lived from 1925 to 2005.

comes steaming from the hog. **C** One winter I knocked a bull calf straight in the brain between the eyes with a sledgehammer

40 and had the meat hung up to chill before nightfall. But of course all this does not show on television. I am the way my daughter would want me to be: a hundred pounds lighter, my skin like an uncooked barley pancake. My hair glistens in the hot bright lights. Johnny Carson has much to do to keep up with my quick and witty tongue.

But that is a mistake. I know even before I wake up. Who ever knew a Johnson with a quick tongue? Who can even imagine me looking a strange white man in the eye? It seems to me I have talked to them always with one foot raised in

50 flight, with my head turned in whichever way is farthest from them. **D** Dee, though. She would always look anyone in the eye. Hesitation was no part of her nature. **E**

IN OTHER WORDS Sometimes I dream that my daughter Dee and I are on a TV program. The TV host tells me what a good daughter I have. I picture myself as my daughter would want me to look and act. In my dream I am beautiful, smart, and I have an answer for everything. In real life I am the opposite of my dream. I am a large woman who works hard all day. I would never look a strange white man in the eye, as I did in my dream. But Dee would look anyone in the eye.

"How do I look, Mama?" Maggie says, showing just enough of her thin body enveloped in pink skirt and red blouse for me to know she's there, almost hidden by the door.

"Come out into the yard," I say.

Have you ever seen a lame animal, perhaps a dog run over by some careless person rich enough to own a car, sidle up to someone who is ignorant enough to be kind to him? **F** That is

60 the way my Maggie walks. She has been like this, chin on chest, eyes on ground, feet in shuffle, ever since the fire that burned the other house to the ground.

D **YOUR TURN**

Literary Focus

Here, the narrator continues to describe herself. What word or words can you now use to describe a **character trait** of the narrator?

_____

E **HERE'S HOW**

Vocabulary

I am not sure what *hesitation* means. I know that Dee will look at anyone, so she must be proud and brave. I looked up *hesitation* in the dictionary, and it means "the act of pausing before saying or doing something." I think this **character trait** shows that Dee is sure of herself.

F **YOUR TURN**

Reading Focus

Sidle means "walk slowly and sideways." What can you **infer** about Maggie because she *sidles*?

_____

_____

_____

_____

Dee is lighter than Maggie, with nicer hair and a fuller figure. She's a woman now, though sometimes I forget. How long ago was it that the other house burned? Ten, twelve years? Sometimes I can still hear the flames and feel Maggie's arms sticking to me, her hair smoking and her dress falling off her in little black papery flakes. Her eyes seemed stretched open, blazed open by the flames reflected in them. **A** And Dee. I see 70 her standing off under the sweet gum tree[2] she used to dig gum out of, a look of concentration on her face as she watched the last dingy gray board of the house fall in toward the red-hot brick chimney. **B** Why don't you do a dance around the ashes? I'd wanted to ask her. She had hated the house that much.

IN OTHER WORDS Maggie is a very shy girl. She walks like she is a scared animal. Maggie has walked like that since our other house burned down in a fire 10 or 12 years ago. I can still remember that fire. I carried Maggie out of the burning house while Dee watched from the yard. Dee had always hated that house.

I used to think she hated Maggie, too. But that was before we raised the money, the church and me, to send her to Augusta to school. She used to read to us without pity, forcing words, lies, other folks' habits, whole lives upon us two, sitting trapped and ignorant underneath her voice. She washed us in a river of 80 make-believe, burned us with a lot of knowledge we didn't necessarily need to know. Pressed us to her with the serious ways she read, to shove us away at just the moment, like dimwits, we seemed about to understand. **C D**

Dee wanted nice things. A yellow organdy[3] dress to wear to her graduation from high school; black pumps to match a green suit she'd made from an old suit somebody gave me. She was determined to stare down any disaster in her efforts. Her eyelids would not flicker for minutes at a time. Often I fought off the

2. A **gum tree** is a type of tree in the Eucalyptus family.
3. **Organdy** (AWR GUHN DEE) is a light, transparent fabric made from cotton.

90 temptation to shake her. At sixteen she had a style of her own: and knew what style was.

I never had an education myself. After second grade the school closed down. Don't ask me why: In 1927 colored asked fewer questions than they do now. Sometimes Maggie reads to me. She stumbles along good-naturedly but can't see well. She knows she is not bright. Like good looks and money, quickness passed her by. She will marry John Thomas (who has mossy teeth in an earnest face), and then I'll be free to sit here and I guess just sing church songs to myself. Although I never was a good singer. Never could carry a tune. I was always better at a man's job. I 100 used to love to milk till I was hooked in the side in '49. Cows are soothing and slow and don't bother you, unless you try to milk them the wrong way.

IN OTHER WORDS I used to think that Dee hated Maggie, just like she hated our other house. But that was before I raised money with the church to send Dee to school. Dee used to read aloud to us even if we did not want her to. She would make us feel stupid, like we were not as good as she was. I stopped school after second grade. Maggie is not smart, either, and she is not pretty like Dee. But Maggie is going to marry John Thomas. Then I will be alone. I could sing church songs to myself, but I'm better at doing men's work on the farm than I am at singing.

I have deliberately turned my back on the house. It is three rooms, just like the one that burned, except the roof is tin; they don't make shingle roofs anymore. There are no real windows, just some holes cut in the sides, like the portholes in a ship, but not round and not square, with rawhide holding the shutters up on the outside. This house is in a pasture, too, like the other one. **F** No doubt when Dee sees it she will want to tear it down. 110 She wrote me once that no matter where we "choose" to live, she will manage to come see us. But she will never bring her friends.

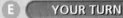

E **YOUR TURN**

Reading Focus

Underline the description of Dee's reading from the previous page. Then circle the description of Maggie's reading in this paragraph. How are they different? What can you **infer** about what each daughter is like?

_____

_____

_____

_____

_____

F **HERE'S HOW**

Vocabulary

I am not sure what a *pasture* is. It sounds like Mama and Maggie live on a farm because Mama has milked cows and killed hogs. I looked up *pasture* and it is "an area with grass for grazing animals." I was right that Mama lives in a rural area and raises animals.

YOUR TURN

Reading Focus

Underline a word or phrase that helps you **infer** what Dee's friends thought about her.

YOUR TURN

Vocabulary

Re-read this paragraph. What is happening with Dee here? Use your understanding of what is happening to help you write a definition for *recompose*.

_____

_____

_____

HERE'S HOW

Reading Focus

Maggie groans when she sees the man. Then Mama says Maggie's groan is like the sound you make when you see a nearby snake. I can **infer** that Maggie is shocked by Dee's companion.

Maggie and I thought about this and Maggie asked me, "Mama, when did Dee ever *have* any friends?"

She had a few. Furtive boys in pink shirts hanging about on washday after school. Nervous girls who never laughed. Impressed with her, they worshiped the well-turned phrase, the cute shape, the humor that erupted like bubbles in lye.[4] She read to them. **A**

When she was courting Jimmy T, she didn't have much time 120 to pay to us but turned all her faultfinding power on him. He *flew* to marry a cheap city girl from a family of ignorant, flashy people. She hardly had time to recompose herself. **B**

When she comes, I will meet—but there they are!

IN OTHER WORDS Our house is small with no real windows, just like the other house that burned. Dee said she would visit us anywhere; but she would not bring her friends. Maggie wondered if Dee had any friends. Dee had a few. She wanted to marry Jimmy T, but he married someone else.

Maggie attempts to make a dash for the house, in her shuffling way, but I stay her with my hand. "Come back here," I say. And she stops and tries to dig a well in the sand with her toe.

It is hard to see them clearly through the strong sun. But even the first glimpse of leg out of the car tells me it is Dee. Her 130 feet were always neat looking, as if God himself shaped them with a certain style. From the other side of the car comes a short, stocky man. Hair is all over his head a foot long and hanging from his chin like a kinky mule tail. I hear Maggie suck in her breath. "Uhnnnh" is what it sounds like. Like when you see the wriggling end of a snake just in front of your foot on the road. "Uhnnnh." **C**

Dee next. A dress down to the ground, in this hot weather. A dress so loud it hurts my eyes. There are yellows and oranges enough to throw back the light of the sun. I feel my whole face

_____

4. **Lye** (LY) is a chemical once used to make soap.

140 warming from the heat waves it throws out. Earrings gold, too, and hanging down to her shoulders. Bracelets dangling and making noises when she moves her arm up to shake the folds of the dress out of her armpits. The dress is loose and flows, and as she walks closer, I like it. I hear Maggie go "Uhnnnh" again. It is her sister's hair. It stands straight up like the wool on a sheep. It is black as night and around the edges are two long pigtails that rope about like small lizards disappearing behind her ears. **D**

IN OTHER WORDS A car pulls up to the house. Dee is here. Maggie tries to run back inside the house, but I make her stay. A man comes out of the car first. He has long hair all over his face and head. Maggie makes a sound like she has seen a snake. Then Dee comes out of the car in a long, bright dress. Maggie makes that sound again when she sees Dee's hair. Dee's hair stands straight up.

"Wa-su-zo-Tean-o![5]" she says, coming on in that gliding way the dress makes her move. The short, stocky fellow with
150 the hair to his navel is all grinning, and he follows up with "Asalamalakim,[6] my mother and sister!" He moves to hug Maggie but she falls back, right up against the back of my chair. I feel her trembling there, and when I look up I see the perspiration falling off her chin. **E**

"Don't get up," says Dee. Since I am stout, it takes something of a push. **F** You can see me trying to move a second or two before I make it. She turns, showing white heels through her sandals, and goes back to the car. Out she peeks next with a Polaroid. She stoops down quickly and lines up picture after
160 picture of me sitting there in front of the house with Maggie cowering behind me. She never takes a shot without making sure the house is included. When a cow comes nibbling around in the edge of the yard, she snaps it and me and Maggie *and* the house.

---

5. **Wa-su-zo-Tean-o** is a greeting used by the Buganda people of Uganda that means "good morning."
6. **Asalamalakim** (AH SUH LAHM AH LAY KOOM) is an Arabic greeting meaning "peace be with you."

D **YOUR TURN**

Literary Focus

Re-read this paragraph. How does Dee's appearance reflect what you already know about her **character traits**?

_____

_____

_____

_____

_____

E **HERE'S HOW**

Reading Focus

Dee and the man speak to Maggie and Mama in other languages. I can **infer** that Dee has made some changes in her life. I also get the feeling that both Dee and the man feel as if they are somehow better than Mama and Maggie.

F **HERE'S HOW**

Vocabulary

I already know that Mama is a large woman, so I think that *stout* means "large." I looked *stout* up in the dictionary, and I was right.

Dee is taking pictures of the house. How does this fit with your idea of how Dee felt about her childhood home?

_____

_____

B HERE'S HOW

Reading Focus

From the way that the man tries to shake Maggie's hand, I can **infer** that he is trying to show off his manners, which are different from Maggie's or Mama's. Mama also calls the man "Asalamalakim," which refers to the man's greeting when he got out of the car. I can infer that Mama calls him this instead of his real name because she does not like him.

C YOUR TURN

Vocabulary

Oppress has the word *press* in it. Imagine a hand pushing down on something. How do you think *oppress* is like *press*? Check your answer by looking up *oppress* in the dictionary.

D HERE'S HOW

Reading Focus

This paragraph says that "Wangero (Dee) was getting tired." I can **infer** that she is impatient with her mother. Wangero does not think Mama is very smart.

Then she puts the Polaroid in the back seat of the car and comes up and kisses me on the forehead. **A**

Meanwhile, Asalamalakim is going through motions with Maggie's hand. Maggie's hand is as limp as a fish, and probably as cold, despite the sweat, and she keeps trying to pull it back. It looks like Asalamalakim wants to shake hands but wants to

170 do it fancy. Or maybe he don't know how people shake hands. Anyhow, he soon gives up on Maggie. **B**

IN OTHER WORDS Dee gets out of the car and says "good morning" in an African language. The short man from the car gives an Arabic greeting. The man moves to hug Maggie but she backs up. Dee grabs a camera from the car and takes pictures of me and Maggie in front of the house. The man tries to shake Maggie's hand, but Maggie, nervous as ever, does not want anything to do with him.

"Well," I say. "Dee."

"No, Mama," she says. "Not 'Dee,' Wangero Leewanika Kemanjo!"[7]

"What happened to 'Dee'?" I wanted to know.

"She's dead," Wangero said. "I couldn't bear it any longer, being named after the people who oppress me." **C**

"You know as well as me you was named after your aunt Dicie," I said. Dicie is my sister. She named Dee. We called her

180 "Big Dee" after Dee was born.

"But who was *she* named after?" asked Wangero.

"I guess after Grandma Dee," I said.

"And who was she named after?" asked Wangero.

"Her mother," I said, and saw Wangero was getting tired. "That's about as far back as I can trace it," I said. Though, in fact, I probably could have carried it back beyond the Civil War through the branches. **D**

"Well," said Asalamalakim, "there you are."

---

7. **Wangero Leewanika Kemanjo** are names from a variety of groups in East Africa.

"Uhnnnh," I heard Maggie say.

190 "There I was not," I said, "before 'Dicie' cropped up in our family, so why should I try to trace it that far back?"

He just stood there grinning, looking down on me like somebody inspecting a Model A[8] car. Every once in a while he and Wangero sent eye signals over my head. **E**

"How do you pronounce this name?" I asked.

"You don't have to call me by it if you don't want to," said Wangero.

"Why shouldn't I?" I asked. "If that's what you want us to call you, we'll call you."

200 "I know it might sound awkward at first," said Wangero.

"I'll get used to it," I said. "Ream it out again." **F**

IN OTHER WORDS Dee says her name is now Wangero. She does not want to be named after slave owners. I tell her that the women in our family have had the name Dee, short for "Dicie," for generations. But I tell Wangero I will call her what she wants to be called.

Well, soon we got the name out of the way. Asalamalakim had a name twice as long and three times as hard. After I tripped over it two or three times, he told me to just call him Hakim-a-barber.[9] I wanted to ask him was he a barber, but I didn't really think he was, so I didn't ask.

"You must belong to those beef-cattle peoples down the road," I said. They said "Asalamalakim" when they met you, too, but they didn't shake hands. Always too busy: feeding the cattle,
210 fixing the fences, putting up salt-lick shelters, throwing down hay. When the white folks poisoned some of the herd, the men stayed up all night with rifles in their hands. I walked a mile and a half just to see the sight.

Hakim-a-barber said, "I accept some of their doctrines, but farming and raising cattle is not my style." **G** (They didn't tell

---

8. **Model A** was a type of car produced by Ford in 1903 and again in 1927.
9. **Hakim-a-barber** is a mispronounced version of the Arabic name Hakim al Baba; Hakim means "leader."

E YOUR TURN

Reading Focus

Inspecting means "looking at closely." What can you **infer** about Wangero and her friend based on the way they are looking at Mama?

_____

_____

_____

_____

F HERE'S HOW

Vocabulary

I am not sure what the expression "ream it out again" means. Mama is asking Dee to repeat her new name, so she can better understand it. The conversation does not seem pleasant, though. I checked a dictionary, and *ream* means "squeeze." Based on this definition and the context of the phrase, I think Mama is asking Dee to say her new name again.

G YOUR TURN

Vocabulary

Doctrines are sets of beliefs held by a religious group. What does this sentence tell you about Hakim-a-barber?

_____

_____

_____

A (HERE'S HOW)

Literary Focus

I can see that Wangero and Hakim-a-barber have different **character traits**. Hakim-a-barber does not eat certain foods, but Wangero likes all of the food from her childhood.

B (YOUR TURN)

Literary Focus

Think about Wangero's **character traits**. Then answer the following question: Why is Wangero delighted by everything?

_____

_____

_____

_____

_____

_____

C (YOUR TURN)

Vocabulary

Re-read these two lines to learn how Uncle Buddy made the churn. Use this information to help you come up with a definition for the word *whittle*. Use a dictionary to check your answer.

_____

_____

_____

me, and I didn't ask, whether Wangero—Dee—had really gone and married him.)

We sat down to eat and right away he said he didn't eat collards[10], and pork was unclean. Wangero, though, went on 220 through the chitlins[11] and corn bread, the greens, and everything else. **A** She talked a blue streak over the sweet potatoes. Everything delighted her. Even the fact that we still used the benches her daddy made for the table when we couldn't afford to buy chairs. **B**

IN OTHER WORDS The man says to call him Hakim-a-barber. There are people who live down the street that use the same Arabic greeting as the man used. One time white people killed their cows. I did not ask if Hakim-a-barber and Wangero were married. We sat down to eat, but Hakim-a-barber did not eat our food. Wangero, though, liked everything.

"Oh, Mama!" she cried. Then turned to Hakim-a-barber. "I never knew how lovely these benches are. You can feel the rump prints," she said, running her hands underneath her and along the bench. Then she gave a sigh, and her hand closed over Grandma Dee's butter dish. "That's it!" she said. "I knew there 230 was something I wanted to ask you if I could have." She jumped up from the table and went over in the corner where the churn[12] stood, the milk in it clabber[13] by now. She looked at the churn and looked at it.

"This churn top is what I need," she said. "Didn't Uncle Buddy whittle it out of a tree you all used to have?" **C**

"Yes," I said.

"Uh huh," she said happily. "And I want the dasher,[14] too."

"Uncle Buddy whittle that, too?" asked the barber.

Dee (Wangero) looked up at me.

---

10. **Collards** (KOL UHRDS) are a vegetable related to the cabbage that has dark green edible leaves.
11. **Chitlins** are the large intestines of a pig, boiled or stewed.
12. A **churn** (CHURN) is a device used to make butter.
13. **Clabber** (KLAB UHR) is thickened or curdled milk, used in making butter.
14. A **dasher** (DASH UHR) is a pole that stirs the milk in a churn.

240   "Aunt Dee's first husband whittled the dash," said Maggie so low you almost couldn't hear her. "His name was Henry, but they called him Stash."

     "Maggie's brain is like an elephant's," Wangero said, laughing. "I can use the churn top as a centerpiece for the alcove table," she said, sliding a plate over the churn, "and I'll think of something artistic to do with the dasher." **D**

     When she finished wrapping the dasher, the handle stuck out. I took it for a moment in my hands. You didn't even have to look close to see where hands pushing the dasher up and down
250 to make butter had left a kind of sink in the wood. In fact, there were a lot of small sinks; you could see where thumbs and fingers had sunk into the wood. It was beautiful light-yellow wood, from a tree that grew in the yard where Big Dee and Stash had lived.

IN OTHER WORDS Dee (Wangero) loved the old benches we sat on. She wanted to take the butter churn with her as a decoration for her house. She saw it as a piece of art, and not the important tool that it was. Uncle Buddy made the churn years ago from a tree. Dee (Wangero) also wanted the pole that stirs the milk inside the churn. You could see where all the hands had used the churn to make butter over the years.

     After dinner Dee (Wangero) went to the trunk at the foot of my bed and started rifling through it. Maggie hung back in the kitchen over the dishpan. Out came Wangero with two quilts. They had been pieced by Grandma Dee, and then Big Dee and me had hung them on the quilt frames on the front porch and quilted them. One was in the Lone Star pattern. The other was
260 Walk Around the Mountain. In both of them were scraps of dresses Grandma Dee had worn fifty and more years ago. Bits and pieces of Grandpa Jarrell's paisley shirts. And one teeny faded blue piece, about the size of a penny matchbox, that was from Great Grandpa Ezra's uniform that he wore in the Civil War. **E**

D   **YOUR TURN**

Literary Focus
Wangero sees the churn as art. She does not think of it as a tool. What **character trait** of Wangero's does this highlight?

_____

_____

_____

E   **QUICK CHECK**

What are these quilts made of?

_____

_____

_____

"Mama," Wangero said sweet as a bird. "Can I have these old quilts?"

I heard something fall in the kitchen, and a minute later the kitchen door slammed. **A**

270 "Why don't you take one or two of the others?" I asked. "These old things was just done by me and Big Dee from some tops your grandma pieced before she died."

"No," said Wangero. "I don't want those. They are stitched around the borders by machine."

"That'll make them last better," I said.

"That's not the point," said Wangero. "These are all pieces of dresses Grandma used to wear. She did all this stitching by hand. Imagine!" She held the quilts securely in her arms, stroking them.

"Some of the pieces, like those lavender ones, come from

280 old clothes her mother handed down to her," I said, moving up to

© The Newark Museum/Art Resource, NY

touch the quilts. Dee (Wangero) moved back just enough so that I couldn't reach the quilts. They already belonged to her.

"Imagine!" she breathed again, clutching them closely to her bosom. **B**

"The truth is," I said, "I promised to give them quilts to Maggie, for when she marries John Thomas."

IN OTHER WORDS Dee (Wangero) went into my room and found two old quilts in my trunk. The quilts were made by Grandma Dee, Aunt Dee, and me. Both quilts had patches of Grandma Dee's old dresses in them, along with pieces of Grandpa Jarrell's shirts and Great Grandpa Ezra's Civil War uniform. Dee asked me if she could have the quilts. I heard Maggie slam the kitchen door. I told Dee to take other, newer quilts that would last longer. But Dee held on to the quilts like she already owned them. I told her that I had already promised to give the quilts to Maggie when she marries John Thomas.

She gasped like a bee had stung her.

"Maggie can't appreciate these quilts!" she said. "She'd probably be backward enough to put them to everyday use." **C**

290 "I reckon she would," I said. "God knows I been saving 'em for long enough with nobody using 'em. I hope she will!" I didn't want to bring up how I had offered Dee (Wangero) a quilt when she went away to college. Then she had told me they were old-fashioned, out of style.

"But they're *priceless!*" she was saying now, furiously; for she has a temper. "Maggie would put them on the bed and in five years they'd be in rags. Less than that!"

"She can always make some more," I said. "Maggie knows how to quilt."

300 Dee (Wangero) looked at me with hatred. "You just will not understand. The point is *these* quilts, these quilts!"

"Well," I said, stumped. "What would *you* do with them?"

B **YOUR TURN**

Reading Focus

Re-read the previous two paragraphs. What can you **infer** about Dee (Wangero) based on her actions? Be sure to list the evidence that supports your inference.

_____

_____

_____

_____

_____

C **LITERARY ANALYSIS**

Re-read lines 285–289. How does the title of this story seem more important now?

_____

_____

_____

_____

_____

_____

_____

_____

_____

_____

_____

A **LITERARY ANALYSIS**

Why does Dee (Wangero) like the quilts?

_____

_____

_____

_____

_____

B **YOUR TURN**

Reading Focus

What can you **infer** about how Mama feels about Maggie? What can you infer about how Mama feels about Dee at this moment? Underline parts of the story that are evidence for your answer.

_____

_____

_____

_____

_____

_____

_____

"Hang them," she said. As if that was the only thing you _could_ do with quilts. **A**

Maggie by now was standing in the door. I could almost hear the sound her feet made as they scraped over each other.

"She can have them, Mama," she said, like somebody used to never winning anything or having anything reserved for her. "I can 'member Grandma Dee without the quilts."

IN OTHER WORDS Dee (Wangero) could not believe that I was going to give the quilts to Maggie. She said Maggie should not have the quilts. I once tried to give Dee one of the quilts but she did not want it back then. She thought it was too old-fashioned. Maggie would use the quilts all the time, but Dee thought the quilts should hang on the walls. Maggie came in and said that Dee could have the quilts. Maggie said she could remember Grandma Dee even if she did not have her quilts.

310   I looked at her hard. She had filled her bottom lip with checkerberry snuff, and it gave her face a kind of dopey, hangdog look. It was Grandma Dee and Big Dee who taught her how to quilt herself. She stood there with her scarred hands hidden in the folds of her skirt. She looked at her sister with something like fear, but she wasn't mad at her. This was Maggie's portion. This was the way she knew God to work.

When I looked at her like that, something hit me in the top of my head and ran down to the soles of my feet. Just like when I'm in church and the spirit of God touches me and I get happy
320   and shout. I did something I never had done before: hugged Maggie to me, then dragged her on into the room, snatched the quilts out of Miss Wangero's hands, and dumped them into Maggie's lap. Maggie just sat there on my bed with her mouth open. **B**

"Take one or two of the others," I said to Dee.

But she turned without a word and went out to Hakim-a-barber.

"You just don't understand," she said, as Maggie and I came out to the car.

330   "What don't I understand?" I wanted to know.

"Your heritage," she said. And then she turned to Maggie, kissed her, and said, "You ought to try to make something of yourself, too, Maggie. **C** It's really a new day for us. But from the way you and Mama still live, you'd never know it."

She put on some sunglasses that hid everything above the tip of her nose and her chin.

Maggie smiled, maybe at the sunglasses. But a real smile, not scared. After we watched the car dust settle, I asked Maggie to bring me a dip of snuff. And then the two of us sat there just

340   enjoying, until it was time to go in the house and go to bed. **D**

IN OTHER WORDS When I saw the way Maggie looked at Dee in fear, something hit me. I did something that I had never done before. I went over to Maggie and I hugged her. I brought her into the room with me. I took the quilts out of Miss Wangero's hands and gave them to Maggie. Maggie just sat on my bed with her mouth open. She was surprised. I told Dee (Wangero) to take one of the other quilts. Dee told me that I just do not understand my heritage. She then told Maggie that it was time for her to make something of herself. Dee put big sunglasses on that hid most of her face. Dee and Hakim-a-barber got in the car and left. Maggie smiled. She was not scared anymore.

C **HERE'S HOW**

Vocabulary

I do not know the exact meaning of the word *heritage*. Based on what I have read, I think *heritage* might have to do with the past. It also has the same root as the verb *inherit*.

D **YOUR TURN**

Literary Focus

What new **character trait** does Maggie show at the end of the story?

_____

_____

_____

_____

_____

_____

Skills Practice

Everyday Use
For Your Grandmama

USE A CHARACTER TRAIT CHART

DIRECTIONS: List the **character traits** that the story reveals about Mama, Maggie, and Dee (Wangero) in the boxes to the right.

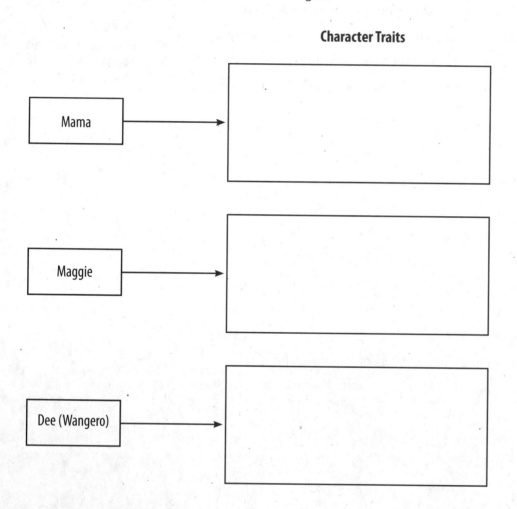

Character Traits

Mama →

Maggie →

Dee (Wangero) →

Applying Your Skills

Everyday Use
For Your Grandmama

LITERARY FOCUS: CHARACTER TRAITS

DIRECTIONS: Choose one of the following characters from the story: Mama, Maggie, or Dee (Wangero). Think about the **character traits** the story reveals about that character. On the lines below, write a short paragraph that describes the character you chose. Use the charts you made on the Skills Practice page to help you.

_____

_____

_____

_____

READING FOCUS: MAKING INFERENCES ABOUT CHARACTERS

DIRECTIONS: Complete the chart below by **making inferences** about the characters in "Everyday Use: For Your Grandmama." One has been provided as an example.

Character	Evidence	Inferences
Maggie	thinks she is unattractive; ashamed; looks at her sister with envy and awe	Maggie feels inferior to Dee. She may be jealous of Dee's good looks.
Mama		
Dee		

VOCABULARY REVIEW

DIRECTIONS: Each sentence below includes an underlined vocabulary word. Circle the sentence in which the underlined word is used correctly.

1. The dictator worked to <u>oppress</u> his people by creating cruel laws.

2. I saw the woman <u>sidle</u> around the track, her hair flying behind her.

Two Kinds

By Amy Tan

LITERARY FOCUS: CHARACTER INTERACTIONS AND MOTIVATION

Motivation is what leads someone to do something. Perhaps your motivation for having a job is so you can buy a car. It is the wish to have a car that motivates you to work. Characters in stories are motivated, too. Sometimes one character is motivated to do something, but another character and his or her motivations get in the way. Conflict results from these **character interactions**. In "Two Kinds," a mother and daughter are motivated to do different things. The story focuses on the conflict that happens between them.

READING FOCUS: MAKING INFERENCES ABOUT MOTIVATION

An **inference** is an educated guess. You make inferences based on information that you have. Inferences can be very helpful when you are trying to figure out a character's motivation. Watch for what the character says, does, and thinks. For example, you might try to infer what motivates a character to wake up at dawn and practice ice skating before leaving for school. You might guess that the student wants to become a professional figure skater. The desire to become a professional might be her motivation.

VOCABULARY

Make flashcards for the words below. On each card, write the word on the front and its definition on the back.

prodigy (PRAHD UH JEE) *n.*: child having extraordinary talent.

listlessly (LIHST LIHS LEE) *adv.*: without energy or interest.

mesmerizing (MEHS MUH RYZ IHNG) *v.* used as *adj.*: spellbinding; fascinating.

discordant (DIHS KAWR DUHNT) *adj.*: clashing; not harmonious.

fiasco (FEE AS KOH) *n.*: total failure.

nonchalantly (NAHN SHUH LUHNT LEE) *adv.*: without interest; indifferently.

INTO THE STORY

The main character in "Two Kinds," Jing-mei, was born in the United States. Her parents were born in China. While the family lives in the United States, they are still very much connected to the parents' way of life in China. As you will read, this connection causes conflict between the two generations.

SKILLS FOCUS

Literary Skills
Understand character interactions; understand character motivation.

Reading Skills
Make inferences about motivation.

TWO KINDS

By Amy Tan

My mother believed you could be anything you wanted to be in America. You could open a restaurant. You could work for the government and get good retirement. You could buy a house with almost no money down. You could become rich. You could become instantly famous.

© Contemplation (2006) by Hao Shiming (b. 1977, He Ze, Shandon Province, China). Chinese ink on silk (90 x 71 cm). Courtesy of the Artist

10 "Of course you can be prodigy, too," my mother told me when I was nine. **A** "You can be best anything. What does Auntie Lindo know? Her daughter, she is only best tricky."

America was where all my mother's hopes lay. She had come here in 1949 after losing everything in China: her mother and father, her family home, her first husband, and two daughters, twin baby girls. But she never looked back with regret. There were so many ways for things to get better.

We didn't immediately pick the right kind of prodigy. At first my mother thought I could be a Chinese Shirley Temple.[1]
20 We'd watch Shirley's old movies on TV as though they were training films. My mother would poke my arm and say, "*Ni kan*"—You watch. And I would see Shirley tapping her feet, or singing a sailor song, or pursing her lips into a very round O while saying, "Oh my goodness." **B**

IN OTHER WORDS The narrator, Jing-mei, begins by telling about her mother's views of America as a land of opportunity. Jing-mei's mother immigrated to America in 1949 after facing

---

1. **Shirley Temple** (1928–): child movie star who was popular during the1930s. Mothers all across the United States tried to set their daughters' hair to look like Shirley Temple's sausage curls.

A **HERE'S HOW**

Vocabulary

I suspect that Jing-mei, the narrator, feels pressured by her mother to do well. Jing-mei is only nine and her mother expects her to become a *prodigy*—"a child having extraordinary talent."

B **HERE'S HOW**

Reading Focus

I can **infer** that Jing-mei's mother wants her daughter to find fame and fortune to make a good life for herself in America.

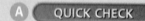

A **QUICK CHECK**

Does Jing-mei's haircut turn out as her mother hoped?

_____

_____

B **HERE'S HOW**

Literary Focus

I think this **character interaction** between Jing-mei and her mother may lead to conflicts, or problems. Jing-mei wants to make her parents proud, but her mother has very high expectations.

much devastation in China. She hopes her daughter will be a prodigy, maybe as a movie star.

"*Ni kan*," said my mother as Shirley's eyes flooded with tears. "You already know how. Don't need talent for crying!"

Soon after my mother got this idea about Shirley Temple, she took me to a beauty training school in the Mission district and put me in the hands of a student who could barely hold 30 the scissors without shaking. Instead of getting big fat curls, I emerged with an uneven mass of crinkly black fuzz. My mother dragged me off to the bathroom and tried to wet down my hair.

"You look like Negro Chinese," she lamented, as if I had done this on purpose. **A**

The instructor of the beauty training school had to lop off these soggy clumps to make my hair even again. "Peter Pan is very popular these days," the instructor assured my mother. I now had hair the length of a boy's, with straight-across bangs that hung at a slant two inches above my eyebrows. I liked the 40 haircut and it made me actually look forward to my future fame.

In fact, in the beginning, I was just as excited as my mother, maybe even more so. I pictured this prodigy part of me as many different images, trying each one on for size. I was a dainty ballerina girl standing by the curtains, waiting to hear the right music that would send me floating on my tiptoes. I was like the Christ child lifted out of the straw manger, crying with holy indignity. I was Cinderella stepping from her pumpkin carriage with sparkly cartoon music filling the air.

In all of my imaginings, I was filled with a sense that 50 I would soon become *perfect*. My mother and father would adore me. I would be beyond reproach. I would never feel the need to sulk for anything. **B**

IN OTHER WORDS Jing-mei's mother takes her for a haircut, but she ends up looking more like Peter Pan than Shirley Temple. Not discouraged, Jing-mei soon becomes excited about becoming a prodigy, too. She tries to be perfect and wants her parents' approval. Jing-mei imagines herself as a ballerina, the Christ child, and Cinderella.

© Photodisc/Superstock

But sometimes the prodigy in me became impatient. "If you don't hurry up and get me out of here, I'm disappearing for good," it warned. "And then you'll always be nothing."

Every night after dinner, my mother and I would sit at the Formica kitchen table. She would present new tests, taking

60 her examples from stories of amazing children she had read in *Ripley's Believe It or Not,* or *Good Housekeeping, Reader's Digest,* and a dozen other magazines she kept in a pile in our bathroom. My mother got these magazines from people whose houses she cleaned. And since she cleaned many houses each week, we had a great assortment. She would look through them all, searching for stories about remarkable children.

The first night she brought out a story about a three-year-old boy who knew the capitals of all the states and even most of the European countries. A teacher was quoted as saying the little boy

70 could also pronounce the names of the foreign cities correctly.

"What's the capital of Finland?" my mother asked me, looking at the magazine story. **C**

All I knew was the capital of California, because Sacramento was the name of the street we lived on in Chinatown. "Nairobi!"[2] I guessed, saying the most foreign word I could think of. She checked to see if that was possibly one way to pronounce "Helsinki" before showing me the answer. **D**

IN OTHER WORDS As time passes, Jing-mei begins to worry that she may not become a prodigy. Jing-mei's mother refuses to give up; she reads many magazine articles about

2. **Nairobi** (NY ROH BEE): capital of Kenya, a nation in Africa.

C YOUR TURN

Reading Focus
What **motivates** Jing-mei's mother to ask her daughter this question?

_____

_____

_____

_____

D LITERARY ANALYSIS

Why does Jing-mei take a wild guess at this question?

_____

_____

_____

_____

_____

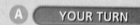

Literary Focus

How would you describe the relationship, or **character interaction**, between Jing-mei and her mother now?

_____

_____

_____

_____

_____

_____

Vocabulary

Re-read this paragraph and think about how Jing-mei treats her mother's tests now. Considering Jing-mei's behavior, what do you think the word *listlessly* means?

_____

_____

_____

The tests got harder—multiplying numbers in my head, finding the queen of hearts in a deck of cards, trying to stand on my head without using my hands, predicting the daily temperatures in Los Angeles, New York, and London.

One night I had to look at a page from the Bible for three minutes and then report everything I could remember. "Now Jehoshaphat had riches and honor in abundance and . . . that's all I remember, Ma," I said.

And after seeing my mother's disappointed face once again, something inside of me began to die. I hated the tests, the raised hopes and failed expectations. Before going to bed that night, I looked in the mirror above the bathroom sink and when I saw only my face staring back—and that it would always be this ordinary face—I began to cry. Such a sad, ugly girl! I made high-pitched noises like a crazed animal, trying to scratch out the face in the mirror.

And then I saw what seemed to be the prodigy side of me—because I had never seen that face before. I looked at my reflection, blinking so I could see more clearly. The girl staring back at me was angry, powerful. This girl and I were the same. I had new thoughts, willful thoughts, or rather thoughts filled with lots of won'ts. I won't let her change me, I promised myself. I won't be what I'm not.

So now, on nights when my mother presented her tests, I performed listlessly, my head propped on one arm. I pretended to be bored. And I was. I got so bored I started counting the bellows of the foghorns out on the bay while my mother drilled me in other areas. The sound was comforting and reminded me of the cow jumping over the moon. And the next day, I played a game with myself, seeing if my mother would give up on me before eight bellows. After a while I usually counted only one, maybe two bellows at most. At last she was beginning to give up hope. **A** **B**

110   Two or three months had gone by without any mention of my being a prodigy again. And then one day my mother was watching *The Ed Sullivan Show* on TV. The TV was old and the sound kept shorting out. Every time my mother got halfway up from the sofa to adjust the set, the sound would go back on and Ed would be talking. As soon as she sat down, Ed would go silent again. She got up, the TV broke into loud piano music. She sat down. Silence. Up and down, back and forth, quiet and loud. It was like a stiff embraceless dance between her and the TV set. Finally she stood by the set with her hand
120   on the sound dial.

She seemed entranced by the music, a little frenzied piano piece with this mesmerizing quality, sort of quick passages and then teasing, lilting ones before it returned to the quick, playful parts. **C**

"*Ni kan*," my mother said, calling me over with hurried hand gestures. "Look here."

I could see why my mother was fascinated by the music. It was being pounded out by a little Chinese girl, about nine years old, with a Peter Pan haircut. The girl had the sauciness of a Shirley Temple. She was proudly modest like a proper Chinese
130   child. **D** And she also did this fancy sweep of a curtsy, so that the fluffy skirt of her white dress cascaded slowly to the floor like the petals of a large carnation.

In spite of these warning signs, I wasn't worried. Our family had no piano and we couldn't afford to buy one, let alone reams of sheet music and piano lessons. So I could be generous in my comments when my mother bad-mouthed the little girl on TV.

C **HERE'S HOW**

Language Coach
Synonyms are words with similar meanings. *Mesmerizing* means "spellbinding" or "fascinating." Knowing this, I think a synonym for *mesmerizing* could be *interesting*.

D **QUICK CHECK**

Why is Jing-mei's mother so excited about this piano player?

_____

_____

_____

_____

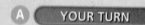

A YOUR TURN

Reading Focus

What was Jing-mei's mother's **motivation** for criticizing the piano player on TV?

_____

_____

_____

_____

B HERE'S HOW

Vocabulary

I am not sure what an *encore* is, but I think it has something to do with performing. I checked my dictionary, and it says that *encore* means "an extra song added to the end of a musical performance because the audience is cheering for more."

C LITERARY ANALYSIS

Why does Jing-mei not want to play piano?

_____

_____

_____

_____

"Play note right, but doesn't sound good! No singing sound," complained my mother.

140   "What are you picking on her for?" I said carelessly. "She's pretty good. Maybe she's not the best, but she's trying hard." I knew almost immediately I would be sorry I said that.

"Just like you," she said. "Not the best. Because you not trying." She gave a little huff as she let go of the sound dial and sat down on the sofa. **A**

The little Chinese girl sat down also to play an encore of "Anitra's Dance" by Grieg.[3] **B** I remember the song, because later on I had to learn how to play it.

Three days after watching *The Ed Sullivan Show*, my mother

150 told me what my schedule would be for piano lessons and piano practice. She had talked to Mr. Chong, who lived on the first floor of our apartment building. Mr. Chong was a retired piano teacher, and my mother had traded housecleaning services for weekly lessons and a piano for me to practice on every day, two hours a day, from four until six.

When my mother told me this, I felt as though I had been sent to hell. I whined and then kicked my foot a little when I couldn't stand it anymore.

"Why don't you like me the way I am? I'm *not* a genius!

160 I can't play the piano. And even if I could, I wouldn't go on TV if you paid me a million dollars!" I cried. **C**

My mother slapped me. "Who ask you be genius?" she shouted. "Only ask you be your best. For you sake. You think I want you be genius? Hnnh! What for! Who ask you!"

IN OTHER WORDS   Jing-mei's mother arranges piano lessons and practice time from a retired piano teacher in exchange for cleaning his apartment. Jing-mei protests this plan and her mother slaps her angrily.

"So ungrateful," I heard her mutter in Chinese. "If she had as much talent as she has temper, she would be famous now."

---

3. **Grieg** (GREEG): Edvard Grieg (1843–1907), Norwegian composer. "Anitra's Dance" is from his *Peer Gynt Suite*.

Mr. Chong, whom I secretly nicknamed Old Chong, was very strange, always tapping his fingers to the silent music of an invisible orchestra. He looked ancient in my eyes. He had lost most of the hair on top of his head and he wore thick glasses and had eyes that always looked tired and sleepy. But he must have been younger than I thought, since he lived with his mother and was not yet married.

I met Old Lady Chong once and that was enough. She had this peculiar smell like a baby that had done something in its pants. **D** And her fingers felt like a dead person's, like an old peach I once found in the back of the refrigerator; the skin just slid off the meat when I picked it up.

I soon found out why Old Chong had retired from teaching piano. He was deaf. "Like Beethoven!" he shouted to me. "We're both listening only in our head!" And he would start to conduct his frantic silent sonatas.[4]

Our lessons went like this. He would open the book and point to different things, explaining their purpose: "Key! Treble! Bass! No sharps or flats! So this is C major! Listen now and play after me!"

And then he would play the C scale a few times, a simple chord, and then, as if inspired by an old, unreachable itch, he gradually added more notes and running trills and a pounding bass until the music was really something quite grand. **E**

IN OTHER WORDS Jing-mei begins piano lessons with Mr. Chong. She quickly realizes that he retired from teaching piano because he is partially deaf and cannot hear very well. Jing-mei finds Mr. Chong a bit odd. He is balding and still lives with his mother, but he is very good at piano.

I would play after him, the simple scale, the simple chord, and then I just played some nonsense that sounded like a cat running up and down on top of garbage cans. Old Chong smiled and applauded and then said, "Very good! But now you must learn to keep time!"

---

4. **Sonatas** (SUH NAHT UHZ) are musical compositions, usually for one or two instruments.

D ▸ YOUR TURN

Vocabulary

Re-read this sentence. What do you think *peculiar* means? Write a definition, below, and then use a dictionary to check your definition.

_____

_____

E ▸ YOUR TURN

Reading Focus

What can you **infer** about Mr. Chong so far? Why does he conduct the silent sonatas in his head?

_____

_____

_____

_____

_____

_____

A **YOUR TURN**

Language Coach

The word *discordant* means "clashing" or "not harmonious." Underline the word in this sentence that is a **synonym** for *discordant*.

B **YOUR TURN**

Reading Focus

What is Jing-mei's **motivation** for not trying at piano?

_____

_____

_____

_____

_____

So that's how I discovered that Old Chong's eyes were too slow to keep up with the wrong notes I was playing. He went through the motions in half-time. To help me keep rhythm, he stood behind me, pushing down on my right shoulder for every beat. He balanced pennies on top of my wrists so I would keep them still as I slowly played scales and arpeggios.[5] He had me curve my hand around an apple and keep that shape when playing chords. He marched stiffly to show me how to make each finger dance up and down, staccato,[6] like an obedient little soldier.

200

He taught me all these things, and that was how I also learned I could be lazy and get away with mistakes, lots of mistakes. If I hit the wrong notes because I hadn't practiced enough, I never corrected myself. I just kept playing in rhythm. And Old Chong kept conducting his own private reverie.[7]

So maybe I never really gave myself a fair chance. I did pick up the basics pretty quickly, and I might have become a good pianist at that young age. But I was so determined not to try, not to be anybody different, that I learned to play only the most earsplitting preludes, the most discordant hymns. **A** **B**

210

IN OTHER WORDS Jing-mei quickly discovers that Mr. Chong cannot tell if she is playing correctly due to his deafness and poor vision. She learns the basics of piano quickly, but she does not like the lessons and decides not to try her hardest.

Over the next year, I practiced like this, dutifully in my own way. And then one day I heard my mother and her friend Lindo Jong both talking in a loud bragging tone of voice so others could hear. It was after church, and I was leaning against the brick wall, wearing a dress with stiff white petticoats. Auntie Lindo's daughter, Waverly, who was about my age, was standing farther down the wall, about five feet away. We had grown up

220

---

5. **Arpeggios** (AHR PEHJ OHS) are chords whose notes are played quickly one after another, rather than at the same time.
6. **Stacatto** (STUH KAHT OH) means with "clear-cut breaks between notes."
7. **Reverie** (REHV UH REE) means "daydream."

together and shared all the closeness of two sisters squabbling over crayons and dolls. In other words, for the most part, we hated each other. I thought she was snotty. Waverly Jong had gained a certain amount of fame as "Chinatown's Littlest Chinese Chess Champion."

"She bring home too many trophy," lamented Auntie Lindo that Sunday. "All day she play chess. All day I have no time do nothing but dust off her winnings." She threw a scolding look at Waverly, who pretended not to see her.

230 "You lucky you don't have this problem," said Auntie Lindo with a sigh to my mother. **C**

And my mother squared her shoulders and bragged: "Our problem worser than yours. If we ask Jing-mei wash dish, she hear nothing but music. It's like you can't stop this natural talent."

And right then, I was determined to put a stop to her foolish pride.

A few weeks later, Old Chong and my mother conspired to have me play in a talent show which would be held in the church hall. **D** By then, my parents had saved up enough to buy me a
240 secondhand piano, a black Wurlitzer spinet with a scarred bench. It was the showpiece of our living room.

IN OTHER WORDS Jing-mei continues practicing half-heartedly for a year. One day at church she hears her mother brag that she is an amazing piano player. Jing-mei decides to put an end to her mother's foolish pride.

For the talent show, I was to play a piece called "Pleading Child" from Schumann's[8] *Scenes from Childhood*. It was a simple, moody piece that sounded more difficult than it was. I was supposed to memorize the whole thing, playing the repeat parts twice to make the piece sound longer. But I dawdled over it, playing a few bars and then cheating, looking up to see what notes followed. I never really listened to what I was playing. I

---

8. **Robert Schumann** (SHOO MAHN) was a German composer who lived from 1810 to 1865.

C **LITERARY ANALYSIS**

When Lindo Jong complains about her daughter's chess playing, what is she really doing? Explain your answer.

_____

_____

_____

_____

_____

D **YOUR TURN**

Language Coach
Re-read this sentence. What do you think *conspired* means? Write a **synonym** for *conspired* on the line below.

_____

A **YOUR TURN**

Literary Focus

What **motivates** Jing-mei to not take her playing seriously?

_____

_____

_____

_____

_____

_____

B **QUICK CHECK**

Why do Jing-mei's parents invite so many people to the talent show?

_____

_____

_____

daydreamed about being somewhere else, about being someone 250 else. **A**

The part I liked to practice best was the fancy curtsy: right foot out, touch the rose on the carpet with a pointed foot, sweep to the side, left leg bends, look up and smile.

My parents invited all the couples from the Joy Luck Club[9] to witness my debut. Auntie Lindo and Uncle Tin were there. Waverly and her two older brothers had also come. **B** The first two rows were filled with children both younger and older than I was. The littlest ones got to go first. They recited simple nursery rhymes, squawked out tunes on miniature violins, 260 twirled Hula-Hoops, pranced in pink ballet tutus, and when they bowed or curtsied, the audience would sigh in unison, "Awww," and then clap enthusiastically.

IN OTHER WORDS Jing-mei's mother enters her in a talent show, and Jing-mei continues to put little effort into her practicing. Her parents invite all of their friends to the performance.

When my turn came, I was very confident. I remember my childish excitement. It was as if I knew, without a doubt, that the prodigy side of me really did exist. I had no fear whatsoever, no nervousness. I remember thinking to myself, This is it! This is it! I looked out over the audience, at my mother's blank face, my father's yawn, Auntie Lindo's stiff-lipped smile, Waverly's sulky expression. I had on a white dress layered with sheets of lace, and 270 a pink bow in my Peter Pan haircut. As I sat down I envisioned people jumping to their feet and Ed Sullivan rushing up to introduce me to everyone on TV.

And I started to play. It was so beautiful. I was so caught up in how lovely I looked that at first I didn't worry how I would sound. So it was a surprise to me when I hit the first wrong note and I realized something didn't sound quite right. And then I hit another, and another followed that. A chill started at the top of

9. **The Joy Luck Club** was a social club to which Jing-mei's mother and three other Chinese mothers belong.

my head and began to trickle down. Yet I couldn't stop playing, as though my hands were bewitched. I kept thinking my fingers would adjust themselves back, like a train switching to the right track. I played this strange jumble through two repeats, the sour notes staying with me all the way to the end.

When I stood up, I discovered my legs were shaking. Maybe I had just been nervous and the audience, like Old Chong, had seen me go through the right motions and had not heard anything wrong at all. I swept my right foot out, went down on my knee, looked up and smiled. The room was quiet, except for Old Chong, who was beaming and shouting, "Bravo! Bravo! Well done!" But then I saw my mother's face, her stricken face. The audience clapped weakly, and as I walked back to my chair, with my whole face quivering as I tried not to cry, I heard a little boy whisper loudly to his mother, "That was awful," and the mother whispered back, "Well, she certainly tried." **C**

IN OTHER WORDS Before performing, Jing-mei feels confident. She plays well at first but soon begins messing up. She hopes no one will notice her mistakes, but the audience barely applauds when she finishes. Jing-mei feels embarrassed and she even hears a little boy say that she was "awful."

And now I realized how many people were in the audience, the whole world it seemed. I was aware of eyes burning into my back. I felt the shame of my mother and father as they sat stiffly throughout the rest of the show.

We could have escaped during intermission. Pride and some strange sense of honor must have anchored my parents to their chairs. **D** And so we watched it all: the eighteen-year-old boy with a fake mustache who did a magic show and juggled flaming hoops while riding a unicycle. The breasted girl with white makeup who sang from *Madama Butterfly*[10] and got honorable

---

10. ***Madama Butterfly*** is an opera that was written by the Italian composer Giacomo Puccini (1858–1924).

C **LITERARY ANALYSIS**

Jing-mei was determined to show her mother that she was no piano prodigy. Why is she not happy that she accomplished that goal?

_____

_____

_____

_____

_____

_____

_____

_____

D **YOUR TURN**

Reading Focus
What **motivates** Jing-mei's family to stay for the rest of the talent show?

_____

_____

_____

_____

A QUICK CHECK

How does Auntie Lindo avoid saying that Jing-mei's performance was bad?

_____

_____

_____

_____

B YOUR TURN

Vocabulary

Knowing what happened at the talent show, what do you think the word *fiasco* means?

_____

_____

_____

mention. And the eleven-year-old boy who won first prize playing a tricky violin song that sounded like a busy bee.

After the show, the Hsus, the Jongs, and the St. Clairs from the Joy Luck Club came up to my mother and father.

"Lots of talented kids," Auntie Lindo said vaguely, smiling broadly. **A**

310 "That was somethin' else," said my father, and I wondered if he was referring to me in a humorous way, or whether he even remembered what I had done.

Waverly looked at me and shrugged her shoulders. "You aren't a genius like me," she said matter-of-factly. And if I hadn't felt so bad, I would have pulled her braids and punched her stomach.

IN OTHER WORDS Even though they are embarrassed, Jing-mei and her family stay for the rest of the talent show. Their conversation with their friends afterwards is awkward but polite, except for Jing-mei's friend Waverly who comes right out and insults Jing-mei.

But my mother's expression was what devastated me: a quiet, blank look that said she had lost everything. I felt the same way, and it seemed as if everybody were now coming 320 up, like gawkers at the scene of an accident, to see what parts were actually missing. When we got on the bus to go home, my father was humming the busy-bee tune and my mother was silent. I kept thinking she wanted to wait until we got home before shouting at me. But when my father unlocked the door to our apartment, my mother walked in and then went to the back, into the bedroom. No accusations. No blame. And in a way, I felt disappointed. I had been waiting for her to start shouting, so I could shout back and cry and blame her for all my misery.

330 I assumed my talent-show fiasco meant I never had to play the piano again. **B** But two days later, after school, my mother came out of the kitchen and saw me watching TV.

"Four clock," she reminded me as if it were any other day. I was stunned, as though she were asking me to go through the talent-show torture again. I wedged myself more tightly in front of the TV.

"Turn off TV," she called from the kitchen five minutes later.

I didn't budge. And then I decided. I didn't have to do what my mother said anymore. I wasn't her slave. This wasn't China. **C** I had listened to her before and look what happened. She was the stupid one.

340

She came out from the kitchen and stood in the arched entryway of the living room. "Four clock," she said once again, louder.

"I'm not going to play anymore," I said nonchalantly. "Why should I? I'm not a genius." **D**

She walked over and stood in front of the TV. I saw her chest was heaving up and down in an angry way.

IN OTHER WORDS After the talent show Jing-mei expects to give up the piano, but her mother insists that she continue. Jing-mei argues that she should stop because she is not a piano "genius."

"No!" I said, and I now felt stronger, as if my true self had finally emerged. So this was what had been inside me all along.

350

"No! I won't!" I screamed.

She yanked me by the arm, pulled me off the floor, snapped off the TV. She was frighteningly strong, half pulling, half carrying me toward the piano as I kicked the throw rugs under my feet. She lifted me up and onto the hard bench. I was sobbing by now, looking at her bitterly. Her chest was heaving even more and her mouth was open, smiling crazily, as if she were pleased I was crying.

"You want me to be someone that I'm not!" I sobbed. "I'll never be the kind of daughter you want me to be!"

360

"Only two kinds of daughters," she shouted in Chinese. "Those who are obedient and those who follow their own mind!

C (YOUR TURN)

Reading Focus

What can you **infer** about Jing-mei's attitude towards China as opposed to America?

_____

_____

_____

_____

_____

D (HERE'S HOW)

Vocabulary

My teacher says that _nonchalantly_ means "without interest" or indifferently." This is about how I would expect Jing-mei to act.

Literary Focus

What is the main cause of tension between Jing-mei and her mother?

_____

_____

_____

_____

_____

_____

_____

B **YOUR TURN**

Literary Focus

Underline Jing-mei's **motivation** for failing her mother so many times.

Only one kind of daughter can live in this house. Obedient daughter!"

"Then I wish I wasn't your daughter. I wish you weren't my mother," I shouted. As I said these things, I got scared. It felt like worms and toads and slimy things crawling out of my chest, but it also felt good, as if this awful side of me had surfaced, at last.

"Too late change this," said my mother shrilly.

370   And I could sense her anger rising to its breaking point. I wanted to see it spill over. And that's when I remembered the babies she had lost in China, the ones we never talked about. "Then I wish I'd never been born!" I shouted. "I wish I were dead! Like them." **A**

IN OTHER WORDS The argument between Jing-mei and her mother turns physical as Jing-mei's mother tries to drag her to the piano bench. In the middle of this fighting, Jing-mei screams that she wishes she were dead like the children her mother lost in China—this is a sensitive subject for Jing-mei's mother.

It was as if I had said the magic words. Alakazam!—and her face went blank, her mouth closed, her arms went slack, and she backed out of the room, stunned, as if she were blowing away like a small brown leaf, thin, brittle, lifeless.

It was not the only disappointment my mother felt in me.

380   In the years that followed, I failed her so many times, each time asserting my own will, my right to fall short of expectations. I didn't get straight A's. I didn't become class president. I didn't get into Stanford.[11] I dropped out of college.

For unlike my mother, I did not believe I could be anything I wanted to be. I could only be me. **B**

And for all those years, we never talked about the disaster at the recital or my terrible accusations afterward at the piano bench. All that remained unchecked, like a betrayal that was now

---

11. Stanford: high-ranking university in Stanford, California.

unspeakable. So I never found a way to ask her why she had

390 hoped for something so large that failure was inevitable.

And even worse, I never asked her what frightened me the most: Why had she given up hope? **C**

For after our struggle at the piano, she never mentioned my playing again. The lessons stopped. The lid to the piano was closed, shutting out the dust, my misery, and her dreams.

IN OTHER WORDS Jing-mei's mention of the dead children shocks her mother and stops the argument. After that, Jing-mei's mother allows her to quit the piano. Unlike her mother, Jing-mei only wanted to be herself, not to live up to others' expectations.

So she surprised me. A few years ago, she offered to give me the piano, for my thirtieth birthday. I had not played in all those years. I saw the offer as a sign of forgiveness, a tremendous burden removed.

400 "Are you sure?" I asked shyly. "I mean, won't you and Dad miss it?"

"No, this your piano," she said firmly. "Always your piano. You only one can play."

"Well, I probably can't play anymore," I said. "It's been years."

"You pick up fast," said my mother, as if she knew this was certain. "You have natural talent. You could been genius if you want to."

"No, I couldn't."

"You just not trying," said my mother. And she was neither 410 angry nor sad. She said it as if to announce a fact that could never be disproved. "Take it," she said.

But I didn't at first. It was enough that she had offered it to me. And after that, every time I saw it in my parents' living room, standing in front of the bay windows, it made me feel proud, as if it were a shiny trophy I had won back.

Last week I sent a tuner over to my parents' apartment and had the piano reconditioned, for purely sentimental reasons. My

C **LITERARY ANALYSIS**

Why do you think Jing-mei never asked her mother why she gave up hope?

_____

_____

_____

_____

_____

_____

Literary Focus

What might be some of the "sentimental reasons" that **motivate** Jing-mei to have the piano tuned?

_____

_____

_____

_____

_____

_____

_____

B (**LITERARY ANALYSIS**)

What significance is there in the titles of the two halves of this song?

_____

_____

_____

_____

_____

_____

_____

mother had died a few months before, and I had been getting things in order for my father, a little bit at a time. **A** I put the jewelry in special silk pouches. The sweaters she had knitted in yellow, pink, bright orange—all the colors I hated—I put those in mothproof boxes. I found some old Chinese silk dresses, the kind with little slits up the sides. I rubbed the old silk against my skin, then wrapped them in tissue and decided to take them home with me.

After I had the piano tuned, I opened the lid and touched the keys. It sounded even richer than I remembered. Really, it was a very good piano. Inside the bench were the same exercise notes with handwritten scales, the same secondhand music books with their covers held together with yellow tape.

I opened up the Schumann book to the dark little piece I had played at the recital. It was on the left-hand side of the page, "Pleading Child." It looked more difficult than I remembered. I played a few bars, surprised at how easily the notes came back to me.

And for the first time, or so it seemed, I noticed the piece on the right-hand side. It was called "Perfectly Contented." I tried to play this one as well. It had a lighter melody but the same flowing rhythm and turned out to be quite easy. "Pleading Child" was shorter but slower; "Perfectly Contented" was longer but faster. And after I played them both a few times, I realized they were two halves of the same song. **B**

(**IN OTHER WORDS**) On Jing-mei's thirtieth birthday, her mother offered her the old piano. Jing-mei turned it down, but she saw the offer as a sign of forgiveness. Years later, Jing-mei's mother died. Jing-mei returned to her parents' apartment to help her father organize things and even hired someone to tune the piano. Sitting down to play the piano for the first time in years, Jing-mei practiced the Schumann piece she had played at the talent show. She played surprisingly well and thought about her childhood happily.

Applying Your Skills

Two Kinds

LITERARY FOCUS: CHARACTER INTERACTIONS AND MOTIVATION

DIRECTIONS: In "Two Kinds," the **motivations** of the narrator and her mother are most obvious during their **interactions**. Read the three motivations listed below. Then find an interaction in the story that shows each motivation. The first row has been filled in for you.

Motivation	Interaction That Shows Motivation
Jing-mei's mother's desire for daughter to be a genius.	Lines 58–62; mother tests daughter for different skills.
Jing-mei's desire to make her mother proud.	
Jing-mei's desire to be loved by her mother.	

READING FOCUS: MAKING INFERENCES ABOUT MOTIVATION

DIRECTIONS: Read the following quotations from "Two Kinds." Then make an **inference** about what that character wants or needs. What is her motivation?

1. "Our problem worser than yours. If we ask Jing-mei wash dish, she hear nothing but music. It's like you can't stop this natural talent."

   Motivation: _____

   _____

2. "Then I wish I wasn't your daughter. I wish you weren't my mother."

   Motivation: _____

   _____

Word Box

prodigy

listlessly

mesmerizing

discordant

fiasco

nonchalantly

VOCABULARY REVIEW

DIRECTIONS: In each exercise, circle the word that does not fit with the others. Explain why you circled this word on the line below.

1. listlessly/nonchalantly/excitedly

   _____

2. genius/fool/prodigy

   _____

MLK's Legacy *and*
A Young Boy's Stand

INFORMATIONAL TEXT FOCUS: SYNTHESIZING SOURCES: DRAWING CONCLUSIONS

The best way to learn more about a subject is to look at several **sources**. Why? One reason is to get as much information as possible. Another reason is to develop a balanced view of the subject. The following selection is a **primary source**—an individual's first-hand account of an experience. "A Young Boy's Stand" is based on a primary source.

Imagine that you are researching the Vietnam War for a history assignment. What would happen if you read only one source, written by someone who supported the war? If you stopped there, you might think everyone supported the war. But if you looked at additional sources, you would discover that there were plenty of people who did not support the war. Knowing all sides of the subject would help you write a balanced essay.

Once you have information from several sources, you need to put it together to see what you've found. This process is called **synthesizing**. When you have synthesized information, you can **draw conclusions** from it. Drawing conclusions means that you make judgments about what you have learned. If you synthesize your sources about the Vietnam War, you will probably conclude that the war was a very emotional time in American history.

When you draw conclusions, follow these steps:

1. Look for the main idea in each source. Look for details that support this main idea. Then write the main idea in your own words.

2. Ask yourself whether you believe the writer's statements. Has he or she given enough information to support the main idea?

3. Ask yourself what conclusions you can draw about the subject.

VOCABULARY

inspiring (IHN SPY RIHNG) *adj.:* awakening; influential.

concussion (KUHN KUSH UHN) *n.:* injury to the brain caused by a fall or a hit.

discrimination (DIHS KRIH MIH NA SHUN) *n.:* biased treatment.

intimidating (IHN TIHM UH DAY TIHNG) *adj.:* overwhelming; frightening.

Informational Text Skills
Synthesize sources; draw conclusions from one or more sources.

MLK's Legacy: An Interview with Congressman John Lewis

from NPR.org

January 14, 1999

npr_host: At this point we'd like to welcome Congressman Lewis.

Congressman_John_Lewis: Good evening. It's great to be here.

npr_host: Can you tell us a bit about your firsthand experience with the Civil Rights Movement? **A**

Congressman_John_Lewis: I was born in Alabama, 50 miles from Montgomery, in southeast Alabama, in a little town of about 13,000 people just outside of Troy. When I would visit the cities of Montgomery or Birmingham, I saw the signs that said white men and white women, I saw the signs that said colored
10 lady, colored men. In 1950 when I was 10 years old I tried to check a book out of the local library, I tried to get a library card and I was told that the library was only for white people and not people of color. It had an unbelievable impact on me. I couldn't understand it. But in 1955 when I was fifteen years old I heard about Martin Luther King Jr. and Rosa Parks.[1] And, three years later I met MLK and a year later I got involved in the Civil Rights Movement.

Congressman_John_Lewis: Dr. King was one of the most inspiring human beings I ever met. He was such a warm,
20 compassionate and loving human being. **B**

npr_host: How was Dr. King inspiring on a personal level, as much as in public?

Congressman_John_Lewis: MLK Jr. taught me how to say no to segregation and I can hear him saying now . . . when you straighten up your back—no man can ride you. He said stand up straight and say no to racial discrimination. **C**

A **HERE'S HOW**

Reading Focus

I see that this is an interview about Congressman John Lewis's first-hand experiences in the Civil Rights Movement. I know that this interview is a **primary source**.

B **HERE'S HOW**

Vocabulary

I am not sure what *inspiring* means. I do know that Congressman Lewis joined the Civil Rights Movement once he met Dr. King. From the way *inspiring* is used, I can guess that Dr. King *influenced* John Lewis.

C **YOUR TURN**

Vocabulary

If you are not sure what *discrimination* means, look at the sentences that came before it. What has Congressman Lewis already told you about Dr. King? What would he have opposed?

_____

_____

From transcript, "MLK's Legacy with Congressman John Lewis (D-GA)" from National Public Radio, January 14, 1999. Copyright © 1999 by **National Public Radio.** Reproduced by permission of the publisher.

A QUICK CHECK

Why did Lewis and other protestors participate in sit-ins at lunch counters?

_____

_____

B HERE'S HOW

Reading Focus

Congressman Lewis says that he and others got into "good trouble" during sit-ins. *Trouble* is usually bad, not good. But Lewis was doing something of which he was proud. I can draw the **conclusion** that he thinks that being arrested for a good cause was worth it.

C HERE'S HOW

Vocabulary

I have heard the word *concussion* used before to describe a brain injury. That makes sense here, because Dr. King wanted to protect Lewis's head.

IN OTHER WORDS

Congressman John Lewis answers questions about how he became involved in the Civil Rights Movement. Denied a library card because of his race, he grew up in a world that needed change. As a teenager, he studied nonviolence, met Martin Luther King, and joined lunch-counter sit-ins to protest against places that refused to serve black customers.

npr_host: You took very quick action. Tell us more, please.

Congressman_John_Lewis: As a young student I got involved in that, studying the philosophy and the discipline of nonvio-
30   lence. And as students—young people, black and white, we would go downtown in Nashville, Atlanta, Birmingham and other cities in the South . . . and we would sit down—we did what we called sit-ins at lunch counters. These places refused to serve black students. And we'd have white students and black students sitting together. And some of the places were like Woolworth stores, where you could go in and buy things, but you couldn't order a hamburger. And while [we were] sitting, sometimes people would come in and beat us, light cigarettes out in our hair, down our backs, throw us off the lunch counter
40   stools, and sometimes kick us and leave us lying down on the floor. **A** We got arrested. When I was growing up I was told over and over again—don't get into trouble. So as students we were getting into trouble—but it was good trouble. **B**

NRP_listener asks: What is the one thing that you remember most about MLK?

Congressman_John_Lewis: Dr. King had a great sense of humor and he loved a good meal. From time to time when we were traveling in the South he would see some restaurant or a hole-in-the-wall place to eat and he would say, we should stop—
50   we should get something to eat, it may be our last chance, we should go on a full stomach.

Congressman_John_Lewis: But on one occasion, on—March 1965 we were walking along, marching, and it started to rain. I didn't have anything on my head. He had a little brown cap he was wearing. He took the cap off his head and gave it to me and he said, "John, you should put this on—you've been hurt." A few days earlier I had been beaten by a group of state troopers and I had a concussion. So he thought it was important that my head be protected. I'll never forget it; it was such an act of compassion
60   and concern. **C**

NRP_listener asks: Was it intimidating meeting MLK? **D**

Congressman_John_Lewis: Well, the first time I met him, I was only eighteen years old in 1958, and he had emerged for me as someone bigger than life. Two miles from where I grew up in Alabama, there was a white college—Troy State College—and I had applied to go there. I never heard anything from the school so I wrote MLK a letter and told him about my desire to go to the school. He wrote me back and sent me a round trip Greyhound bus ticket and invited me to come to Montgomery

70 to meet with him. One Saturday, my father drove me to the Greyhound bus station, I traveled the 50 miles from my home. A young black lawyer met me at the bus station in Montgomery and drove me to the First Baptist Church—that was Rev. Abernathy . . . a friend of Dr. King and a leader in the local movement with Dr. King. We entered the office of the church and MLK stood up from behind a desk and he said something like, "Are you the boy from Troy? Are you John Lewis?" **E**

Congressman_John_Lewis: I was scared, I was nervous, I didn't know what I was going to say. And I said—Dr. King, I am John

80 Robert Lewis. I gave my whole name, I didn't want there to be any mistake.

Congressman_John_Lewis: That was the beginning of our relationship. We became friends. We became brothers in a struggle. He was my leader. He was my hero.

NRP_listener asks: Why did you decide to run for congress?

Congressman_John_Lewis: When I would make trips to D.C. during the height of the Civil Rights Movement . . . I had a chance to meet many members of Congress and I had been involved in getting people to register (to vote) and I thought

90 somehow and someway I could make a contribution by being involved in politics. **F**

NRP_listener asks: How does one keep struggling for social change in this environment? How does one keep [one's] spirits up?

Congressman_John_Lewis: You must never, ever give up. Let me give you an example. I just finished a book called *Walking*

D **YOUR TURN**

Vocabulary

Intimidating appears in line 61. If you look closely, you can see the word *timid* in *intimidating*. *Timid* means "lacking in courage." Knowing this, what do you think *intimidating* means?

_____

_____

_____

E **HERE'S HOW**

Reading Focus

From this paragraph I can **draw the conclusion** that Dr. King may have been impressed by Lewis's determination to go to Troy State College. Maybe Dr. King wanted Lewis to join his efforts to end discrimination.

F **HERE'S HOW**

Language Coach

I know *contribution* is the noun form of the verb *contribute*. Contribute means "give." *Contribution* means "the act of giving." *Contribution* and *contribute* are called **related words**.

IN OTHER WORDS

Congressman Lewis recalls meeting Martin Luther King for the first time after writing Dr. King a letter about his desire to go to college. Lewis decided to run for office after meeting members of Congress during the Civil Rights Movement.

Dr. King was Congressman Lewis's inspiration in the 1960s. Lewis believes that Dr. King can still be an inspiration to people today. Why does Lewis feel this way?

_____

_____

_____

_____

B **YOUR TURN**

Reading Focus

You can **conclude** that John Lewis hopes that people today will learn from experiences of those in the past. He wants people to take action. Underline evidence in his final statement that supports that conclusion.

IN OTHER WORDS

In a book he wrote about the Civil Rights Movement, Congressman Lewis tells a story from his childhood about a terrible storm that seemed about to destroy his aunt's home. His aunt, the only adult there, gathered the children and they held hands and survived the storm together. Lewis says that if Martin Luther King were alive today, he would want the country to focus on the needs of people. Lewis urges young people to study the past for inspiration and know that they can act too.

with the Wind: A Memoir of the Movement; it's published by Simon and Schuster. In the prologue of the book, I tell a story about when I was growing up and I was only about seven or eight years old, but I remember like it was yesterday.

100   **Congressman_John_Lewis:** One Saturday afternoon a group of my sisters and brothers, along with some of my first cousins, about twelve or fifteen of us—young children were outside playing in the yard, and a storm came up . . . an unbelievable storm occurred and the only adult around was my aunt who lived in this old house. A shotgun house—a house with a tin roof, small . . . The wind started blowing, the lightning started flashing and we were all in the house. My aunt was terrified, she thought the house would blow away. So she suggested we should hold hands and we were crying, all of us.

110   **Congressman_John_Lewis:** So when one side of the house appeared to be lifted from its foundation we'd try and hold it down with our little bodies . . . and when the other corner of the house appeared to be lifting up we'd walk over there . . . trying to hold it down. Thunder may roll, lightning may flash . . . but we may never leave the house.

NRP_listener asks: How do you think MLK would fare in today's political arena?

Congressman_John_Lewis: Today, MLK would be the undisputed moral leader in America. If he were here today . . . he'd
120   say we're majoring in minor things. He'd be very disappointed that we're wasting so much of our time, so much of our energy and resources on investigation rather than dealing with the basic needs of people.

NRP_listener asks: If there is any advice you could give to our generation, what would it be?

Congressman_John_Lewis: This generation should study contemporary history: read the books, listen to the tapes, watch the video, study the early days of the Civil Rights Movement and be inspired. They too can act. **A** **B**

A YOUNG BOY'S STAND ON A NEW ORLEANS STREETCAR

Based on an interview from StoryCorps, December 1, 2006

> **INTO THE INTERVIEW**
>
> StoryCorps was created in 2003 to record the oral history of ordinary people. Booths and recording studios around the country are available for people to interview friends and family members about their life experiences. These oral histories are then stored in the Library of Congress.

Jerome Smith was ten years old when he removed the screen that separated white and black passengers on a New Orleans streetcar. "People became very angry," Smith recalls.

The event took place five years before Rosa Parks refused to give up her bus seat to a white passenger in Montgomery, Alabama. Parks's actions on December 1, 1955, helped spark the Civil Rights Movement.

Smith was sitting in the white section of the street car when an older black woman came up from the rear of the car. She hit
10 him so hard that "it felt like there was a bell ringing in my head," Smith says.

The woman loudly said she'd teach the boy a lesson. "You should never disrespect white people," she said. "You have no business trying to sit with them."

She forced Smith off the streetcar. But once they were out of sight, the woman's tone changed.

"Never, ever stop," the woman told Smith. She began to cry. "I'm proud of you. Don't you ever quit." **A**

© Story Corps

A HERE'S HOW

Reading Focus

I know that the woman seemed angry on the bus. Yet she encouraged Jerome Smith once they were off the bus. I can **draw the conclusion** that she was actually very proud of what he did.

"A Young Boy's Stand on a New Orleans Streetcar," adapted from "StoryCorps: Recording America," January 24, 2007, from *National Public Radio* Web site, accessed November 30, 2007, at http://www.npr.org/templates/story/story.php?storyId=6562915. Copyright © 2007 by **Story-Corps®**. Retold by Holt, Rinehart and Winston. Reproduced by permission of the publisher.

A YOUR TURN

Reading Focus

Just like Congressman John Lewis did in the previous selection, Smith explains how one person affected his involvement in the Civil Rights Movement. By **synthesizing** this information, what **conclusion** can you draw about the power of the Movement?

_____

_____

_____

_____

_____

_____

B HERE'S HOW

Language Coach

The last sentence of the selection includes the noun *partipation*. I can come up with a verb that is related to that noun. The verb *participate* and the noun *participation* are **related words**.

20   Smith went on to help found the New Orleans chapter of CORE, The Congress of Racial Equality. He says that moment made him who he is today. **A**

"Even though I didn't know the words 'civil rights' then," Smith says, "that opened up the door."

Today Smith directs the Tambourine and Fan, a New Orleans organization that teaches young people about civil rights, leadership and political participation. **B**

Applying Your Skills

MLK's Legacy *and* A Young Boy's Stand

INFORMATIONAL TEXT FOCUS: SYNTHESIZING SOURCES: DRAWING CONCLUSIONS

DIRECTIONS: After you read information from two **sources**, you need to **synthesize** it before you can **draw conclusions**. Fill in the graphic organizers below with the conclusions you reached by synthesizing the information provided.

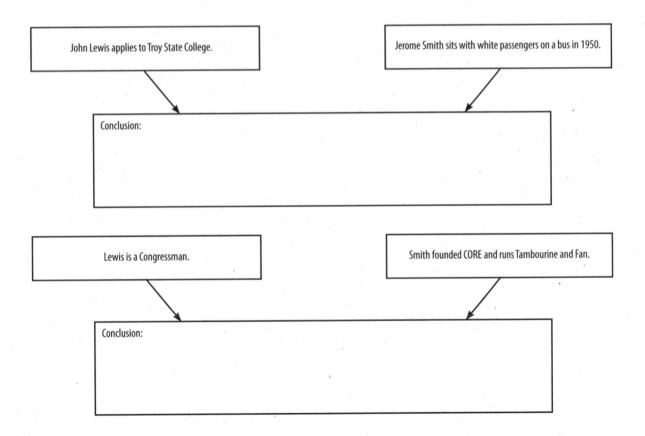

John Lewis applies to Troy State College.

Jerome Smith sits with white passengers on a bus in 1950.

Conclusion:

Lewis is a Congressman.

Smith founded CORE and runs Tambourine and Fan.

Conclusion:

VOCABULARY REVIEW

DIRECTIONS: Match each word on the left with its definition on the right. Write the correct letters on the blank.

_____ **1.** inspiring   **a.** overwhelming; frightening

_____ **2.** concussion   **b.** awakening; influential

_____ **3.** intimidating   **c.** biased treatment

_____ **4.** discrimination   **d.** brain injury

Collection 2

VOCABULARY REVIEW

DIRECTIONS: In the chart below, the left column lists Collection 2 vocabulary words. The right column lists the definitions of these words. Fill in any blanks in the chart using the Word Box and definitions you have already learned. Not all words will be used.

Word Box

sidle

cowering

furtive

oppress

inspiring

concussion

discordant

prodigy

fiasco

discrimination

intimidating

Word	Definition
intimidating	
	hold down unfairly
cowering	
discrimination	
	move in a slow, sideways manner
discordant	
	total failure

Skills Review

Collection 2

LANGUAGE COACH: RELATED WORDS

Sometimes you can guess the meaning of an unfamiliar word by thinking of **related words** you already know. For example, consider the word *oppress*. You already know that *press* means "to push down." Using that knowledge and the way *oppress* is used in a sentence, you can probably guess that *oppress* means "hold down unfairly."

DIRECTIONS: Each sentence below includes a boldface word. Look for a smaller word you know within each boldface word. Then use this knowledge and the way the word is used in the sentence to guess its meaning.

1. I felt **indebted** to my brother after he saved my life.
   What word do you recognize in *indebted*? What does this word mean?

   _____

   Knowing this, re-read the sentence. What do you think *indebted* means?

   _____

   Now look up *indebted* in a dictionary. Write its definition here.

   _____

2. I thought that turning on the radio might **enliven** the dull party.
   What word do you recognize in *enliven*? What does this word mean?

   _____

   Knowing this, re-read the sentence. What do you think *enliven* means?

   _____

   Now look up *enliven* in a dictionary. Write its definition here.

   _____

WRITING ACTIVITY

DIRECTIONS: Write a brief paragraph in which you identify three **character traits** belonging to Jing-mei in the story "Two Kinds." Explain how you **inferred** each trait by listing at least one piece of evidence from the story. Your evidence can be a quotation or a summary of an event in the story.

_____

_____

_____

_____

_____

Narrator and Voice

© Dream Child (1990) by Graham Arnold

Literary and Academic Vocabulary for Collection 3

LITERARY VOCABULARY

narrator (NAR UH TUHR) *n.:* the person telling a story.

The details provided by the narrator made the story very realistic.

omniscient narrator (AHM NISH EHNT NAR UH TUHR) *n:* a narrator who knows what all the characters are thinking and feeling.

The story was told by an omniscient narrator, so it was easy to figure out what each character was thinking.

third-person limited narrator (THUHRD PUHR SUHN LIH MIH TEHD NAR UH TUHR) *n.:* a narrator who tells the story in the third person and reveals the thoughts and feelings of only one character.

The third-person limited narrator gave me a look at the protagonist's feelings, but I had to draw conclusions about the rest of the characters.

ACADEMIC VOCABULARY

complex (KUHM PLEHKS) *adj.:* complicated; made up of many parts.

Although the story may seem simple, its characters are actually quite complex.

correspond (KAWR UH SPAHND) *v.:* agree or be in harmony; be similar.

Often a character's voice corresponds to his actions.

perceive (PUR SEEV) *v.:* be aware of; sense; observe.

By paying attention to details, you will be able to perceive a lot about characters.

incorporate (IHN KOHR PUH RAYT) *v.:* make something a part of something else.

A writer may incorporate details from her own background into her writing.

The Storyteller

Based on the short story by Saki

LITERARY FOCUS: OMNISCIENT NARRATOR

Omniscient means "all-knowing." Some stories are told by an **omniscient narrator**. This kind of narrator knows exactly what all of the characters are thinking and feeling—even if they do not reveal it themselves. By sharing this information, and sometimes making comments, omniscient narrators let you in on the thoughts and attitudes of all the characters.

READING FOCUS: IDENTIFYING WRITER'S PURPOSE

When you read a story, it is important to keep asking yourself, "Why did the author write this?" Amusing stories, such as "The Storyteller," often seem to be just that—amusing and written simply for entertainment. However, the author often has a more serious **purpose**. For example, a funny story about a rabbit that always lies might actually be the author's way of encouraging readers to always tell the truth. In the story you are about to read, the author is making a point by poking fun at different characters. To discover what the author's point is, look for parts of the story that reveal the narrator's attitude toward the characters.

VOCABULARY

With a partner, practice using these words in complete sentences.

persisted (PUHR SIHS TIHD) *v.:* stubbornly continued.

scowled (SKOWLD) *v.:* made a facial expression of displeasure.

undermined (UHN DUHR MYND) *v.:* weakened.

INTO THE SHORT STORY

This story takes place in the early 1900s. At that time, many people traveled by train. Trains were different than they are today. They were divided into closed, often stuffy compartments. Passengers sat in these small spaces with people they did not know. In this story, an aunt and three children travel by train. A bachelor, or an unmarried man, sits in the compartment with them.

SKILLS FOCUS

Literary Skills
Understand omniscient narrator.

Reading Skills
Determine the writer's purpose or intent as a strategy for comprehension.

THE STORYTELLER

Based on the short story by Saki

The railway carriage was terribly hot. The next stop was almost an hour away. In the carriage were two small girls, and a small boy. The children's aunt sat in one corner seat. In another corner sat a bachelor who was not part of their group. The aunt and the children kept talking in an annoying way. Most of what the aunt said started with "Don't," and almost everything the children said began with "Why?"

"Don't, Cyril," cried the aunt, as the small boy hit the seat cushions. The child moved to the window. "Where are those

10   sheep going?" he asked.

"They are going to another field where there is more grass," said the aunt.

"But there is lots of grass in that field," protested the boy.

"Perhaps the grass in the other field is better," suggested the aunt. She tried to change the subject. "Oh, look at those cows!"

"Why is the grass in the other field better?" persisted Cyril. **B**

The bachelor scowled. He was a hard, mean man, the aunt thought.

20   The smaller girl began to recite a poem. She only knew the first line, but she repeated it over and over. The bachelor scowled toward them again.

A **HERE'S HOW**

Literary Focus

I can already tell that this story has an **omniscient narrator**. I know this because the narrator has told me that "the children kept talking in an annoying way." No character said or thought this, so it is the observation of an omniscient narrator.

B **HERE'S HOW**

Vocabulary

I do not know the word *persisted* in line 16. I do know that the boy is asking a lot of questions, even after his aunt changes the subject. *Persisted* must have something to do with not giving up. I checked my dictionary and *persisted* means "stubbornly continued."

Literary Focus

Re-read lines 20–29. Underline any details that prove there is an **omniscient narrator**. How is the narrator giving you a better idea of the aunt's personality?

_____

_____

_____

How did the bachelor end up telling the children a story?

_____

_____

_____

Reading Focus

I can see that the children's attitudes in lines 41–48 change. The change happens once the bachelor describes the girl in his story as "horribly good." I think the **writer's purpose** here is to show me that the bachelor knows exactly what the children do and do not want to hear.

Language Coach

I know the word *park* can have **multiple meanings**. It can be a verb, as it is in the phrase, "Park your car." Here, I think it is a noun, meaning "an area of land for recreation."

"Come listen to a story," said the aunt. In a low voice, she told an uninteresting story about a good little girl who made friends with everyone. The little girl was finally saved from a mad bull by rescuers who admired her moral goodness.

"Wouldn't they have saved her if she hadn't been good?" asked one girl. It was exactly the question that the bachelor wanted to ask. **A**

30   "Well, yes," admitted the aunt.

"It's the stupidest story I've ever heard," said the bigger girl.

"You don't seem to be a success as a storyteller," said the bachelor.

"It's very difficult to tell stories for children," answered the aunt.

"I don't agree with you," said the bachelor.

"Perhaps you would like to tell them a story," said aunt.

"Tell us a story," begged the bigger girl.

"Once upon a time," began the bachelor, "there was a little

40   girl called Bertha, who was very, very good." **B**

The children were instantly bored. It seemed as if all stories were alike.

"She did everything that she was told," said the bachelor. "She always told the truth. She kept her clothes clean, learned her lessons perfectly, and had beautiful manners. In fact, she was horribly good."

Suddenly the story seemed more interesting. The word horrible in connection with goodness was new and surprising. **C**

"She was so good," continued the bachelor, "that she won

50   several medals for goodness. She always wore them pinned onto her dress. There was a medal for doing as she was told, another medal for being on time, and a third for good behavior. No other child in town had three medals, so everybody knew that she must be an extra good child."

"Horribly good," repeated Cyril.

"Everybody talked about her goodness. The Prince heard about it, and invited her to walk in his park. **D** It was a beautiful

park, and no children were ever allowed in it. So it was a great
honor for Bertha."

60   "Were there any sheep in the park?" demanded Cyril.

"No," said the bachelor, "there were no sheep in the park,
but there were lots of little pigs."

"What color were they?"

"Black with white faces, white with black spots, black all
over, gray with white patches, and some were white all over."

"Bertha was sorry that there were no flowers in the park.
She had promised her aunts that she would not pick any of the
Prince's flowers. So it made her feel silly to find that there were
no flowers to pick." **E**

70   "Why weren't there any flowers?"

"The pigs had eaten them all," answered the bachelor. "You
can't have both pigs and flowers, so the Prince decided to have
just pigs."

The children liked the Prince's choice. Most people would
have preferred flowers. **F**

"In the park there were ponds with gold and blue and green
fish. There were trees with parrots that said clever things, and
hummingbirds that hummed popular tunes. Bertha thought to
herself: 'If I were not so very good I would not have been invited

80 to this beautiful park.' Her three medals clinked against one
another as she walked. They reminded her how very good she
really was. Just then an enormous wolf came into the park to see
if it could catch a fat little pig for supper." **G**

"What color was the wolf?" asked the children.

"Mud-color, with a black tongue and gray eyes. The first
thing that it saw in the park was Bertha. Her dress was so white
and clean that it could be seen from a great distance. Bertha saw
the wolf and began to wish that she had never come into the
park. She ran as hard as she could until she reached some bushes

90 where she could hide. As the wolf came toward the branches,
Bertha was terrified. She thought: 'If I had not been so very good
I would be safe in town.' The bushes were so thick that the wolf
couldn't see her. Bertha was trembling with fear, however. As she

E   YOUR TURN

Literary Focus

As he tells the story about
Bertha, the bachelor is
actually acting as an
omniscient narrator. Re-read
lines 49–69. Circle key words
or phrases that prove that
the bachelor is an omniscient
narrator.

F   YOUR TURN

Reading Focus

Why does the bachelor fill
the park with pigs instead
of flowers? Does his choice
of pigs seem to fit with the
writer's purpose from the
previous page? Explain your
answer.

_____

_____

_____

_____

_____

G   HERE'S HOW

Reading Focus

I think the bachelor is making
fun of Bertha and how good
she is. Earlier in the story, I
felt that the **writer's purpose**
was to make fun of the aunt.
Maybe Saki has the bachelor
tell the story about Bertha to
mock the way adults expect
children to act.

Vocabulary

Look at the word *undermined* in line 105. You can tell that the aunt is not pleased with the bachelor's story. Knowing this, what do you think *undermined* means here?

What was the bachelor's purpose in telling the story he told? Is it possible that he had more than one purpose? Explain your answer.

trembled, her medals clinked against each other. The wolf heard the sound of the medals clinking. He found Bertha, dragged her out and ate her up. All that was left were her shoes, bits of clothing, and the three medals for goodness."

"Were any of the little pigs killed?"

"No, they all escaped."

100   "The story began badly," said the smaller girl, "but it had a beautiful ending."

"It is the most beautiful story that I ever heard," said the bigger girl.

The aunt disagreed. "What an improper story to tell children! You have undermined years of careful teaching." **A**

"At any rate," said the bachelor, "I kept them quiet for ten minutes, which was more than you could do." He gathered his belongings and left the train.

"Poor woman!" he thought as he walked away. "Now those 110   children will always be begging her in public for an improper story!" **B**

Applying Your Skills

The Storyteller

LITERARY FOCUS: OMNISCIENT NARRATOR

DIRECTIONS: Imagine that "The Storyteller" did *not* have an **omniscient narrator**. Write a brief paragraph discussing how the story would be different without an omniscient narrator. Would you still know what the characters were thinking and feeling?

_____

_____

_____

_____

_____

_____

READING FOCUS: IDENTIFYING WRITER'S PURPOSE

DIRECTIONS: Various sections of the story are described in the left-hand column of the table below. In the right-hand column, explain what you think the **writer's purpose** was in writing each section.

Section	I think the writer's purpose was to:
Lines 32–37: first conversation between the aunt and the bachelor	
Lines 39–99: bachelor's story about Bertha	
Lines 104–108: second conversation between the aunt and the bachelor	

Word Box

persisted

scowled

undermined

VOCABULARY REVIEW

DIRECTIONS: Antonyms are words with opposite meanings. For example, *hot* is an antonym of *cold*. Determine which vocabulary words from the Word Box are antonyms of the words listed below. Write your answers on the blanks.

1. grinned: _____

2. strengthened: _____

3. stopped: _____

Evacuation Order No. 19

Based on the short story by Julie Otsuka

LITERARY FOCUS: THIRD-PERSON LIMITED NARRATOR

The story you are about to read has a **third-person limited narrator**. This kind of narrator tells you about the actions, thoughts, and feelings of only one character. The narrator still describes other characters, but you only get to know one character's point of view. Imagine that your friend Pamela has told you a story about scoring a goal in a recent soccer game and how it made her feel. If you then go home and tell your brother about Pamela's goal, you are acting as a third-person limited narrator. You tell the story about Pamela in the third person, but you still reveal her thoughts and feelings.

READING FOCUS: DRAWING CONCLUSIONS

A narrator does not always tell you why a character behaves the way he or she does. As a reader, you have to **draw conclusions** about the character's actions. For example, imagine that the narrator tells you that a character receives a phone call and then immediately drives to the hospital. However, you do not know what was said during the phone call. This means that you need to draw a conclusion. Here is a possible conclusion that you might draw from what you do know: During the phone call, the character found out that someone was in the hospital.

VOCABULARY

evacuation (IH VAK YOO AY SHUHN) *n.:* removal or withdrawal.

streetcar (STREET KAHR) *n.:* a train-car-like vehicle that runs on rails on city streets; a popular mode of transportation in San Francisco, California.

shuddered (SHUH DUHRD) *v.:* trembled or shivered.

INTO THE SHORT STORY

On December 7, 1941, Japanese forces bombed Pearl Harbor. In response, the United States declared war on Japan. On February 19, 1942, President Roosevelt ordered Japanese-Americans to be moved to internment camps. The camps were like prison camps. While Japanese-Americans were not charged with any crimes, the government believed they might be dangerous. By September, 1942, 120,000 people were living in these camps.

SKILLS FOCUS

Literary Skills
Understand third-person limited narrator.

Reading Skills
Draw conclusions.

EVACUATION ORDER NO. 19 Ⓐ

Based on the short story by Julie Otsuka

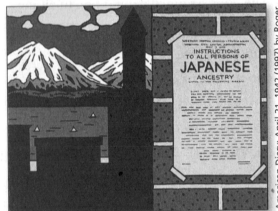

American Diary: April 21, 1942 (1997) by Roger Shimomura. Acrylic. 11 × 4 inches. Collection of Esther Weissman. Courtesy the Artist.

Overnight the sign had appeared. It hung on billboards, trees, bus stop benches, and every other telephone pole along University Avenue. It was a sunny day in Berkeley[1] in the spring of 1942. Mrs. Hayashi read the sign from top to bottom. Then she went home and began to pack. Ⓑ

Nine days later, she pulled on her white silk gloves and walked to the Rumford Pharmacy. She bought several bars of soap and a large jar of face cream. Then she went into Lundy's Hardware. "Nice glasses," Joe Lundy said the moment she entered.

10 "You think?" she asked. "I'm not used to them yet."

"How's your roof?" he asked.

"It just sprung another leak."

"It's been a wet year."

Mrs. Hayashi nodded. She picked out two rolls of tape and a ball of string and brought them to the register. Ⓒ She put two quarters on the counter.

Joe Lundy pushed the quarters back toward her across the counter. He did not look at her. "You can pay me later," he said.

"I can pay you now," she said.

20 "Don't worry about it." He reached into his shirt pocket and gave her two caramel candies. "For the children," he said.

---

1. **Berkeley** is a city in California along the shore of San Francisco Bay.

Ⓐ **HERE'S HOW**

Vocabulary

The word *evacuation* appears in the title. If I look closely, I can see that it contains another word that looks familiar: *evacuate*. I know that *evacuate* means "remove or withdraw." Knowing this, I am going to guess that *evacuation* means "a removal process." I will keep reading to learn more.

Ⓑ **HERE'S HOW**

Reading Focus

I see that two things happen in the first paragraph: Mrs. Hayashi reads the sign and then she begins to pack. However, the story does not say *why* Mrs. Hayashi begins to pack. I do know that she only starts packing after she reads the sign. I can **conclude**, then, that the sign said she had to leave.

Ⓒ **HERE'S HOW**

Language Coach

I know that the word ending *-ed* is not always pronounced as a separate syllable. In the word *nodded* it is a separate syllable, but in the word *picked* it is not. Recognizing different pronunciations is important for building **oral fluency**.

"Evacuation Order No. 19," adapted from *When the Emperor Was Divine: A Novel* by Julie Otsuka. Copyright © 2002 by Julie Otsuka, Inc. Retold by Holt, Rinehart and Winston. Reproduced by permission of **Alfred A. Knopf, Inc., a division of Random House, Inc.**

A YOUR TURN

Reading Focus

Why do you think Joe Lundy compliments Mrs. Hayashi and offers to let her pay later? Think about what has already happened in the story, then **draw a conclusion.**

_____

_____

_____

_____

_____

B HERE'S HOW

Literary Focus

I see that in lines 26–29 the narrator tells us about Mrs. Hayashi's feelings. But the narrator says nothing about Joe Lundy's feelings. I think that is because the story is told by a **third-person limited narrator.**

 C YOUR TURN

Reading Focus

Why do you think the duffel bags are sold out? **Draw a conclusion** as to why so many people need duffel bags.

_____

_____

_____

_____

She slipped the caramels into her purse but left the money. She thanked him for the candy and walked out of the store.

"That's a nice red dress," he called out after her.

She turned around. "Thank you," she said. "Thank you, Joe." The door slammed behind her. In all the years she had been going to Joe Lundy's store she had never once called him by his name until now. Joe. It sounded strange to her. She wished she had said it earlier. **A** **B**

30　　She took the streetcar downtown. At J. F. Hink's department store she asked the salesman if they had any duffel bags but they did not. They were all sold out. All the stores in town were sold out of duffel bags. **C**

When she got home she had to finish packing. She took down the mirrors and the curtains. She carried the tiny bonsai tree[2] out to the yard and set it down where it would get just the right amount of sun and shade. She brought the record player and the chime clock to the basement.

Upstairs, in the boy's room, she wrapped up his stamp 40　collection, and the painted wooden Indian he had won at the State Fair. She pulled his comic books from under the bed. She emptied the drawers. She left the clothes out for him to pack later. She placed his baseball glove on his pillow. The rest of his things she put into boxes in the sunroom.

The door to the girl's room was closed. Above the doorknob was a note that had not been there the day before. It said, "Do Not Disturb." Mrs. Hayashi did not open the door. She went downstairs and removed a picture from the wall: Millet's _The Gleaners_.[3] She looked at the picture. It bothered her, the way 50　those peasants were forever bent over above that endless field of wheat. She set the picture outside with the garbage.

In the living room she emptied all the books from the shelves. In the kitchen she emptied the cupboards. She set aside a few things for later that evening. Everything else—the

---

2.　A **bonsai tree** is a miniature tree.

3.　**Millet's _The Gleaners_** is a famous painting by the French artist Jean Millet (1814–1875) showing three peasants bending over to gather kernels of wheat.

good dishes, the silverware, the ivory chopsticks—she put into boxes.

She taped the boxes shut with the tape from Lundy's Hardware Store and carried them one by one to the sunroom. Tomorrow she and the children would be leaving. She did not know where they were going or how long they would be gone or who would look after the house.

There were things they could take with them: bedding, a few dishes, clothes. Pets were not allowed. That was what the sign said.

It was the fourth week of the fifth month of the war. Mrs. Hayashi gave the cat to the Greers next door. **D**

By early afternoon Mrs. Hayashi was hot and tired. She put two rice balls into a blue bowl. She cracked an egg over the bowl and added some salmon. She brought the bowl outside to the back porch. Her back ached but she stood up straight and clapped her hands three times. **E**

A small white dog came out of the trees.

"Eat up, White Dog," she said. White Dog was old and sick but he knew how to eat. When the bowl was empty he looked up at her. One of his eyes was clouded over. She rubbed his stomach and his tail thumped against the wooden steps.

"Good dog," she said.

She stood up and walked across the yard. White Dog followed her. She had not mowed the grass for months. Her husband Junior usually did that. Last December Junior had been arrested and sent to Missoula, Montana, on a train. Now he was in Lordsburg, New Mexico. Every few days he sent her a letter. He told her about the weather. The weather in Lordsburg was fine. On the back of every envelope was stamped "Enemy Mail." **F**

Mrs. Hayashi sat down on a rock. "White Dog," she said, "look at me." White Dog raised his head. She put on her white silk gloves and took out a roll of string. She tied White Dog to the tree. "You've been a good dog," she said. "You've been a good white dog."

White Dog barked. "Hush," she said. White Dog grew quiet. "Play dead," she said. White Dog rolled over, turned his head

60
70
80
90

D QUICK CHECK

Why does Mrs. Hayashi give the family's cat to her neighbors?

_____

_____

E YOUR TURN

Literary Focus

What has the **narrator** told you about Mrs. Hayashi in lines 66–70 that you might not know otherwise?

_____

_____

_____

F YOUR TURN

Reading Focus

What kind of **conclusion** can you draw about why Mrs. Hayashi's husband was arrested? Think about what you already know about Junior and his letters. Does this information give you any clues about the arrest?

_____

_____

_____

A YOUR TURN

Vocabulary

The narrator says that White Dog *shuddered,* then stopped moving. What do you think *shuddered* means?

_____

_____

_____

B LITERARY ANALYSIS

Before she killed him, how did Mrs. Hayashi treat White Dog? Knowing this, why do you think she killed him?

_____

_____

_____

C YOUR TURN

Reading Focus

What can you **conclude** about the boy's feelings for his father? Underline the evidence that leads you to that conclusion.

_____

_____

to the side, and closed his eyes. Mrs. Hayashi picked up a large shovel. She lifted it high in the air with both hands. Then she slammed the shovel swiftly down onto the dog's head. White Dog's body shuddered twice. Then he grew still. A She untied him and let out a deep breath.

She dug a hole under a tree in the yard. She picked up White Dog and dropped him into the hole. She pulled off her gloves and dropped them into the hole, too. Then she filled up the hole. Mrs. Hayashi was forty-one and tired. B

100 When the children came home from school she reminded them that early the next morning they would be leaving. They could only bring with them what they could carry.

"I already know that," said the girl. She knew how to read signs on trees. She tossed her books onto the sofa. She was ten years old and she knew what she liked. Boys and black licorice and her pet bird.

The boy went out to the porch and clapped his hands three times.

"White Dog!" he yelled. He called out several more times,

110 then went back inside. "That dog gets deafer every day," he said.

He sat down. "It's so hot in here," he said.

"Take off your hat then," said Mrs. Hayashi, but the boy refused. The hat was a present from Junior. It was too big but he wore it every day. She poured the boy a glass of cold water. He drank it all in one gulp. C

The girl came into the kitchen and went to the bird's cage. She leaned over and put her face close to the bars. "Tell me something," she said.

"Take off your hat," said the bird.

120 The girl sat down. Mrs. Hayashi gave her a glass of cold water too.

"Is there anything wrong with my face?" she asked.

"Why?" said Mrs. Hayashi.

"People were staring."

"Let me look at you," said Mrs. Hayashi.

"You took down the mirrors," the girl said.

"I had to. I had to put them away."

"Tell me how I look."

"You have the most beautiful face I have ever seen."

130 "You're just saying that."

"No, I mean it."

The girl sat down. She drank her water. **D**

Mrs. Hayashi told the girl it was time to practice the piano for Thursday's lesson.

"Do I have to?"

Mrs. Hayashi thought for a moment. "No," she said.

"Tell me I have to."

"I can't." **E**

They were eating supper at the table. Outside it was dusk.

140 The boy asked Mrs. Hayashi where they were going the next day.

"I don't know," she said.

The girl left the table. She sat down at the piano and began to play a piece from memory. When she began to play it a second time the boy got up and went to his room and began to pack.

The first thing he put in his suitcase was his baseball glove. Then he threw in his clothes. He sat on top of the suitcase. It was very full. The lid sank down slowly as the air hissed out. **F**

Mrs. Hayashi stood in the kitchen, washing her hands. The children had gone to bed and the house was quiet. She could see

150 a full moon through the branches of the young maple tree. Junior had planted that tree for her four summers ago.

Literary Focus

In lines 122–132, Mrs. Hayashi and her daughter have a conversation. The **narrator** tells us nothing about Mrs. Hayashi's thoughts or feelings during this conversation. What do you learn about her anyway?

_____

_____

E HERE'S HOW

Reading Focus

I know that Mrs. Hayashi's daughter usually has piano lessons on Thursdays. But she does not force her daughter to practice. I know that the family is getting ready to move. I can **conclude** that Mrs. Hayashi does not force her daughter to practice because she knows that the family will move before her daughter's lesson on Thursday.

F YOUR TURN

Literary Focus

Imagine that the **third-person limited narrator** in this story were to let you know the thoughts and feelings of the son, instead of Mrs. Hayashi. What do you think the narrator would say in lines 145–147?

_____

_____

Reading Focus

Look what Mrs. Hayashi does with the bird on lines 152–172. Then think about what she did with the family's cat and dog. What can you **conclude** about how long Mrs. Hayashi expects to be away from home?

_____

_____

_____

_____

Pause at line 180. Think about why Mrs. Hayashi laughs. Does her laughing have to do with only the painting or something else? Explain your answer.

_____

_____

_____

_____

She went to the bird cage and undid the door. "Come on out," she said. The bird stepped cautiously onto her finger and looked at her. "It's only me," she said. He blinked.

"Get over here," he said, "get over here now." He sounded just like Junior. If she closed her eyes she could easily imagine that Junior was right there in the room with her.

Mrs. Hayashi did not close her eyes. She knew exactly where Junior was. He was sleeping somewhere in a tent in Lordsburg. 160 She pictured him lying there and kissed the bird's head.

She gave the bird a sunflower seed. "Get over here," he said again.

She opened the window and set the bird outside on the ledge.

"You're all right," the bird said.

She stroked his chin. "Silly bird," she whispered. Then she closed the window and locked it. Now the bird was outside. He tapped the glass three times with his claw. He said something but she could not hear him.

170 "Go," she said. The bird flapped his wings and flew up into the maple tree. She went outside and shook the branches of the tree. "Go," she shouted. "Get on out of here." A

The bird spread his wings and flew off into the night.

She went back inside the kitchen and took out a bottle of plum wine. Without the bird, the house felt empty. She put the bottle to her lips. She swallowed once and looked at the place on the wall where *The Gleaners* had hung. She began to laugh quietly, but soon she was doubled over and gasping for breath. She laughed until the tears were running down her cheeks. She 180 drank from the bottle again. B She put the cork back into the bottle. She hid the bottle in the basement behind the old furnace. No one would ever find it there.

Except for the sound of the rain the house was quiet. The boy was chewing in his sleep. Mrs. Hayashi wondered if he was hungry. Then she remembered the candy in her purse. She had forgotten about the caramels. She closed her eyes. She would give the caramels to the children in the morning.

In a few hours the boy and the girl and Mrs. Hayashi would report to the Civil Control Station at the First Congregational Church. They would pin their identification numbers to their collars and grab their suitcases and climb onto the bus. The bus would head out of town. Through the dusty window Mrs. Hayashi would see the boarded-up grocery store. It had a new sign in front of it that said, "Thank you for your business. God be with you until we meet again." She would see the Rumford Pharmacy and her house with its gravel walkway. The bus would turn left onto Route 80, then cross the Bay Bridge and take them away. **C** **D**

Three years and four months later they would return. The war would be over. The furniture in the house would be gone but the house would still be theirs. The sunroom would be empty. The bonsai tree would be dead but the maple would be alive. Six months later Junior would come home from New Mexico a tired and sick old man. The following summer Junior would have a stroke and Mrs. Hayashi would go to work for the first time in her life. For five and sometimes six days a week she would clean other people's houses. Her back would grow strong and the years would go by quickly. Junior would have two more strokes and then die. The children would grow up. The boy would become a lieutenant colonel in the army and the girl would become my mother. She would tell me many things but she would never speak of the war. The bottle of plum wine would continue to gather dust behind the furnace in the basement. It would grow darker and sweeter with every passing year. The leak in the roof has still, to this day, not been properly fixed. **E**

© Russell Lee/Library of Congress

C **YOUR TURN**

Literary Focus

The **narrator** suddenly jumps ahead, giving you a glimpse of what will happen to Mrs. Hayashi and her family in a few hours. What effect does this look at the future have on your reading?

_____

_____

_____

D **HERE'S HOW**

Reading Focus

The narrator does not say why the store is boarded up. I can **conclude** it is boarded up because the owners also had to follow the instructions on the sign from the beginning of the story. They have probably recently left on another bus.

E **YOUR TURN**

Literary Focus

What do you find out about the narrator in lines 209–215? Now that you know her relationship to Mrs. Hayashi, does it make sense that she would be a **third-person limited narrator**? Explain your answer.

_____

_____

_____

Skills Practice

Evacuation Order No. 19

USE A CONCLUSIONS CHART

The narrator in the story does not always explain why Mrs. Hayashi and other characters do what they do. You have to **draw conclusions** based on the information you do know—as well as the information you do *not* know.

DIRECTIONS: Details from the story appear in the left column of the table below. Use this information to draw a conclusion about what is happening in the story. Write your conclusion in the right column. The first row has been filled in as an example.

What I Know:	My Conclusion:
Mrs. Hayashi reads a sign, then begins packing.	The sign said that people like Mrs. Hayashi have to leave town. I am guessing it is because she is Japanese.
Mrs. Hayashi goes to buy duffel bags, but they are sold out.	1.
Mrs. Hayashi feeds White Dog, then kills and buries him.	2.
Mrs. Hayashi's daughter does not have to practice piano, yet she does.	3.
Mrs. Hayashi looks at where the painting was and laughs hysterically.	4.

Applying Your Skills

Evacuation Order No. 19

LITERARY FOCUS: THIRD-PERSON LIMITED NARRATOR

DIRECTIONS: Read the excerpts listed below. Now that you know that Mrs. Hayashi's granddaughter is the story's **narrator**, describe what you think she is trying to explain about her grandmother in each section listed below.

Excerpt	What narrator is trying to explain:
"In all the years she had been going to Joe Lundy's store she had never once called him by his name until now. Joe. It sounded strange to her. She wished she had said it earlier." (lines 26–29)	
"Mrs. Hayashi did not close her eyes. She knew exactly where Junior was. He was sleeping somewhere in a tent in Lordsburg. She pictured him lying there and kissed the bird's head." (lines 158–160)	

READING FOCUS: DRAWING CONCLUSIONS

DIRECTIONS: List details from the story to support the two **conclusions** below.

Conclusion 1:	Conclusion 2:
Mrs. Hayashi does not want her family's pets to suffer.	**Mr. and Mrs. Hayashi have difficult lives after the internment.**

VOCABULARY REVIEW

DIRECTIONS: Write one sentence that correctly uses the following words:
shuddered and *evacuation*: _____

_____

Islam in America

Based on the magazine article by Patricia Smith

We Are Each Other's Business

Based on the web essay by Eboo Patel

INFORMATIONAL TEXT FOCUS: ANALYZING AUDIENCE AND PURPOSE

Writers always have a reason, or **purpose**, for writing a particular text. This purpose may be to tell a story or express feelings. It could also be to provide information or persuade readers of something. For example, someone writing an advertisement for a new product wants to persuade readers to buy the product. The author of an editorial in a newspaper wants to express feelings on a local or national issue.

Writers must also consider their **audiences**—the people that will read their work. A writer's word choice and **tone**, or attitude, will reflect the audience he or she is writing for. Someone who writes stories for young children, for example, will use simpler words than someone who writes for adults.

As you read the following selections, try to figure out the writers' audience. It might help to ask yourself these questions:

1. What does the author believe readers know about the topic? Does the selection explain basic or more complex ideas?

2. What is the tone of the text? What is the writer's attitude towards the subject or the audience?

3. Who would be interested in reading the text? Who would *not* be interested?

SKILLS FOCUS

Informational Text Skills
Determine a writer's audience; understand author's purpose.

VOCABULARY REVIEW

observant (UHB ZUHR VUHNT) *adj.:* following the rules of a religion closely.

stereotypes (STEHR EE OH TYPS) *n.:* standard, usually negative ideas about groups of people.

melded (MEHLD IHD) *v.:* blended or mixed together.

applicable (UH PLIHK UH BUHL) *adj.:* useful in a specific situation.

humiliated (HYOO MIHL EE AYT IHD) *adj.:* ashamed; embarassed.

ISLAM IN AMERICA

Based on the magazine article by Patricia Smith

© Steve Raymer/Corbis

INTO THE MAGAZINE ARTICLE
In 1965, President Lyndon Johnson signed an immigration bill that allowed more people to move to the United States. Many of these new immigrants were from the Middle East. This article is about American Muslims, a group of people with a Middle Eastern background, who are now a major part of American society.

Like most American teenagers, 17-year-old Sana Haq enjoys hanging out with her friends and going to the movies. She just got her driver's license, and she's worried about college applications. But Sana, a high school senior from Norwood, N.J., is an observant Muslim. **(A)** That makes her different from most of her friends.

She prays five times a day, as Islam requires. She wears only modest clothing—no shorts, no bathing suits, no tight jeans.

Islam affects every aspect of her life. "If you ask me to
10 describe myself in one word, that word would be Muslim," says Sana. "It's the most important thing to me."

Islam is one of the fastest growing religions in the U.S. The number of American Muslims is hard to pin down, but estimates range from 1.5 million to 9 million.

The Muslim community in the U.S. is very diverse. According to a 2004 poll, South Asians (from countries like India, Pakistan, and Bangladesh) are the largest group. They are followed by Arabs and African-Americans. (Starting in the 1960s, many blacks in the U.S. converted to Islam.) Thirty-six percent
20 of American Muslims were born in the U.S. The other 64 percent come from 80 different countries. **(B)**

Creating an American Muslim identity is a challenge for young Muslims. They are creating a culture "that blends

A HERE'S HOW

Vocabulary

I see the word *observant* in line 5. I know *observe* can be a verb, meaning "watch." In this case though, I do not think Sana is watching something. I think the author is saying that Sana is very dedicated to her religious beliefs.

B HERE'S HOW

Reading Focus

Lines 12–21 include statistics about Muslims in the United States. The author probably assumes that the **audience** does not know much about American Muslims.

"Islam in America" by Patricia Smith, adapted from *The New York Times: Upfront*, vol. 138, no. 8, January 9, 2006. Copyright © 2006 by **Scholastic Inc.** Retold by Holt, Rinehart and Winston. Reproduced by permission of the publisher.

A QUICK CHECK

In lines 22–26, the author states a major main idea in her article. What is it?

_____

_____

_____

B HERE'S HOW

Reading Focus

In the first section of the article, the author gives statistics on American Muslims. In this section, she talks about growing up Muslim in America. Knowing this, I think her **purpose** is to give readers a close look at American Muslims' lives.

C YOUR TURN

Reading Focus

Re-read lines 32–46. The author has included a lot of basic information about Islam. What does she assume about her **audience**?

_____

_____

_____

_____

_____

_____

their American way of . . . living with Islamic guidelines," says Tayyibah Taylor, the editor of a Muslim women's magazine published in Atlanta. **A**

Contrast with Europe

As a group, American Muslims have a higher income than most Americans, and they vote in higher numbers. In addition, they are contributing to American culture. They are forming Muslim
30 comedy groups, rap groups, Scout troops, magazines, and other media.

At Dearborn High School in Dearborn, Mich., about one third of the students on the football team are Muslims. This year, Ramadan[1] coincided with football season. During the holy month of Ramadan, Muslims do not eat or drink between sunrise and sunset. So Muslim players had to wake up at 4:30 for breakfast, go through classes without eating or drinking, and start most Friday night games before darkness allowed them to eat.

"You get to football at the end of the day," says Hassan
40 Cheaib, a 17-year-old senior. "You know you've been faithful. . . . After fasting all day, you feel like a warrior."

Some of Islam's rules are very different from American norms. For example, Sana doesn't date. "Dating means spending intimate time with someone, and for me, that's not allowed," she explains. "But it's not that I don't talk to guys. I have guy friends." **B** **C**

Impact of 9/11

The terrorist attacks of Sept. 11, 2001, had a big impact on Muslims in America. On the one hand, anti-Muslim feeling has increased. On the other hand, many Muslims have taken more
50 interest in their religion. They are also reaching out to more non-Muslims.

---

1. **Ramadan** is the month every year during which Muslims fast between dawn and sunset.

Ishan Bagby is a professor of Islamic Studies at the University of Kentucky. He explains that after September 11, many American Muslims faced negative responses from other Americans. He says, "Muslims have come to the conclusion that . . . if people don't know you it's easy for them to accept the worst stereotypes." **D**

According to one poll in 2003, 63 percent of Americans say they do not have a good understanding of Islam. Many young

60 Muslims are trying to correct common misunderstandings about their religion. For example, Islam does not approve terrorism. It does not deny women equal rights (though many majority-Muslim cultures and countries do). **E**

Ibrahim Elshamy, 18, is a freshman at Dartmouth College in Hanover, N.H. Two days after he arrived on campus, he contacted the Muslim student group. And five times a day, he returns to his dorm room to say his prayers.

In college, Ibrahim has found a Muslim community in which he feels at home. The mosque he and his Egyptian father

70 attended in Manchester attracted many Arab, Asian, and African immigrants. The problem with that, he says, was that people melded their cultural traditions with their practice of Islam. As an American-born Muslim, he found that frustrating. **F**

"Here at Dartmouth, it was extremely refreshing," he says. "I was finally around Muslims who were exactly like me."

Professor Bagby says many young Muslims distinguish between Islam's teachings and the cultural traditions often associated with Islam. Nothing in the Koran forbids women from fully participating (in religion or in life). American women

80 are increasingly demanding equal participation and leadership in the mosque. **G**

'More American'

Samiyyah Ali, 17, grew up in Atlanta. She describes herself as a practicing Muslim. Islam guides her but she doesn't worry about following every rule.

D **YOUR TURN**

Vocabulary

One definition of a *stereotype* is "a simplified definition of a group of people." Most stereotypes are negative. How can stereotypes be harmful?

_____

_____

_____

E **HERE'S HOW**

Reading Focus

In lines 58–63, the author corrects stereotypes about Islam that are wrong. I think she assumes that some members of her **audience** believe those stereotypes.

F **YOUR TURN**

Vocabulary

Find the word *melded* in line 72. Then re-read this paragraph. What do you think *melded* means? (Hint: Think about the differences between Ibrahim's experiences in Manchester and Hanover.)

_____

_____

_____

G **HERE'S HOW**

Language Coach

A **suffix** is a word part added to another word to change that word's meaning. The suffix *–tion* suggests a new state of being. So, *Participation* means "take part in something."

Islam in America **117**

Other than her name, there's not much about Samiyyah that would tell a stranger she is Muslim. She's a cheerleader at Westminster Academy, on the varsity track and field team, in the dance club, and on the school newspaper staff. And she does date.

90 She views the Koran as a historical document that should be understood in context. "A lot of stuff is still applicable—honor and respect is always applicable," says Samiyyah. "But other things . . . are cultural—even ideas about sex. Back then people got married when they were fourteen." Samiyyah says that her family is not so strict. **A**

Most American mosques were formed by first-generation immigrants. As their American-born children take over, the norms are changing.

"Islam in America will feel a lot different in the next 100 40 years," Professor Bagby says. "It'll feel more American."

WE ARE EACH OTHER'S BUSINESS

Based on the web essay by Eboo Patel

> **INTO THE WEB ESSAY**
> *Pluralism* is a situation in which minority groups can maintain their identities within a larger society. American Muslims, for example, can keep their identity as Muslims. They can also see themselves as Americans.

I am an American Muslim. I believe in Pluralism. In the Holy Quran[1], God tells us, "I created you into diverse nations and tribes that you may come to know one another." I believe America is our best chance to make God's wish a reality. **(A)**

In my office hangs a picture called *Freedom of Worship*. A Muslim holding a Quran stands near a Catholic woman holding rosary beads. They stand together, with other praying figures. They are comfortable with each other and yet apart. The picture shows a group living in peace with its diversity, yet not exploring it.

10　　Many forces seek to divide us. To overcome them, we must do more than stand next to one another in silence. **(B)**

I attended high school in the western suburbs of Chicago. The group I ate lunch with included a Jew, a Mormon, a Hindu, a Catholic and a Lutheran. We almost never talked about religion. Someone at the table would announce that they couldn't eat a certain kind of food, or any food at all, for a period of time. We all knew religion hovered behind this, but nobody ever offered any explanation.

A few years after we graduated, my Jewish friend reminded
20　　me of an experience we both wish had never happened. A group

---

1.　The **Holy Quran** is the main religious text of Islam (sometimes spelled Koran).

"We Are Each Other's Business" by Eboo Patel, adapted from *This I Believe: The Personal Philosophies of Remarkable Men and Women*, edited by Jay Allison and Dan Gediman with John Gregory and Viki Merrick. Copyright © 2006 by This I Believe, Inc. Retold by permission of Holt, Rinehart and Winston. Reproduced by permission of **Henry Holt and Company, LLC.**

A **HERE'S HOW**

Reading Focus

In lines 1–4, the author clearly states what he believes. I am guessing that his **purpose** for writing has something to do with persuading people to "come to know one another." I will keep reading carefully to see if this is actually what he ends up explaining.

B **YOUR TURN**

Reading Focus

The author refers to "us" in line 10. What **audience** does he assume is reading his essay?

_____

_____

_____

Vocabulary

I do not recognize the word *humiliated* in line 27. From its context, I can tell *humiliated* suggests the author felt bad in some way. I looked it up, and *humiliated* means "embarrassed."

B   **YOUR TURN**

Reading Focus

What does the story about the author's Jewish friend have to do with his overall **purpose**? How does that story connect to the idea of pluralism?

_____

_____

_____

_____

_____

C   **HERE'S HOW**

Language Coach

My teacher says that the **etymology**, or root, of the word *suffering* comes from the old French *sufrir,* meaning "endure."

D   **YOUR TURN**

Reading Focus

Now that you have finished reading, is the intended **audience** the same as you thought it was earlier?

_____

_____

of thugs in our high school had started writing anti-Jewish insults on classroom desks and shouting them in the hallway.

I did not confront them. I did not comfort my Jewish friend. Instead I looked away.

My friend told me he feared coming to school those days. He felt abandoned when his close friends did nothing. I feel humiliated that I did nothing to stop my friend's suffering. **A**

My friend needed more than my silent presence at the lunch table. I realize now that to believe in pluralism means

30   I need the courage to act on it. In the words of the American poet Gwendolyn Brooks: "We are each other's business." **B**

I cannot go back in time and take away the suffering of my Jewish friend, but through action I can prevent it from happening to others. **C D**

© Curtis Publishing

Applying Your Skills

Islam in America *and* We Are Each Other's Business

INFORMATIONAL TEXT FOCUS: ANALYZING AUDIENCE AND PURPOSE

DIRECTIONS: Complete the chart below by filling in the **audience** and overall **purpose** for "Islam in America" and "We Are Each Other's Business."

Selection	Audience	Purpose
"Islam in America"		
"We Are Each Other's Business"		

VOCABULARY REVIEW

DIRECTIONS: Fill in the blanks with the correct words from the Word Box.

Word Box

observant
stereotypes
melded
applicable
humiliated

1. Instead of learning more about the neighborhood, my uncle insists on believing _____ about that part of the city.

2. I am 15 years old, so the Children Under 16 discount is _____.

3. Since she is a(n) _____ Muslim, she makes sure to pray five times a day.

4. I was so _____ when the other players began making fun of me.

5. Once we _____ my ideas with hers, the project became much more successful.

Skills Review

Collection 3

VOCABULARY REVIEW

DIRECTIONS: Fill in the blanks with the correct words from the Word Box. Not all words will be used.

Word Box

humiliated

perceive

undermined

stereotypes

persisted

scowled

observant

applicable

evacuation

melded

incorporate

shuddered

1. The employees _____ in asking their boss questions they knew she could not answer.

2. Two things that have been _____ have been blended or mixed together.

3. Some _____ Muslim women wear headscarves.

4. _____ about a certain group of people are often misinformed and incorrect.

5. I hope to _____ some new ideas into the group's presentation.

6. I felt that his laughter _____ the serious topic of conversation.

7. Officials called for a(n) _____ of the school once the fire alarms started.

8. He _____ at the other driver after she cut in front of him.

9. I was _____ to realize that I was wearing two different colored socks.

10. The woman _____ every time she walked by the haunted house.

Skills Review

Collection 3

LANGUAGE COACH: SUFFIXES

A **suffix** is a word part that is added to the end of a word to change that word's meaning. Sometimes a few other letters also need to be dropped or added. Think of the word *fearless*. To make this word, the suffix *–less* (meaning "without") is added to the word *fear*. *Fearless* means "without fear." Study the Suffix Meanings Chart below.

Suffix Meanings Chart	
-less: without	*-ary* or *-ic*: relating to
-ness: state of being	*-ful*: full of

DIRECTIONS: For each word listed below, circle the suffix. Then, using the Suffix Meanings Chart, write a definition for the word. Use a dictionary if necessary.

1. boastful _____

2. budgetary _____

3. academic _____

4. lawlessness _____

5. How would you form a word that means "without emotion"?

_____

6. How would you form a word that means "a state of being happy"?

_____

7. How would you form a word that means "relating to caution"?

_____

ORAL LANGUAGE ACTIVITY

DIRECTIONS: Think of an event in your life that made you very happy. It can be an afternoon with friends, or a memory of a baseball game, or even a birthday when you got a great gift. Now, tell a partner the story of your happy event. Tell the story as a **third-person limited narrator** describing the emotions of the main character—you!

Symbolism and Irony

Literary and Academic Vocabulary for Collection 4

LITERARY VOCABULARY

symbol (SIHM BUHL) *n.:* a person, place, thing or event that stands for something else.

A common symbol in many stories is a dove that represents peace.

irony (Y RUH NEE) *n.:* the use of words to suggest a meaning that is opposite and contrary to the words' literal meaning.

There are many examples of irony in the story A Very Old Man with Enormous Wings. *One example is when the townspeople see the angel as a "disaster waiting to happen."*

generalization (JEHN UHR UH LUH ZAY SHUHN) *n.:* a broad statement based on details from a story.

After reading A Very Old Man with Enormous Wings, *I can make the generalization that the townspeople were not understanding and not very friendly.*

ACADEMIC VOCABULARY

derive (DIH RYV) *v.:* obtain from a source.

You can derive meaning from symbols used in a story.

function (FUHNGK SHUHN) *v.:* act in a specific manner; work.

Elements in a story, like symbolism, function in different ways and have different effects on a story.

interact (IHN TUHR AKT) *v.:* act towards each other.

You can tell a lot about the characters in a story by looking at how they interact with one another.

significant (SIHG NIHF UH KUHNT) *adj.:* important; full of meaning.

When you read, pay attention to significant details.

Through the Tunnel

By Doris Lessing

LITERARY FOCUS: SYMBOLISM

A **symbol** is a person, place, thing, or event that stands for something else. For example, the Statue of Liberty is a symbol for freedom. Many stories include symbols. By studying these symbols, you can find the deeper meaning within a story. The tunnel in this story is a real tunnel. As you read, however, think about what the tunnel might symbolize. What deeper meaning might the tunnel have?

READING FOCUS: MONITORING YOUR READING

While reading a selection, it is important to check to make sure that you understand what you are reading. After you finish a paragraph or page in a story, there are several ways you can **monitor your reading**:

1. Ask questions, such as "What will happen next?" and "Why did the character do that?"

2. Analyze important details. Think about why the author included a certain detail. Decide if a detail might be a symbol of something else.

3. Re-read parts of the story that you did not understand.

VOCABULARY

Practice saying the following vocabulary words aloud.

contrition (KUHN TRIHSH UHN) *n.:* sense of guilt at having done wrong.

defiant (DIH FY UHNT) *adj.:* challenging authority.

inquisitive (IHN KWIHZ UH TIHV) *adj.:* questioning.

minute (MY NOOT) *adj.:* very small; tiny.

incredulous (IHN KREHJ UH LUHS) *adj.:* skeptical; disbelieving.

INTO THE SHORT STORY

This story takes place in a beach resort where many British people take vacations. The main character is British. He is on vacation with his mother. The exact location of the resort is never given, but the author implies that it is somewhere exotic, like along the Mediterranean Sea.

SKILLS FOCUS

Literary Skills
Understand symbolism.

Reading Skills
Monitor your reading or comprehension; identify details.

THROUGH THE TUNNEL

By Doris Lessing

Courtesy the Mary Robertson/George Krevsky Gallery

Going to the shore on the first morning of the vacation, the young English boy stopped at a turning of the path and looked down at a wild and rocky bay and then over to the crowded beach he knew so well from other years. His mother walked on in front of him, carrying a bright striped bag in one hand. Her other arm, swinging loose, was very white in the sun. The boy watched that white naked arm and turned his eyes, which had a frown behind them, toward the bay and back again to his mother. When she felt he was not with her, she swung around. "Oh, there you are, Jerry!" she said. She looked impatient, then smiled. "Why, darling, would you rather not come with me? Would you rather—" She frowned, conscientiously worrying over what amusements he might secretly be longing for, which she had been too busy or too careless to imagine. He was very familiar with that anxious, apologetic smile. Contrition sent him running after her.  And yet, as he ran, he looked back over his shoulder at the wild bay; and all morning, as he played on the safe beach, he was thinking of it.

"Through the Tunnel" from *The Habit of Loving* by Doris Lessing. Copyright © 1955 by Doris Lessing. Reproduced by permission of **HarperCollins Publishers, Inc.** and electronic format by permission of **Jonathan Clowes Ltd., London, on behalf of Doris Lessing.**

10

A **HERE'S HOW**

Vocabulary

I wonder what *contrition* means? If I re-read lines 10–16, I see that the mother thinks her son is daydreaming about doing something wild. The son can tell that his mother is worried about what he might want to do by the look on her face. Her worried look leads him to forget about his thoughts and follow his mother. This makes me think that *contrition* must mean "a sense of guilt."

B **HERE'S HOW**

Literary Focus

I think the safe beach might be a **symbol**. I think the beach stands for the safety a child feels with his mother. I think the wild bay is a symbol of growing up and taking chances on your own.

A · YOUR TURN

Literary Focus

This is the second time the author has mentioned the mother's bare arm. Think about how a young son often holds his mother's hand while they walk. What do you think the mother's arm is a **symbol** of?

_____

_____

_____

B · YOUR TURN

Vocabulary

Circle the word in this sentence that has the opposite meaning of the phrase "lacking in devotion." If necessary, use a dictionary for help.

20   Next morning, when it was time for the routine of swimming and sunbathing, his mother said, "Are you tired of the usual beach, Jerry? Would you like to go somewhere else?"

"Oh, no!" he said quickly, smiling at her out of that unfailing impulse of contrition—a sort of chivalry[1]. Yet, walking down the path with her, he blurted out, "I'd like to go and have a look at those rocks down there."

She gave the idea her attention. It was a wild-looking place, and there was no one there, but she said, "Of course, Jerry. When you've had enough, come to the big beach. Or just go straight back to the villa, if you like." She walked away, that bare arm, now

30   slightly reddened from yesterday's sun, swinging. And he almost ran after her again, feeling it unbearable that she should go by herself, but he did not. **A**

She was thinking, Of course he's old enough to be safe without me. Have I been keeping him too close? He mustn't feel he ought to be with me. I must be careful.

He was an only child, eleven years old. She was a widow. She was determined to be neither possessive nor lacking in devotion. **B** She went worrying off to her beach.

IN OTHER WORDS   Jerry and his mother have spent vacation on the same beach for many years. As they were walking to the beach, Jerry saw a nearby beach with big rocks and wild waters that he wanted to go to. He was a little bit scared, but with his mother's permission, he headed to the wild beach. As she walked to the larger, calmer beach, the mother wondered if she had been babying Jerry for too long.

As for Jerry, once he saw that his mother had gained her

40   beach, he began the steep descent to the bay. From where he was, high up among red-brown rocks, it was a scoop of moving bluish green fringed with white. As he went lower, he saw that it spread among small promontories and inlets of rough, sharp rock, and

---

1. **Chivalry** (SHIHV UHL REE) is the act of being polite.

the crisping, lapping surface showed stains of purple and darker blue. **C** Finally, as he ran sliding and scraping down the last few yards, he saw an edge of white surf and the shallow, luminous movement of water over white sand and, beyond that, a solid, heavy blue.

50 He ran straight into the water and began swimming. He was a good swimmer. He went out fast over the gleaming sand, over a middle region where rocks lay like discolored monsters under the surface, and then he was in the real sea—a warm sea where irregular cold currents from the deep water shocked his limbs.

When he was so far out that he could look back not only on the little bay but past the promontory that was between it and the big beach, he floated on the buoyant surface and looked for his mother. There she was, a speck of yellow under an umbrella that looked like a slice of orange peel. He swam back to shore, relieved at being sure she was there, but all at once very lonely. **D**

60 On the edge of a small cape that marked the side of the bay away from the promontory was a loose scatter of rocks. Above them, some boys were stripping off their clothes. They came running, naked, down to the rocks. The English boy swam toward them but kept his distance at a stone's throw. They were of that coast; all of them were burned smooth dark brown and speaking a language he did not understand. To be with them, of them, was a craving that filled his whole body. He swam a little closer; they turned and watched him with narrowed, alert dark eyes. Then one smiled and waved. It was enough. In a minute, he

70 had swum in and was on the rocks beside them, smiling with a desperate, nervous supplication[2]. They shouted cheerful greetings at him; and then, as he preserved his nervous, uncomprehending smile, they understood that he was a foreigner strayed from his own beach, and they proceeded to forget him. But he was happy. He was with them.

---

2. In this sentence, the author is explaining that Jerry was shy. He was using his body language to show **supplication** (SUHP LUH KAY SHUHN), or a request to be accepted even though he felt he was not worthy.

C HERE'S HOW

Vocabulary

I know from the beginning of this paragraph that Jerry is climbing down a steep rock formation toward the bay. Therefore, I think that *promontories* are high pieces of land that jut out over water.

D HERE'S HOW

Reading Focus

I will **monitor my reading** to make sure I understand this paragraph. I will ask myself a question about it: Why does Jerry feel relieved, but lonely when he sees his mother? I think Jerry still feels conflicted about whether he wants to be on his own or to feel the security of being with his mother.

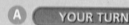

A YOUR TURN

Reading Focus

Re-read this paragraph. Then, **monitor your reading** by answering the following question: Why does Jerry dive off the high cliff?

_____

_____

_____

B QUICK CHECK

What are the shapes moving around in the water?

_____

_____

They began diving again and again from a high point into a well of blue sea between rough, pointed rocks. After they had dived and come up, they swam around, hauled themselves up, and waited their turn to dive again. They were big boys—men, 80 to Jerry. He dived, and they watched him; and when he swam around to take his place, they made way for him. He felt he was accepted and he dived again, carefully, proud of himself. **A**

Soon the biggest of the boys poised himself, shot down into the water, and did not come up. The others stood about, watching. Jerry, after waiting for the sleek brown head to appear, let out a yell of warning; they looked at him idly and turned their eyes back toward the water. After a long time, the boy came up on the other side of a big dark rock, letting the air out of his lungs in a sputtering gasp and a shout of triumph. Immediately 90 the rest of them dived in. One moment, the morning seemed full of chattering boys; the next, the air and the surface of the water were empty. But through the heavy blue, dark shapes could be seen moving and groping. **B**

IN OTHER WORDS Jerry climbed down a big rock formation to get to the bay. Once he got there, he began to swim out. He floated over to make sure he could see his mother on the shore. Once he spotted her, he swam back to shore. From there he saw a group of boys jumping off of high peaks into the water. He swam over to them and they greeted him. Jerry overcame feeling a bit shy and jumped off the peaks just as they did. He felt happy and accepted when they watched him jump. Then the biggest boy jumped in and did not come right back up to the surface. Jerry called out a warming but the boys ignored him. Soon, the biggest boy surfaced looking happy and satisfied with himself. The other boys jumped in and they all disappeared under the water.

Jerry dived, shot past the school of underwater swimmers, saw a black wall of rock looming at him, touched it, and bobbed up at once to the surface, where the wall was a low barrier he could see across. There was no one visible; under him, in the water, the dim shapes of the swimmers had disappeared. Then one and then another of the boys came up on the far side of the barrier of rock, and he understood that they had swum through some gap or hole in it. He plunged down again. He could see nothing through the stinging salt water but the blank rock. When he came up, the boys were all on the diving rock, preparing to attempt the feat again. And now, in a panic of failure, he yelled up, in English, "Look at me! Look!" and he began splashing and kicking in the water like a foolish dog.

They looked down gravely, frowning. He knew the frown. At moments of failure, when he clowned to claim his mother's attention, it was with just this grave, embarrassed inspection that she rewarded him. Through his hot shame, feeling the pleading grin on his face like a scar that he could never remove, he looked up at the group of big brown boys on the rock and shouted, *"Bonjour! Merci! Au revoir! Monsieur, monsieur!"*[3] while he hooked his fingers round his ears and waggled them. **C**

Water surged into his mouth; he choked, sank, came up. The rock, lately weighted with boys, seemed to rear up out of the water as their weight was removed. **D** They were flying down past him now, into the water; the air was full of falling bodies. Then the rock was empty in the hot sunlight. He counted one, two, three . . .

At fifty, he was terrified. They must all be drowning beneath him, in the watery caves of the rock! At a hundred, he stared around him at the empty hillside, wondering if he should yell for help. He counted faster, faster, to hurry them up, to bring them to the surface quickly, to drown them quickly—anything rather than the terror of counting on and on into the blue emptiness of the morning. And then, at a hundred and sixty, the water beyond the rock was full of boys blowing like brown whales. They swam back to the shore without a look at him.

---

3. ***Bonjour! Merci! Au revoir! Monsieur monsieur!*** are French for "Hello! Thank you! Goodbye! Mister, mister!"

C (HERE'S HOW)

Reading Focus

I think this is an important detail in the story. Let me take a moment to analyze it and **monitor my reading.** Jerry wants to feel more like a grownup. But here he is acting like a child to try to get the attention of the older boys. I think that Jerry is not quite ready to be a grownup yet.

D (YOUR TURN)

Vocabulary

The word *rear* has many different meanings. What is the meaning of *rear* as it is used here? Use a dictionary to help you.

_____

_____

He climbed back to the diving rock and sat down, feeling the hot roughness of it under his thighs. The boys were gathering up their bits of clothing and running off along the shore to another promontory. They were leaving to get away from him.

He cried openly, fists in his eyes. There was no one to see him, and he cried himself out.

IN OTHER WORDS Jerry plunged deep into the water to imitate the other boys. He dived down, touched the rock, and came back up. He shouted to the boys so that they would pay attention to him, but they just frowned at him and Jerry felt like a failure. He made childish faces at the boys and called out the only French words he knew. The boys dived back into the water and disappeared for even longer. Jerry worried and wondered if he should call for help. But the boys popped up on the other side of the rock. They swam back to shore and headed off. Jerry thought they were leaving to get away from him and he cried.

It seemed to him that a long time had passed, and he swam out to where he could see his mother. Yes, she was still there, a yellow spot under an orange umbrella. He swam back to the big rock, climbed up, and dived into the blue pool among the fanged and angry boulders. Down he went, until he touched the wall of rock again. But the salt was so painful in his eyes that he could not see.

He came to the surface, swam to shore, and went back to the villa to wait for his mother. Soon she walked slowly up the path, swinging her striped bag, the flushed, naked arm dangling beside her. "I want some swimming goggles," he panted, defiant and beseeching. **A**

She gave him a patient, inquisitive look as she said casually, "Well, of course, darling." **B**

But now, now, now! He must have them this minute, and no other time. He nagged and pestered until she went with him to a shop. As soon as she had bought the goggles, he grabbed them

---

A YOUR TURN

Vocabulary

Use a dictionary to find the definitions of *defiant* and *beseeching*. Then, re-write the sentence in which they are used in your own words.

_____

_____

_____

_____

B HERE'S HOW

Language Coach

My teacher says that the **origin** of the word *inquisitive* is the Latin word *quaerere*, which means "seek." This makes sense because *inquisitive* means "questioning."

from her hand as if she were going to claim them for herself, and was off, running down the steep path to the bay. 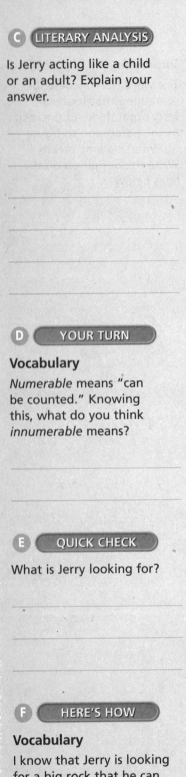**C**

Jerry swam out to the big barrier rock, adjusted the goggles, and dived. The impact of the water broke the rubber-enclosed vacuum, and the goggles came loose. He understood that he must swim down to the base of the rock from the surface of the water. He fixed the goggles tight and firm, filled his lungs, and floated, face down, on the water. Now he could see. It was as if he had eyes of a different kind—fish eyes that showed everything clear and delicate and wavering in the bright water.

Under him, six or seven feet down, was a floor of perfectly clean, shining white sand, rippled firm and hard by the tides. Two grayish shapes steered there, like long, rounded pieces of wood or slate. They were fish. He saw them nose toward each other, poise motionless, make a dart forward, swerve off, and come around again. It was like a water dance. A few inches above them the water sparkled as if sequins were dropping through it. Fish again—myriads of minute fish, the length of his fingernail— were drifting through the water, and in a moment he could feel the innumerable tiny touches of them against his limbs. **D** It was like swimming in flaked silver. The great rock the big boys had swum through rose sheer out of the white sand—black, tufted lightly with greenish weed. He could see no gap in it. He swam down to its base. **E**

Again and again he rose, took a big chestful of air, and went down. Again and again he groped over the surface of the rock, feeling it, almost hugging it in the desperate need to find the entrance. And then, once, while he was clinging to the black wall, his knees came up and he shot his feet out forward and they met no obstacle. He had found the hole.

He gained the surface, clambered about the stones that littered the barrier rock until he found a big one, and with this in his arms, let himself down over the side of the rock. **F** He dropped, with the weight, straight to the sandy floor. Clinging tight to the anchor of stone, he lay on his side and looked in under the dark shelf at the place where his feet had gone. He

160

170

180

C LITERARY ANALYSIS

Is Jerry acting like a child or an adult? Explain your answer.

_____

_____

_____

_____

D YOUR TURN

Vocabulary

Numerable means "can be counted." Knowing this, what do you think *innumerable* means?

_____

_____

E QUICK CHECK

What is Jerry looking for?

_____

_____

_____

F HERE'S HOW

Vocabulary

I know that Jerry is looking for a big rock that he can take down into the water with himself. I think the word *clambered* means "crawled around clumsily."

Vocabulary

The word *clammy* describes something that touches Jerry's mouth. Read the rest of the paragraph to figure out what *clammy* means. Write the definition on the lines below.

_____

_____

© Ali Kabas/Alamy

could see the hole. It was an irregular, dark gap; but he could not
190 see deep into it. He let go of his anchor, clung with his hands to
the edges of the hole, and tried to push himself in.

He got his head in, found his shoulders jammed, moved
them in sidewise, and was inside as far as his wrist. He could see
nothing ahead. Something soft and clammy touched his mouth;
he saw a dark frond[4] moving against the grayish rock, and panic
filled him. **A** He thought of octopuses, of clinging weed. He
pushed himself out backward and caught a glimpse, as he
retreated, of a harmless tentacle of seaweed drifting in the mouth
of the tunnel. But it was enough. He reached the sunlight, swam
200 to shore, and lay on the diving rock. He looked down into the
blue well of water. He knew he must find his way through that
cave, or hole, or tunnel, and out the other side.

IN OTHER WORDS Jerry realized that he would need
goggles to find the underwater tunnel the boys swam through.
He begged his mother to buy him goggles immediately.
He returned to the bay and dived into the water with the
goggles on. He saw many fish in the bay. He felt around
on the underwater rock to try to find the opening the boys

---

4. A **frond** is a large leaf or leaf-like part of seaweed.

swam through. Once he found it, he returned to the surface. He grabbed a large rock that would help him sink quickly down to the opening in the rock. He tried to squeeze through the opening as seaweed brushed his face. He could not get through. He returned to the surface and thought about how he wanted to get through the tunnel.

First, he thought, he must learn to control his breathing. He let himself down into the water with another big stone in his arms, so that he could lie effortlessly on the bottom of the sea. He counted. One, two, three. He counted steadily. He could hear the movement of blood in his chest. Fifty-one, fifty-two. . . . His chest was hurting. He let go of the rock and went up into the air. He saw that the sun was low. He rushed to the villa and found his

210 mother at her supper. She said only, "Did you enjoy yourself?" and he said, "Yes."

All night the boy dreamed of the water-filled cave in the rock, and as soon as breakfast was over, he went to the bay.

That night, his nose bled badly. For hours he had been underwater, learning to hold his breath, and now he felt weak and dizzy. His mother said, "I shouldn't overdo things, darling, if I were you."

That day and the next, Jerry exercised his lungs as if every-thing, the whole of his life, all that he would become, depended

220 upon it. Again his nose bled at night, and his mother insisted on his coming with her the next day. It was a torment to him to waste a day of his careful self-training, but he stayed with her on that other beach, which now seemed a place for small children, a place where his mother might lie safe in the sun. It was not his beach. **B**

He did not ask for permission, on the following day, to go to his beach. He went, before his mother could consider the complicated rights and wrongs of the matter. A day's rest, he dis-covered, had improved his count by ten. The big boys had made

230 the passage while he counted a hundred and sixty. He had been counting fast, in his fright. Probably now, if he tried, he could get

B **YOUR TURN**

Literary Focus
What does Jerry think his mother's beach is a **symbol** of?

_____

_____

_____

_____

YOUR TURN A

Vocabulary
Write a definition for *incredulous*. If necessary, check a dictionary.

_____

_____

HERE'S HOW B

Reading Focus
I am going to analyze the details in this paragraph to **monitor my reading.** They show me that Jerry is behaving more like an adult as he practices to reach his goal. When I compare this to his earlier childish behavior, I can see that he is changing.

through that long tunnel, but he was not going to try yet. A curious, most unchildlike persistence, a controlled impatience, made him wait. In the meantime, he lay underwater on the white sand, littered now by stones he had brought down from the upper air, and studied the entrance to the tunnel. He knew every jut and corner of it, as far as it was possible to see. It was as if he already felt its sharpness about his shoulders.

240   He sat by the clock in the villa, when his mother was not near, and checked his time. He was incredulous and then proud to find he could hold his breath without strain for two minutes. **A** The words "two minutes," authorized by the clock, brought close the adventure that was so necessary to him. **B**

IN OTHER WORDS Jerry spent the day training himself to hold his breath longer. That night his nose started bleeding as a result of his training. His mother warned him not to overdo it. He ignored her warning and returned to the bay the next day to train more. That night his nose bled again. The following day Jerry's mother insisted that he come to the beach with her. He obeyed and found that when he returned to the bay the next day, the rest helped him to hold his breath longer.

In another four days, his mother said casually one morning, they must go home. On the day before they left, he would do it. He would do it if it killed him, he said defiantly to himself. But two days before they were to leave–a day of triumph when he increased his count by fifteen—his nose bled
250   so badly that he turned dizzy and had to lie limply over the big rock like a bit of seaweed, watching the thick red blood flow onto the rock and trickle slowly down to the sea. He was frightened. Supposing he turned dizzy in the tunnel? Supposing he died there, trapped? Supposing—his head went around, in the hot sun, and he almost gave up. He thought he would return to the house and lie down, and next summer, perhaps, when he had another year's growth in him—then he would go through the hole.

But even after he had made the decision, or thought he had, he found himself sitting up on the rock and looking down into the water; and he knew that now, this moment, when his nose had only just stopped bleeding, when his head was still sore and throbbing—this was the moment when he would try. If he did not do it now, he never would. **C** He was trembling with fear that he would not go; and he was trembling with horror at the long, long tunnel under the rock, under the sea. Even in the open sunlight, the barrier rock seemed very wide and very heavy; tons of rock pressed down on where he would go. If he died there, he would lie until one day—perhaps not before next year—those big boys would swim into it and find it blocked. **D**

He put on his goggles, fitted them tight, tested the vacuum. His hands were shaking. Then he chose the biggest stone he could carry and slipped over the edge of the rock until half of him was in the cool enclosing water and half in the hot sun. He looked up once at the empty sky, filled his lungs once, twice, and then sank fast to the bottom with the stone. He let it go and began to count. He took the edges of the hole in his hands and drew himself into it, wriggling his shoulders in sidewise as he remembered he must, kicking himself along with his feet.

Soon he was clear inside. He was in a small rock-bound hole filled with yellowish-gray water. The water was pushing him up against the roof. The roof was sharp and pained his back. He pulled himself along with his hands—fast, fast—and used his legs as levers. **E** His head knocked against something; a sharp pain dizzied him. Fifty, fifty-one, fifty-two . . . He was without light, and the water seemed to press upon him with the weight of rock. Seventy-one, seventy-two . . . There was no strain on his lungs. He felt like an inflated balloon, his lungs were so light and easy, but his head was pulsing.

He was being continually pressed against the sharp roof, which felt slimy as well as sharp. Again he thought of octopuses, and wondered if the tunnel might be filled with weed that could tangle him. He gave himself a panicky, convulsive kick forward, ducked his head, and swam. **F** His feet and hands moved freely,

C YOUR TURN

Reading Focus

Answer the following question to **monitor your reading:** Why is it so important to Jerry to swim through the tunnel now?

_____

_____

_____

D YOUR TURN

Reading Focus

What questions do you have about what will happen next? Write them below to **monitor your reading.**

_____

_____

_____

E HERE'S HOW

Vocabulary

I am not sure what *levers* are. When I see the context, I think *levers* might be tools to move something, since Jerry is using his legs that way. I checked a dictionary, and I was right.

F YOUR TURN

Vocabulary

What do you think *convulsive* means?

_____

_____

Literary Focus

Jerry made it through the tunnel. The tunnel is a **symbol**. What does it represent? What "passage" has Jerry gone through?

_____

_____

_____

_____

_____

_____

as if in open water. The hole must have widened out. He thought he must be swimming fast, and he was frightened of banging his head if the tunnel narrowed.

A hundred, a hundred and one . . . The water paled. Victory filled him. His lungs were beginning to hurt. A few more strokes and he would be out. He was counting wildly; he said a hundred and fifteen and then, a long time later, a hundred and fifteen

300 again. The water was a clear jewel-green all around him. Then he saw, above his head, a crack running up through the rock. Sunlight was falling through it, showing the clean, dark rock of the tunnel, a single mussel[5] shell, and darkness ahead.

He was at the end of what he could do. He looked up at the crack as if it were filled with air and not water, as if he could put his mouth to it to draw in air. A hundred and fifteen, he heard himself say inside his head—but he had said that long ago. He must go on into the blackness ahead, or he would drown. His head was swelling, his lungs cracking. A hundred and fifteen, a

310 hundred and fifteen, pounded through his head, and he feebly clutched at rocks in the dark, pulling himself forward, leaving the brief space of sunlit water behind. He felt he was dying. He was no longer quite conscious. He struggled on in the darkness between lapses into unconsciousness. An immense, swelling pain filled his head, and then the darkness cracked with an explosion of green light. His hands, groping forward, met nothing; and his feet, kicking back, propelled him out into the open sea.

He drifted to the surface, his face turned up to the air. He was gasping like a fish. He felt he would sink now and drown;

320 he could not swim the few feet back to the rock. Then he was clutching it and pulling himself up onto it. He lay face down, gasping. He could see nothing but a red-veined, clotted dark. His eyes must have burst, he thought; they were full of blood. He tore off his goggles and a gout[6] of blood went into the sea. His nose was bleeding, and the blood had filled the goggles. **A**

---

5. A **mussel** (MUHS UHL) is a type of shellfish. It is similar to a clam or an oyster.
6. A **gout** (GOWT) is a large glob.

He scooped up handfuls of water from the cool, salty sea, to splash on his face, and did not know whether it was blood or salt water he tasted. After a time, his heart quieted, his eyes cleared, and he sat up. He could see the local boys diving and playing half

330   a mile away. He did not want them. He wanted nothing but to get back home and lie down. **B**

In a short while, Jerry swam to shore and climbed slowly up the path to the villa. He flung himself on his bed and slept, waking at the sound of feet on the path outside. His mother was coming back. He rushed to the bathroom, thinking she must not see his face with bloodstains, or tearstains, on it. He came out of the bathroom and met her as she walked into the villa, smiling, her eyes lighting up.

"Have a nice morning?" she asked, laying her hand on his

340   warm brown shoulder a moment.

"Oh, yes, thank you," he said.

"You look a bit pale." And then, sharp and anxious, "How did you bang your head?"

"Oh, just banged it," he told her.

She looked at him closely. He was strained; his eyes were glazed-looking. She was worried. And then she said to herself, Oh, don't fuss! Nothing can happen. He can swim like a fish.

They sat down to lunch together.

"Mummy," he said, "I can stay underwater for two

350   minutes—three minutes, at least." It came bursting out of him.

"Can you, darling?" she said. "Well, I shouldn't overdo it. I don't think you ought to swim anymore today."

She was ready for a battle of wills, but he gave in at once. It was no longer of the least importance to go to the bay. **C**

IN OTHER WORDS Jerry's mother told him they must go home soon. One day after practicing a while, Jerry's nose bled as he sat on the rock. When it stopped, he decided to go through the tunnel right at that moment. Part of the way into his journey, he wondered if he could make it. He felt like he could not hold his breath any longer and he occasionally lost

B **HERE'S HOW**

Literary Focus

I wonder why Jerry is no longer interested in being friends with the local boys. Maybe they were a **symbol** of what Jerry wanted to become. Now that he has gone through the tunnel, the boys do not matter any more.

C **LITERARY ANALYSIS**

Why is it no longer important to Jerry to go to the bay?

_____

_____

_____

consciousness. But he made it through and pulled himself up onto the rock. He lay there while his nose bled. He saw the boys playing in the distance and had no desire to go play with them. He returned home. After a nap, he had lunch with his mother and told her he can hold his breath for two or three minutes. She told him he should not swim any more that day and he agrees. He did not feel the need to go back.

Applying Your Skills

Through the Tunnel

LITERARY FOCUS: SYMBOLISM

DIRECTIONS: What do you think each of these elements in the story **symbolizes**? Write your answers in the right column.

wild bay	**1.**
rocks	**2.**
safe beach	**3.**
tunnel	**4.**
Jerry's passage through the tunnel	**5.**

READING FOCUS: MONITORING YOUR READING

DIRECTIONS: Think back to how you read the story. Write a brief paragraph discussing when you used one of these **monitoring** strategies: **1.** Asking questions; **2.** Analyzing important details; **3.** Re-reading parts of the story you did not understand.

_____

_____

_____

_____

Word Box

contrition

defiant

inquisitive

minute

incredulous

VOCABULARY REVIEW

DIRECTIONS: Fill in the blanks with the correct words from the Word Box. Not all words will be used.

1. Scientists have to pay very close attention to their work. Even the smallest, most _____ details must be noted.

2. After the boy broke the window, he felt a sense of _____.

3. It is good for students to be _____ and to ask many questions.

A Very Old Man with Enormous Wings

by Gabriel García Márquez

LITERARY FOCUS: MAGIC REALISM AND IRONY

Magic realism is a style of fiction. In magic realism, elements of fantasy are placed into realistic settings. In this story, for example, an old man falls into a courtyard. The old man also happens to have wings. Magic realism is filled with this kind of meeting between the normal and the very strange. The authors who write in this style ask us to rethink or question our own ideas about what is normal and what is make-believe.

Irony is the difference between what is expected and what actually happens. Irony can also be the difference between appearances and reality. Magic realists use irony to help us see the real part of fantasy, and the fantasy part of reality.

READING FOCUS: ANALYZING DETAILS

When you watch a movie, you are presented with many visual **details**. When you read, though, you have to imagine what things look like. Writers help you do that by including descriptive details that appeal to your five senses. These details bring settings and characters to life. Gabriel García Márquez includes many such details. As you read, try to imagine what the characters and the setting are like.

VOCABULARY

ranting (RANT IHNG) *v.:* speaking wildly.

standoffish (STAND AWF IHSH) *adj.:* unfriendly.

annoyance (UH NOY UNHS) *n.:* something that causes discomfort or trouble.

INTO THE SHORT STORY

Gabriel García Márquez sets many of his stories in the imaginary town of Macondo. In many ways, Macondo shares similarities with the small Colombian town of Aracataca, where García Márquez grew up. In this story, Pelayo and Elisenda find an old man with wings lying in the mud in their courtyard. The author introduces elements of fantasy into a very real setting.

SKILLS FOCUS

Literary Skills
Understand irony; understand elements of style.

Reading Skills
Identify and analyze sensory details.

A Very Old Man with Enormous Wings

by Gabriel García Márquez

On the third day of rain they had killed so many crabs inside the house that Pelayo had to cross his drenched courtyard and throw them into the sea, because <u>the newborn child had a temperature all night and they thought it was due to the stench</u>. The world had

10 been sad since Tuesday. <u>Sea and sky were a single ash-gray thing</u>, and the sands of the beach, which on March nights glimmered like powdered light, had become a stew of mud and rotten shellfish. The light was so weak at noon that when Pelayo was coming back to the house after throwing away the crabs, <u>it was hard for him to see what it was that was moving and groaning</u> in the rear of the courtyard. **A** He had to go very close to see that it was an old man, a very old man, lying face down in the mud, who, in

20 spite of his tremendous efforts, couldn't get up, impeded by his enormous wings. **B**

Frightened by that nightmare, Pelayo ran to get Elisenda, his wife, who was putting compresses on the sick child, and he took her to the rear of the courtyard. They both looked at the fallen body with mute stupor.[1] He was dressed like a ragpicker. There were only a few faded hairs left on his bald skull and very

Courtesy of the artist, Clifford Goodenough

---

1. **stupor** (STOO PUHR): dullness of the mind and senses.

"A Very Old Man with Enormous Wings" from *Leaf Storm and Other Stories* by Gabriel García Márquez, translated by Gregory Rabassa. Copyright © 1971 by Gabriel García Márquez. Reproduced by permission of **HarperCollins Publishers, Inc.** and electronic format by permission of **Agencia Literaria Carmen Balcells, S.A.**

A **HERE'S HOW**

Reading Focus

I have underlined the **details** the author includes to help me see, smell, and feel the setting.

B **YOUR TURN**

Reading Focus

What are some **details** in lines 22–39 that help you imagine what the old man looks like?

_____

_____

_____

_____

_____

How do Pelayo and Elisenda react to the fact that this man has wings? What do they think he is?

_____

_____

_____

_____

_____

How does the neighbor explain the old man's wings?

_____

_____

_____

_____

few teeth in his mouth, and his pitiful condition of a drenched great grandfather had taken away any sense of grandeur he might have had. His huge buzzard wings, dirty and half plucked, were 30 forever entangled in the mud. They looked at him so long and so closely that Pelayo and Elisenda very soon overcame their surprise and in the end found him familiar. Then they dared speak to him, and he answered in an incomprehensible dialect with a strong sailor's voice. That was how they skipped over the inconvenience of the wings and quite intelligently concluded that he was a lonely castaway from some foreign ship wrecked by the storm. **A** And yet, they called in a neighbor woman who knew everything about life and death to see him, and all she needed was one look to show them their mistake.

40 "He's an angel," she told them. "He must have been coming for the child, but the poor fellow is so old that the rain knocked him down." **B**

IN OTHER WORDS In the courtyard of their house, Pelayo and Elisenda discover an old man with large wings. The old man is dressed in rags; he is almost bald and has very few teeth. They stare at him for so long that he starts to look familiar. He speaks in an unfamiliar language, and they think he must be a sailor from a foreign ship. However, their neighbor thinks he is an angel.

On the following day everyone knew that a flesh-and-blood angel was held captive in Pelayo's house. Against the judgment of the wise neighbor woman, for whom angels in those times were the fugitive survivors of a celestial conspiracy,[2] they did not have the heart to club him to death. Pelayo watched over him all afternoon from the kitchen, armed with his bailiff's[3] club, and before going to bed, he dragged him out of the mud and locked

2. **celestial conspiracy:** According to the Book of Revelation in the Bible (12:7–9), Satan—the devil—originally was an angel who led a rebellion in Heaven. As a result, he and his followers, called the fallen angels, were cast out of Heaven.
3. **bailiff's** (BAY LIHFS): A bailiff is a minor local official.

50 him up with the hens in the wire chicken coop. In the middle of
the night, when the rain stopped, Pelayo and Elisenda were still
killing crabs. A short time afterward the child woke up without a
fever and with a desire to eat. Then they felt magnanimous[4] and
decided to put the angel on a raft with fresh water and provisions
for three days and leave him to his fate on the high seas. But
when they went out into the courtyard with the first light of
dawn, they found the whole neighborhood in front of the chicken
coop having fun with the angel, without the slightest reverence,[5]
tossing him things to eat through the openings in the wire as if he
60 weren't a supernatural creature but a circus animal. **C**

Father Gonzaga arrived before seven o'clock, alarmed at the
strange news. By that time onlookers less frivolous than those
at dawn had already arrived and they were making all kinds of
conjectures[6] concerning the captive's future. The simplest among
them thought that he should be named mayor of the world. Others
of sterner mind felt that he should be promoted to the rank of
five-star general in order to win all wars. Some visionaries hoped
that he could be put to stud in order to implant on earth a race
of winged wise men who could take charge of the universe. **D**

70 But Father Gonzaga, before becoming a priest, had been a robust
woodcutter. Standing by the wire, he reviewed his catechism[7]
in an instant and asked them to open the door so that he could
take a close look at that pitiful man who looked more like a huge
decrepit hen among the fascinated chickens. He was lying in a
corner drying his open wings in the sunlight among the fruit peels
and breakfast leftovers that the early risers had thrown him. Alien
to the impertinences[8] of the world, he only lifted his antiquarian[9]
eyes and murmured something in his dialect when Father

---

4. **magnanimous** (MAG NAN UH MUHS): generous; noble.
5. **reverence** (REV UHR UHNS): attitude or display of deep respect and awe.
6. **conjectures** (KUHN JEHK CHURZ): guesses not completely supported by
   evidence.
7. **catechism** (KAT UH KIHZ UHM): book of religious doctrine, consisting of
   a series of questions and answers.
8. **impertinences** (IHM PUR TUH NEHNS EHZ): insults; disrespectful acts or
   remarks.
9. **antiquarian** (AN TUH KWAR EE UHN): ancient.

C **HERE'S HOW**

Literary Focus
The man with the wings appears to be an angel. I would expect people to treat an angel well. It is **ironic** that people treat him badly.

D **QUICK CHECK**

What are some things the people think the angel should become?

_____

_____

_____

_____

A **READING FOCUS**

What are some of the **details** the writer uses to describe the old man in this paragraph?

_____

_____

_____

_____

_____

B **HERE'S HOW**

Literary Focus

The setting of this story is very realistic. I can picture the town as a very real place and the characters as real people. However, the author introduces elements of **magic realism** with the descriptions of the "angel" and how the people view him. Father Gonzaga brings the story back into the real world, as he questions whether the old man is actually an angel.

Gonzaga went into the chicken coop and said good morning

80 to him in Latin. The parish priest had his first suspicion of an impostor when he saw that he did not understand the language of God or know how to greet His ministers. Then he noticed that seen close up, he was much too human: He had an unbearable smell of the outdoors, the back side of his wings was strewn with parasites and his main feathers had been mistreated by terrestrial[10] winds, and nothing about him measured up to the proud dignity of angels. **A** Then he came out of the chicken coop and in a brief sermon warned the curious against the risks of being ingenuous.[11] He reminded them that the devil had the bad habit of making use

90 of carnival tricks in order to confuse the unwary. He argued that if wings were not the essential element in determining the difference between a hawk and an airplane, they were even less so in the recognition of angels. Nevertheless, he promised to write a letter to his bishop so that the latter would write to his primate[12] so that the latter would write to the Supreme Pontiff[13] in order to get the final verdict from the highest courts. **B**

IN OTHER WORDS The neighbor thinks the angel should be killed, because he must be one of the angels who rebelled against God. Pelayo just locks him in the chicken coop. The next morning all the neighbors are watching the old man angel and teasing him. The village priest and some others have more serious ideas about what is in the angel's future. When the priest gets near the angel, the angel seems all too human because he isn't very clean. The priest decides he should write to his superiors about what should happen to the so-called angel.

His prudence fell on sterile hearts. The news of the captive angel spread with such rapidity that after a few hours the courtyard had the bustle of a marketplace, and they had to call in troops with

---

10. **terrestrial** (TUH REHS TREE UHL): earthly.
11. **ingenuous** (IHN JEHN YOO UHS): too trusting; tending to believe too readily.
12. **primate:** here, an archbishop or highest-ranking bishop in a country or province.
13. **Supreme Pontiff:** pope, head of the Roman Catholic Church.

100　fixed bayonets to disperse the mob that was about to knock the house down. Elisenda, her spine all twisted from sweeping up so much marketplace trash, then got the idea of fencing in the yard and charging five cents admission to see the angel.

The curious came from far away. A traveling carnival arrived with a flying acrobat, who buzzed over the crowd several times, but no one paid any attention to him because his wings were not those of an angel but, rather, those of a sidereal[14] bat. The most unfortunate invalids on earth came in search of health: a poor woman who since childhood had been counting her heartbeats

110　and had run out of numbers; a Portuguese man who couldn't sleep because the noise of the stars disturbed him; a sleepwalker who got up at night to undo the things he had done while awake; and many others with less serious ailments. In the midst of that shipwreck disorder that made the earth tremble, Pelayo and Elisenda were happy with fatigue, for in less than a week they had crammed their rooms with money and the line of pilgrims waiting their turn to enter still reached beyond the horizon.

IN OTHER WORDS So many people come to see the angel that soldiers have to be called in to keep order. Elisenda decides that she and Pelayo should charge admission to see the angel. The visitors include a traveling carnival with an acrobat with wings, but his wings are not angel wings. Different people hope the angel can cure their problems or diseases. Pelayo and Elisenda make lots of money, and the crowds continue to come.

The angel was the only one who took no part in his own act. He spent his time trying to get comfortable in his borrowed nest,
120　befuddled by the hellish heat of the oil lamps and sacramental candles that had been placed along the wire. **C** At first they tried to make him eat some mothballs, which, according to the wisdom of the wise neighbor woman, were the food prescribed for angels. But he turned them down, just as he turned down the

14. **sidereal** (SY DIHR EE UHL): relating to the stars or constellations.

C **LANGUAGE COACH**

A **suffix** is a group of letters that is added to the end of a word to change its meaning. For example, the word *showed* contains the suffix *–ed*. Identify the suffix and the root of the word *hellish*. What do you think this word means?

_____

_____

_____

papal[15] lunches that the penitents[16] brought him, and they never found out whether it was because he was an angel or because he was an old man that in the end he ate nothing but eggplant mush. His only supernatural virtue seemed to be patience. Especially during the first days, when the hens pecked at him, searching for stellar[17] parasites that proliferated[18] in his wings, and the cripples pulled out feathers to touch their defective parts with, and even the most merciful threw stones at him, trying to get him to rise so they could see him standing. The only time they succeeded in arousing him was when they burned his side with an iron for branding steers, for he had been motionless for so many hours that they thought he was dead. He awoke with a start, ranting in his hermetic[19] language and with tears in his eyes, and he flapped his wings a couple of times, which brought

130

---

15. **papal** (PAY PUHL): here, fit for the pope.
16. **penitents** (PEHN UH TUHNTS): people who repent their sins.
17. **stellar** (STEHL UHR): having to do with the stars.
18. **proliferated** (PROH LIHF UH RAYT IHD): quickly increased in number.
19. **hermetic** (HUR MEHT IHK): difficult to understand; mysterious.

on a whirlwind of chicken dung and lunar dust and a gale of
panic that did not seem to be of this world. **A** Although many
thought that his reaction had been one not of rage but of pain,
from then on they were careful not to annoy him, because the
majority understood that his passivity was not that of a hero
taking his ease but that of a cataclysm[20] in repose. **B**

IN OTHER WORDS The angel doesn't really do anything.
He just tries to get comfortable, but he is confused by his
surroundings. He won't eat anything except eggplant mush.
He is patient when the hens peck at him, when people throw
stones at him, and when some pull out his feathers. When he
is burned by a branding iron, however, he becomes very angry
and seems dangerous. After this happens, people are careful
not to bother him.

Father Gonzaga held back the crowd's frivolity[21] with
formulas of maidservant inspiration while awaiting the arrival
of a final judgment on the nature of the captive. But the mail
from Rome showed no sense of urgency. They spent their time
finding out if the prisoner had a navel, if his dialect had any
connection with Aramaic,[22] how many times he could fit on the
head of a pin, or whether he wasn't just a Norwegian with wings.
Those meager letters might have come and gone until the end of
time if a providential[23] event had not put an end to the priest's
tribulations.[24] **C**

It so happened that during those days, among so many other
carnival attractions, there arrived in town the traveling show of the
woman who had been changed into a spider for having disobeyed
her parents. The admission to see her was not only less than the
admission to see the angel, but people were permitted to ask her all

---

20. **cataclysm** (KAT uh KLIHZ uhm): disaster; sudden, violent event.
21. **frivolity** (FRIH VAHL uh TEE): silly behavior.
22. **Aramaic:** ancient Middle Eastern language spoken by Jesus and his disciples.
23. **providential** (PRAHV uh DEHN shuhl): fortunate; like something caused by a divine act.
24. **tribulations** (TRIHB yuh LAY shuhnz): conditions of great unhappiness, sometimes caused by oppression.

A **HERE'S HOW**

Vocabulary

I am not sure what *ranting* means. Based on the context, it seems to mean "screaming or talking wildly." I checked my dictionary to be sure, and I was right.

B **HERE'S HOW**

Word Study

It is **ironic** that people see an angel as "a cataclysm in repose," or a disaster waiting to happen. Angels are supposed to be good! I think the author is poking fun at the people who cannot see that.

C **YOUR TURN**

Literary Focus

Re-read lines 151–154. What is **ironic**, or unexpected about the questions from Rome? How is the irony mocking?

_____

_____

_____

_____

_____

_____

_____

_____

_____

A Very Old Man with Enormous Wings   **149**

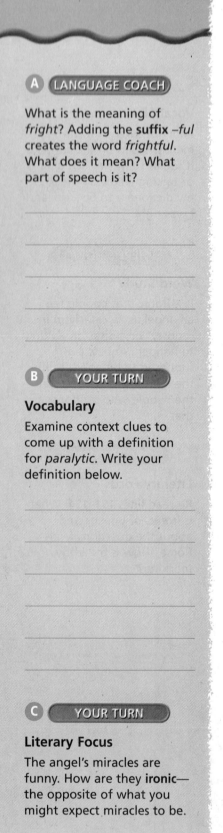

160 manner of questions about her absurd state and to examine her up and down so that no one would ever doubt the truth of her horror. She was a frightful tarantula the size of a ram and with the head of a sad maiden. **A** What was most heart-rending, however, was not her outlandish shape but the sincere affliction[25] with which she recounted the details of her misfortune. While still practically a child, she had sneaked out of her parents' house to go to a dance, and while she was coming back through the woods after having danced all night without permission, a fearful thunderclap rent the sky in two and through the crack came the lightning bolt of

170 brimstone that changed her into a spider. Her only nourishment came from the meatballs that charitable souls chose to toss into her mouth. A spectacle like that, full of so much human truth and with such a fearful lesson, was bound to defeat without even trying that of a haughty angel who scarcely deigned to look at mortals. Besides, the few miracles attributed to the angel showed a certain mental disorder, like the blind man who didn't recover his sight but grew three new teeth, or the paralytic who didn't get to walk but almost won the lottery, or the leper whose sores sprouted sunflowers. **B** Those consolation miracles, which were more like

180 mocking fun, had already ruined the angel's reputation when the woman who had been changed into a spider finally crushed him completely. **C** That was how Father Gonzaga was cured forever of his insomnia and Pelayo's courtyard went back to being as empty as during the time it had rained for three days and crabs walked through the bedrooms.

IN OTHER WORDS The priest tries to keep the crowd from doing silly things while he waits to hear from his superiors. Then a new show arrives in town: a woman who has been changed into a spider for disobeying her parents. People can see her for less money than it takes to see the angel, and they can also ask her questions. She is much more appealing than the proud angel, whose only miracles were more like bad jokes. The priest feels much better, and Pelayo's courtyard is empty again.

---

25. **affliction** (UH FLIHK SHUHN): suffering; distress.

The owners of the house had no reason to lament. With the money they saved they built a two-story mansion with balconies and gardens and high netting so that crabs wouldn't get in during the winter, and with iron bars on the windows so that angels wouldn't get in. Pelayo also set up a rabbit warren close to town and gave up his job as bailiff for good, and Elisenda bought some satin pumps with high heels and many dresses of iridescent silk, the kind worn on Sunday by the most desirable women in those times. The chicken coop was the only thing that didn't receive any attention. If they washed it down with creolin and burned tears of myrrh[26] inside it every so often, it was not in homage to the angel but to drive away the dung-heap stench that still hung everywhere like a ghost and was turning the new house into an old one. At first, when the child learned to walk, they were careful that he not get too close to the chicken coop. But then they began to lose their fears and got used to the smell, and before the child got his second teeth, he'd gone inside the chicken coop to play, where the wires were falling apart. The angel was no less standoffish with him than with other mortals, but he tolerated the most ingenious infamies[27] with the patience of a dog who had no illusions. **D** They both came down with chickenpox at the same time. The doctor who took care of the child couldn't resist the temptation to listen to the angel's heart, and he found so much whistling in the heart and so many sounds in his kidneys that it seemed impossible for him to be alive. What surprised him most, however, was the logic of his wings. They

26. **myrrh** (MUHR): sweet-smelling substance used in making perfume.
27. **infamies** (IHN FUH MEEZ): disrespectful acts; insults.

D HERE'S HOW

Vocabulary
I'm not sure what *standoffish* means. Based on how it is used, it sounds as if it means the angel was unfriendly and not very interested in the people.

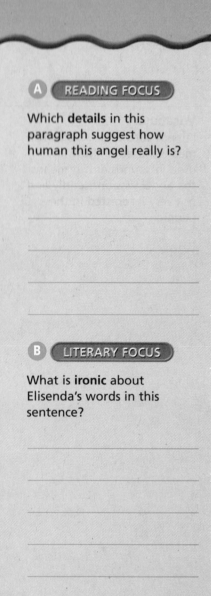

seemed so natural on that completely human organism that he couldn't understand why other men didn't have them too. **A**

IN OTHER WORDS Pelayo and Elisenda don't mind. With the money they saved from charging people to see the angel, they build a new house. Pelayo quits his job, and Elisenda buys new shoes and dresses. They don't pay any attention to the chicken coop or the angel, but the smell from the old building is everywhere. At first, they try to keep their child away from the angel, but eventually he goes inside the chicken coop to play. The angel puts up with him, but he is still very distant. When the boy and the angel get chicken pox at the same time, the doctor examines the angel along with the boy. The doctor thinks the angel is in very poor health, but the wings seem perfectly normal to him.

When the child began school, it had been some time since the sun and rain had caused the collapse of the chicken coop. The angel went dragging himself about here and there like a stray dying man. They would drive him out of the bedroom with a broom and a moment later find him in the kitchen. He seemed to be in so many places at the same time that they grew to think that

220 he'd been duplicated, that he was reproducing himself all through the house, and the exasperated and unhinged Elisenda shouted that it was awful living in that hell full of angels. **B** He could scarcely eat and his antiquarian eyes had also become so foggy that he went about bumping into posts. All he had left were the bare cannulae[28] of his last feathers. Pelayo threw a blanket over him and extended him the charity of letting him sleep in the shed, and only then did they notice that he had a temperature at night and was delirious with the tongue twisters of an old Norwegian. That was one of the few times they became alarmed, for they

230 thought he was going to die and not even the wise neighbor woman had been able to tell them what to do with dead angels.

And yet he not only survived his worst winter but seemed improved with the first sunny days. He remained motionless for

---

28. **cannulae** (KAN yoo lee): here, tubes that hold the feathers.

---

several days in the farthest corner of the courtyard, where no one would see him, and at the beginning of December some large, stiff feathers began to grow on his wings, the feathers of a scarecrow, which looked more like another misfortune of decrepitude.[29] But he must have known the reason for those changes, for he was quite careful that no one should notice them, that no one should

240 hear the sea chanteys that he sometimes sang under the stars. One morning Elisenda was cutting some bunches of onions for lunch when a wind that seemed to come from the high seas blew into the kitchen. Then she went to the window and caught the angel in his first attempts at flight. They were so clumsy that his fingernails opened a furrow in the vegetable patch and he was on the point of knocking the shed down with the ungainly flapping that slipped on the light and couldn't get a grip on the air. But he did manage to gain altitude. Elisenda let out a sigh of relief, for herself and for him, when she saw him pass over the last houses, holding himself

250 up in some way with the risky flapping of a senile vulture. She kept watching him even when she was through cutting the onions and she kept on watching until it was no longer possible for her to see him, because then he was no longer an annoyance in her life but an imaginary dot on the horizon of the sea. **C D**

IN OTHER WORDS After the chicken coop collapses, the angel drags himself all over the new house. Elisenda is very angry that the angel seems to be everywhere, and Pelayo finally lets him sleep in the shed. They notice he is very sick and worry about what they will do with him if he dies. The angel survives, however, and even seems to improve. Feathers grow back on his wings. One morning Elisenda sees him trying to fly. He is clumsy at first, but he keeps going up. Elisenda watches him fly away until she cannot see him. The angel is no longer a bother to her; he is just an imaginary dot in the distance.

---

29. **decrepitude** (DIH KREHP UH TOOD): feebleness; weakness usually due to old age.

C (HERE'S HOW)

Vocabulary
I think an *annoyance* is something that is annoying and causes discomfort or trouble. It is ironic that Elisenda no longer sees the angel as annoying, since she had felt that way for the whole story.

D (YOUR TURN)

Literary Focus
Now that you have read the whole story, did you enjoy the author's use of **magic realism**? How did the author's use of elements of fantasy add to the story?

_____

_____

_____

_____

_____

_____

_____

_____

_____

_____

_____

A Very Old Man with Enormous Wings

USE A COMPARISON CHART

DIRECTIONS: Details make it possible for you to picture characters and settings. They also contribute to how you feel about the people and places in a story. In the box below, fill in two details about the old man and two details about the setting. Then write a sentence describing how you feel about each.

Setting	Old Man
Details: 1. 2.	Details: 1. 2.
How I feel about the setting:	How I feel about the old man:

Applying Your Skills

A Very Old Man with Enormous Wings

LITERARY FOCUS: MAGIC REALISM AND IRONY

DIRECTIONS: Find three places in the story that use **irony**. List them on the lines below and explain what you find entertaining or shocking about each of them.

1. _____

_____

2. _____

_____

3. _____

_____

READING FOCUS: ANALYZING DETAILS

DIRECTIONS: Details help bring characters to life. Complete the exercise below by providing three details about the townspeople in the story.

1. _____

2. _____

3. _____

4. When you look at the details that you listed, what do you think about the townspeople? _____

_____

VOCABULARY REVIEW

Directions: Fill in the blanks with the correct words from the Word Box. Not all words will be used.

Word Box
ranting
standoffish
annoyance

1. The old man was _____ and yelling very loudly.

2. The fly buzzing around the picnic table was an _____, and I just wanted it to go away.

R.M.S. Titanic

Based on the historical article by Hanson W. Baldwin

A Fireman's Story

Based on the eyewitness account by Harry Senior

From a Lifeboat

Based on the eyewitness account by Mrs. D. H. Bishop

INFORMATIONAL TEXT FOCUS: PRIMARY AND SECONDARY SOURCES

When you research a historical subject, you will find two types of information:

- When someone writes about something he or she experienced firsthand, it is called a **primary source**. For example, "A Fireman's Story" and "From a Lifeboat" are primary sources because they are both accounts of the sinking of the *Titanic* that were written by actual passengers aboard the famous ship. Primary sources have not been interpreted by other writers, but they have some disadvantages as well. The main problem is that they share only one person's perspective. Primary sources can also be **subjective**, or based on emotion or opinion rather than hard facts.

- A **secondary source** is a writing based on other sources. The author of "R.M.S. Titanic," for instance, was not actually on the *Titanic*, but he did research for his article by reading other sources on the subject. Secondary sources lack the personal insights that primary sources provide, but they also give broader perspectives. However, keep in mind that authors of secondary sources may also include their own opinions in their writing. For the most part, secondary sources are more **objective**, or factual.

VOCABULARY

Look for these words and their context as you read the selections.

slabs (SLABS) *n.:* thick pieces of some solid material.

muster (MUHS TUHR) *v.:* move toward; gather.

stern (STURN) *n.:* the back of a boat.

SKILLS FOCUS

Informational Text Skills
Synthesize information from several sources on a single topic; understand primary and secondary sources; identify objectivity and subjectivity in a text.

R.M.S. TITANIC

Based on the article by Hanson W. Baldwin

> **INTO THE HISTORICAL ARTICLE**
> This article, written in 1934, is about the sinking of the *Titanic*, which happened in 1912. Hanson W. Baldwin did thorough research by reviewing interviews, ship's logs, and other records. Since the publication of Baldwin's article, the *Titanic* has continued to catch other investigators' interest.

I

The *Titanic*, the largest ship ever, began her maiden[1] voyage on Wednesday, April 10, 1912. **A** She was not only the largest ship afloat, but was believed to be the safest, even unsinkable.

At 9:00 A.M. Sunday, a wireless[2] message from the *Caronia* warned the *Titanic* of an ice field in her path. At least five wireless ice warnings reached the ship that day. The *Titanic* did not slow down.

At 11:30 P.M. in the crow's-nest,[3] lookout Frederick Fleet gazed down at the dark, silent, cold water. He searched the darkness for the dreaded ice, but saw only stars and sea.

A wire[4] from the *Californian* warned that it was stuck in pack ice.[5] The *Titanic* commanded the *Californian* to stay off the air.

II

Then, about 11:40 . . . a vast, dim, white, monstrous shape rose directly in the *Titanic*'s path. Frantically, Fleet struck three

A (HERE'S HOW)

Reading Focus
The author begins by stating some facts. I know the first sentence is **objective**.

---

1. Here, **maiden** (MAY DUHN) means "first."
2. **Wireless** (WYR LIHS) means sent by radio waves instead of electric wires.
3. A **crow's-nest** is a small closed-in platform near the top of a ship's mast.
4. A **wire** is a telegram.
5. **Pack ice** is a large area of floating pieces of ice, frozen together.

"R.M.S. Titanic" by Hanson W. Baldwin, adapted from *Harper's Magazine*, January 1934. Copyright © 1934 by Hanson W. Baldwin. Retold by Holt, Rinehart and Winston. Reproduced by permission of **Curtis Brown, Ltd.**

A YOUR TURN

Reading Focus

Even though this is a **secondary source**, the author may still put his own twist on some details. Underline words in this paragraph that show that the author is giving his opinion.

B HERE'S HOW

Language Coach

I know that writers sometimes place **context clues** in a text to help the reader understand certain words. Here, I do not know what *slabs* are, but I do know what *chunks* of ice are. I think the two words are very similar. I checked my dictionary, and *slabs* are "thick pieces of solid material," like ice.

C HERE'S HOW

Reading Focus

Over fifty years after this article was published, scientists investigating the *Titanic's* remains found no evidence of a "three-hundred foot slash in the ship's bottom." While the author was trying to be **objective** here, in this case he was misinformed.

bells[6]—meaning something was straight ahead. He telephoned the bridge.[7] **A**

"Iceberg! Right ahead!"

The first officer ordered a turn. The bow[8] swung slowly left. The monster was almost upon them.

First Officer Murdoch leaped to the engine-room telegraph.[9] Bells clanged. In the engine room the indicators swung to "Stop!" Frantically, the engineers turned great valve[10] wheels and answered the bells . . . There was a slight shock, a brief scraping, a small tilting left. Slabs and chunks of ice fell on the deck. **B** Slowly the *Titanic* stopped.

Captain Smith hurried to the deck. Murdoch reported the ship had struck an iceberg.

In and around the boiler rooms, men could see that the *Titanic's* damage was deadly. In ten seconds the iceberg had ripped a three-hundred-foot slash in the ship's bottom. **C**

---

6. Here, the **three bells** are a warning signal.
7. Here, a **bridge** (BRIHJ) is a raised part of a ship where the captain controls the ship's movements.
8. The **bow** (BOW) is the front part of a ship.
9. An **engine-room telegraph** (TEHL UH GRAF) is the apparatus that allows messages to be sent from the engine room to other parts of the ship.
10. A **valve** is a device that controls the flow of liquids.

The call for help went out. Miles away, ships heard it.

The sea surged into the *Titanic's* hold. At 12:20 the water burst into the seamen's quarters.[11] Pumps strained in the engine rooms, but the water rose steadily.

The lifeboats were prepared. Because there had been no lifeboat drill,[12] many of the crew did not know where to go.

12:25 A.M. The *Titanic's* position[13] is sent to a fleet of ships: "Come at once. We have struck a berg."

12:30 A.M. The word is passed: "Women and children in the
40 boats." Stewards[14] wake the last passengers. The *Carpathia* radios, "Coming hard." The alarm changes the course of many ships— but not of the *Californian*. The operator of the *Californian*, nearby, has put down his earphones and gone to bed.

12:45 A.M. Lifeboats are lowered, but at first, women hang back. They hesitate to leave the unsinkable ship for a lifeboat ride on an icy sea. **D** One boat, with room for sixty-five passengers, has only twenty-eight. The band plays ragtime, popular music of the day. **E**

1:00 A.M. Slowly the water creeps higher. The "Millionaires'
50 Special" lifeboat, with room for forty, leaves with twelve wealthy passengers while poor immigrants[15] race for space on a boat. The band plays ragtime.

1:20 A.M. Half-filled lifeboats are ordered to take on more passengers, but the boats are never filled. Some boats head for another ship's lights miles away. The lights disappear. The unknown ship steams off. On the *Titanic*, the water rises. The band plays ragtime.

1:30 A.M. As one boat is lowered into the sea, a boat officer fires his gun to stop a rush of poor people from the lower decks.
60 A woman tries to take her Great Dane on a lifeboat. When she is refused, she steps out of the boat to die with her dog.

---

11. **Quarters** (KWAWR TUHRZ) are the part of the ship where the sailors slept.
12. Here, a **drill** is a training exercise.
13. **Position** (PUH ZIHSH UHN) means "location; where something is."
14. **Stewards** (STOO IJRDZ) are shipboard servants.
15. **Immigrants** (IHM UH GRUHNTZ) are people who come into a country
    to live.

D QUICK CHECK

Why are some people hesitant to get in the lifeboats?

_____

_____

_____

E YOUR TURN

Language Coach
Use **context clues** to write a definition for *ragtime* music.

_____

_____

Illustrations by Ken Marschall © 1992 from TITANIC: AN ILLUSTRATED HISTORY, a Hyperion/Madison Press Book

A **YOUR TURN**

Reading Focus

Is this sentence **objective** or **subjective**? Explain your answer.

_____

_____

_____

_____

_____

_____

_____

1:40 A.M. Major Butt helps women into the last boats. Colonel John Jacob Astor put his young wife in a boat, saying "I'll join you later." Another woman chooses to stay with her husband.

2:00 A.M. The *Titanic* is dying now. Her front goes deeper, her back higher. Below, the sweaty firemen[16] keep steam up for the engines.

660 people are in boats with 1,500 still on the sinking ship. **A**

In the radio shack, the operator, sends "SOS—"[17]

70   The tired captain appears at the radio-room door. "Men, you have done your full duty. Now, it's every man for himself."

2:10 A.M. The band plays "Nearer My God to Thee." The water creeps over the bridge where the *Titanic*'s master stands; he steps out to meet it.

---

16. **Firemen** were men who tended the fires that heated the boilers in the ship. The boilers made steam, which drove the ship's engine.
17. An **SOS** is a call for help in code.

2:17 A.M. The lights flicker out. The engineers have lost their battle.

2:18 A.M. People leap into the night and are swept into the sea.

The *Titanic* stands on end. She slides to her grave—slowly at first, and then faster.

80   2:20 A.M. The greatest ship in the world has sunk. **B**

III

The lifeboats pulled safely away from the sinking ship, from the people freezing in the water. Only a few lifeboats were fully loaded. Most half-empty ones did not try to pick anyone up. People on some lifeboats beat away the freezing swimmers.

Only a few lifeboats had lights. Only No. 2 had a light that helped the *Carpathia*, coming to the rescue. Other ships were rushing to help too, but not the *Californian*.

At 2:40 the *Carpathia* sighted boat lights. At 4:10 she picked up the first boat and learned that the *Titanic* had sunk. About

90 that time, the *Californian*'s radio operator put on his earphones and learned of the disaster. **C**

IV

On Thursday night, when the *Carpathia* reached New York, thirty thousand people jammed the streets as the first survivor[18] stepped down the gangway.

Thus ended the maiden voyage of the *Titanic*.

V

Eventually, people learned the *Titanic* had carried lifeboats for only one third of her load. The boats had been only partly full. Boat crews had been slow in reaching their stations. Warnings of ice ahead had reached the *Titanic*. Her speed was excessive.[19]

100 The posted lookout was inadequate.[20]

The *Carpathia* was highly praised; the *Californian* was not. Reports showed that she was probably five to ten miles away from

---

18. A **survivor** (SUHR VY vuhr) is someone who stays alive.
19. **Excessive** (EHK SEHS ihv) means "too great."
20. **Inadequate** (IHN AD uh KWIHT) means "not enough."

B QUICK CHECK

About how much time passed between when the *Titanic* first hit the iceberg and when it actually sunk?

_____

_____

C YOUR TURN

Reading Focus

Remember that a **secondary source** (like this one) is based on other sources. What sources do you think the author might have used to find the information in this paragraph?

_____

_____

_____

_____

the sinking *Titanic*. She had seen the lights and the rockets. She had not received the wires because her radio operator was asleep.

A report stated, "When she first saw the rockets,[21] the *Californian* could have pushed through the ice to the open water easily and so helped the *Titanic*. Had she done so she might have saved many if not all of the lives that were lost." **A**

"She made no attempt."

---

21. Rockets are flares shot up in the air as a signal of distress.

A Fireman's Story

Based on the eyewitness account by Harry Senior

© Mary Evans Picture Library/Alamy

INTO THE EYEWITNESS ACCOUNT

The *Titanic* carried about 2,200 people. But the ship only had enough lifeboats for less than one-third of them. When the *Titanic* sank, 1,517 people died. Many of them were poor passengers who were far below deck. Harry Senior worked on the *Titanic*. This is his memory of what happened.

A **HERE'S HOW**

Vocabulary

I am not sure what *muster* means. Based on its context, I can guess that it means "go somewhere" or "gather together." I checked my dictionary, and I was right.

I was in my bunk when I felt a bump. One man said, "She has been struck." I went on deck and saw a great pile of ice on the deck. But we all thought the ship would last some time. Then one of the firemen came running down and yelled, "All muster for the lifeboats." **A** I ran on deck, and the captain said, "All firemen keep down. If a man comes up, I'll shoot him."

Then I saw the first lifeboat lowered. Thirteen people were on board, eleven men and two women. Three were millionaires.

Reading Focus

This story is a **primary source**—meaning it is told by someone who was there when the *Titanic* sank. Re-read this paragraph. How might the paragraph be different if it had been written by a reporter (who would be **objective**) rather than by someone who was there?

_____

_____

_____

_____

_____

_____

Reading Focus

Re-write one of the sentences in this paragraph as if you were a reporter describing the scene. How is your sentence (which is now a **secondary source**) different from the original?

_____

_____

_____

_____

_____

_____

10   Then I ran up onto the hurricane deck and helped to throw one of the boats onto the lower deck. I saw an Italian woman holding two babies. I took one of them and made the woman jump overboard with one baby. I did the same with the other. When I came to the surface, the baby in my arms was dead. I saw the woman start to swim, but a boiler burst on the Titanic and started a big wave. When the woman saw that wave, she gave up. The child was dead, so I let it sink too. **A**

I swam around for about half an hour. I was still swimming on my back when the *Titanic* went down. I tried to get aboard a boat, but someone hit me on the head with an oar. There were 20   too many people in the boat. I went around to the other side and climbed in. **B**

FROM A LIFEBOAT

Based on the eyewitness account by Mrs. D. H. Bishop

> **INTO THE EYEWITNESS ACCOUNT**
> Mrs. Bishop was a passenger on the *Titanic*. She survived by escaping on one of the lifeboats. As you read her memoir, think about how Mrs. Bishop's experience was different from Harry Senior's experience. Why do you think their experiences were so different?

© Don Lynch Collection

A (**HERE'S HOW**)

Reading Focus
I see that the person telling this story is already on a lifeboat. She is watching the *Titanic* sink from a mile away, so I know this is a **primary source**.

We did not begin to understand the situation till we were a mile or more away from the *Titanic*. Then we could see the rows of lights along the decks begin to slant upward. Very slowly, the lines of light began to point down. The sinking was so slow that you could not see the lights of the deck changing their position. The slant seemed to be greater about every fifteen minutes. **A**

In a couple of hours, the fearful sight began. The people in the ship were just beginning to realize how great their danger was. When the forward part of the ship suddenly dropped faster,

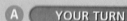

Vocabulary

What do you think the word *stern* means? What makes you think so? Check a dictionary to see if you are right.

_____

_____

_____

Reading Focus

Why do you think Mrs. Bishop included this last sentence? Is her statement **objective** or **subjective**?

_____

_____

_____

_____

_____

_____

10 there was a sudden rush of passengers toward the stern. **A** It was like a wave. We could see the crowd of people sweeping to the rear part of the boat and fleeing to the upper decks. The night was clear. From about a mile away, we could see everything.

This panic went on for an hour. Then suddenly the ship seemed to shoot up out of the water. It seemed to us that it stood upright in the water for four full minutes.

Then it began to slide gently downward. Its speed increased as it went down headfirst.

The lights continued to burn till it sank. We could see the
20 people packed tightly in the stern till it was gone.

As the ship sank, we could hear the screaming a mile away. Slowly it died away. Some of the lifeboats had extra room. If they went back to rescue more people, though, then everyone in the water would have swarmed aboard and sunk them. **B**

© Stockbyte/Punchstock

Applying Your Skills

R.M.S. Titanic, A Fireman's Story, From a Lifeboat

INFORMATIONAL TEXT FOCUS: PRIMARY AND SECONDARY SOURCES

DIRECTIONS: Complete the chart below by deciding if the following excerpts are **objective** (factual) or **subjective** (reflecting some of the author's opinions).

Text	Objective or Subjective?
"At 9:00 A.M. Sunday, a wireless message from the *Caronia* warned the *Titanic* of an ice field in her path." (*R.M.S. Titanic*, lines 4–5)	**1.**
"Frantically, the engineers turned great valve wheels and answered the bells . . . There was a slight shock, a brief scraping, a small tilting left." (*R.M.S. Titanic*, lines 22–24)	**2.**
"I was in my bunk when I felt a bump. One man said, 'She's been struck.'" (*A Fireman's Story*, lines 1–2)	**3.**
"The people in the ship were just beginning to realize how great their danger was." (*From a Lifeboat*, lines 7–9)	**4.**

VOCABULARY REVIEW

DIRECTIONS: Write "Yes" after each sentence if the boldfaced vocabulary word is being used correctly. Write "No" if it is not being used correctly.

1. **Slabs** of passengers rushed for the lifeboats. _____

2. The fireman could barely **muster** the strength to swim. _____

3. The **stern** of the *Titanic* struck the iceberg first. _____

Skills Review

Collection 4

DIRECTIONS: Draw a line between each word in the left column and its correct meaning in the right column.

1. ranting   obtain from a source

2. minute   act in a specific manner; work

3. stern   very important

4. significant   move toward

5. annoyance   the back of a boat

6. inquisitive   very small

7. contrition   speaking wildly

8. derive   something that causes discomfort

9. function   sense of guilt at having done wrong

10. muster   questioning

Collection 4

LANGUAGE COACH: SUFFIXES

A **suffix** is a word part that is added to the end of a word to create another word. The new word is related to the first word. For example, you can add the suffix -ful to peace and get the word peaceful, which means "full of peace."

The suffixes -ence and -ance turn verbs or adjectives into nouns. For example, the verb confer becomes the noun conference.

DIRECTIONS: For each word below, write down its part of speech. Then add -ence or -ance to the word to make it into a noun. Use a dictionary to see if you have spelled the words correctly.

1. deliver _____

2. differ _____

3. perform _____

4. allow _____

5. exist _____

ORAL LANGUAGE ACTIVITY

A **symbol** is something that stands for something else. Think about the chart that you made on the Applying Your Skills Page from the story "Through the Tunnel."

DIRECTIONS: With a partner, talk about "A Very Old Man with Enormous Wings." What do you think are some symbols in that story? After you have talked with your partner, write down the symbols and their meanings on the lines below.

_____

_____

_____

_____

_____

Form and Style

Fish Pond, 1993 (oil on linen), Culler, Pat/
The Bridgeman Art Library International

Literary and Academic Vocabulary for Collection 5

LITERARY VOCABULARY

biography (BY AH GRUH FEE) *n.*: an account of one person's life written by
someone else.
I read a biography to learn about the life of Abraham Lincoln.

autobiography (AH TOH BY AH GRUH FEE) *n.*: a writer's account of his or her
own life.
The famous mathematician wrote an autobiography about her life.

memoir (MEHM WAHR) *n.*: a type of autobiography that deals with an
important event or period of the writer's life.
The memoir is about the writer's year-long battle with cancer.

journalist (JUHR NUHL IHST) *n.*: a writer for a magazine or newspaper
that uses facts, statistics, and statements from others to write a
straightforward account of something.
The author of Into Thin Air *is a journalist who writes for a magazine.*

style (STY UHL) *n.*: the way a writer uses language.
Every writer uses his or her own style in a given text.

diction (DIHK SHUHN) *n.*: writer's specific choice of words.
*A writer's diction may be different when he or she goes from writing
about a funny situation to a sad situation.*

ACADEMIC VOCABULARY

component (KUHM POH NUHNT) *n.*: necessary part of something.
Language is one component of literary style.

subsequent (SUHB SUH KWUHNT) *adj.*: coming next; following.
*In the subsequent paragraphs, the author describes how her feelings
changed over the years.*

equivalent (IH KWIHV UH LUHNT) *adj.*: equal in value, strength, or force.
*Synonyms are words that have equivalent meanings but may be used
in different contexts.*

technique (TEHK NEEK) *n.*: method used to do something.
The climber uses careful technique to reach the top of the mountain.

Typhoid Fever

Based on an excerpt from *Angela's Ashes* by Frank McCourt

LITERARY FOCUS: STYLE—DICTION, TONE, AND VOICE

Every writer has his or her own **style**, or particular use of language. Elements of style include a writer's **diction** (word choice), **sentence structure** (whether sentences are long or short, simple or complicated, and so forth), **tone** (attitude), and **voice** (distinct use of language).

For example, Frank McCourt uses a unique voice to tell his painful story of growing up poor in Ireland. As you read this selection, McCourt's voice should stand out as strong and truthful.

READING FOCUS: EVALUATING WORD CHOICE

In "Typhoid Fever," McCourt chooses his **words** very carefully. For instance, how the characters speak can reveal important information about them. As you read McCourt's story, pay close attention to his word choice to discover additional insights about the characters.

VOCABULARY

Look for these words and their context as you read the selection.

pagan (PAY GUHN) *adj.*: having little or no religion.

privilege (PRIHV LIHJ) *n.*: a special opportunity.

INTO THE AUTOBIOGRAPHY

"Typhoid Fever" is based on an event in Frank McCourt's boyhood. McCourt grew up poor in Ireland in the 1930s and 1940s. He lived in a crowded slum where diseases like typhoid fever and diphtheria were common. People catch typhoid fever by eating food or drinking water that contains the germs that cause the disease. They catch diphtheria by being in contact with people that already have it.

Both diseases are easy to catch, so sick people are kept away from healthy people. In McCourt's Ireland, the sick were kept in "fever hospitals." As in his story, the Roman Catholic Church ran most of those hospitals, and nuns cared for patients. McCourt caught typhoid fever when he was ten years old. Like other sick people, he was sent to a fever hospital.

SKILLS FOCUS

Literary Skills
Understand elements of style, including diction, sentence structure, and tone; understand voice.

Reading Skills
Analyze word choice.

TYPHOID FEVER

Based on an excerpt from *Angela's Ashes* by Frank McCourt

One morning a girl's voice from the next room says, "Boy with the typhoid, are you awake?"

"I am."

"What's your name?"

"Frank."

"My name is Patricia Madigan. How old are you?"

"Ten."

"Oh." She sounds disappointed.

"But I'll be eleven next month."

"Well, that's better than ten. I'll be fourteen in September." **A**

She tells me she is in the Fever Hospital with diphtheria and "something else," nobody knows what.

Soon Sister Rita is lecturing about no talking between rooms and telling us we should be saying the rosary[1] and giving thanks for our recoveries.

She leaves and Patricia whispers, "Give thanks, Francis, and say your rosary." I laugh so hard the stern nurse from County Kerry[2] runs in to see if I'm all right. She scolds me for laughing and says, "No laughing because you'll damage your internal apparatus!" **B**

Courtesy of David Prifti

1. The **rosary** is a group of prayers that Roman Catholics say while holding a string of beads.
2. **County Kerry:** The nurse's accent is different from that of the children.

Adapted from *Angela's Ashes* by Frank McCourt. Copyright © 1996 by Frank McCourt. Retold by Holt, Rinehart and Winston. Reproduced by permission of **Scribner, an imprint of Simon & Schuster Adult Publishing Group** and audio format by permission of **Scribner and Simon & Schuster Audio, divisions of Simon & Schuster Adult Publishing Group.**

A (**HERE'S HOW**)

Literary Focus

The author keeps his **sentences** short and crisp while Frank and Patricia are meeting each other. I will keep reading to see if he changes his sentence structure as the story goes on.

B (**HERE'S HOW**)

Reading Focus

The nun from County Kerry seems very strict. I think the author may be using his **word choice** to really show how he felt about nuns as a young boy.

Literary Focus

How would you describe the author's **tone** in this paragraph?

_____

_____

_____

_____

B YOUR TURN

Reading Focus

By examining the author's **word choice**, how do you think he feels about Sister Rita?

_____

_____

_____

_____

_____

C HERE'S HOW

Vocabulary

I looked up the word *pagan* in the dictionary and it means "having little or no religion."

D HERE'S HOW

Language Coach

I know that every word has a **denotation** (dictionary definition) and a **connotation** (feeling or association attached to it). I think Sister Rita uses the word *pagan* with a negative connotation.

After she plods out, Patricia whispers again in a heavy Kerry accent, "No laughing, Francis, and pray for your internal apparatus."

30 Mam visits me on Thursdays. She says my father is back at work at Rank's Flour Mills and please God this job will last a while with the war on and the English desperate for flour. **A**

Patricia gives Seamus, the man who mops the floors, a short history of England for me. He tries to sing me a song, but the Kerry nurse threatens to report him to Sister Rita.

The book tells about all the kings and queens of England. It includes the first bit of Shakespeare I ever read. I don't know what it means, but it's like having jewels in my mouth when I say the words.

Patricia reads me a verse from "The Highwayman"
40 every day. I can't wait to learn a new verse and find out what's happening to the highwayman and the landlord's red-lipped daughter. I love the poem because it's exciting and almost as good as my two lines of Shakespeare.

Patricia's ready to read the last few verses when in comes the nurse from Kerry shouting at us. "I told ye there was to be no talking between rooms. Diphtheria is never allowed to talk to typhoid and visa versa." And she makes Seamus take me upstairs.

He whispers, "I'm sorry, Frankie," as he slips the book under
50 my shirt and lifts me from the bed.

Sister Rita stops us to say I'm a great disappointment to her and that I'll have plenty of time to reflect on my sins in the big ward upstairs and I should beg God's forgiveness for my disobedience reciting a pagan English poem about a thief on a horse when I could have been praying. **B C D**

There are twenty beds in the ward, all white, all empty. The nurse tells Seamus to put me at the far end of the ward to make sure I don't talk to anyone, which is very unlikely since there isn't another soul on this whole floor. She tells me this was the fever
60 ward during the Great Famine[3] long ago. She says, "'Twould break your heart to think of what the English did to us, no pity at

---

3. The **Great Famine** was a time when potato crops failed in 1845–1847. About one million people in Ireland starved to death as a result.

all for the little children with their mouths all green from trying to eat the grass, God bless us and save us."

The nurse takes my temperature. "'Tis up a bit. Have a good sleep for yourself now that you're away from the chatter with Patricia Madigan below who will never know a gray hair." **E**

Nurses and nuns never think you know what they're talking about. You can't show you understood that Patricia is going to die. You can't show you want to cry over this girl who taught you a lovely poem which the nun says is bad.

Seamus tells me the nurse is a right ol' witch for running to Sister Rita and complaining about the poem going between the two rooms. "Anyway, Frankie, you'll be outa here one of these fine days," he says, "and you can read all the poetry you want though I don't know about Patricia below, God help us."

He knows about Patricia in two days because she collapsed and died in the bathroom. There are tears on his cheeks when he says, "She told me she was sorry she had you reciting that poem and getting you shifted from the room, Frankie. She said 'twas all her fault."

"It wasn't, Seamus."

"I know and didn't I tell her that."

Now I'll never know what happened to the highwayman and Bess, the landlord's daughter. Seamus says he'll ask the men in his local pub where there's always someone reciting something and he'll bring it back to me.

I can't sleep because I see people in the other beds all dying and green around their mouths and moaning for soup Protestant soup any soup and I cover my face with the pillow hoping they won't come and stand around the bed howling for bits of my chocolate bar. **F**

I can't have any more visitors. Sister Rita says after my bad behavior with Patricia and that poem I can't have the privilege anymore. **G** She says I'll be going home in a few weeks and I must concentrate on getting better.

E QUICK CHECK

What does Sister Rita mean when she says that Patricia "will never know a gray hair"?

_____

_____

F YOUR TURN

Literary Focus

In this paragraph, Frank imagines starving children surrounding him. Underline the portion of the paragraph that makes the **tone** more lighthearted.

G YOUR TURN

Vocabulary

What does the word *privilege* mean?

_____

_____

_____

_____

I don't want to be in this
empty ward with ghosts of
children and no Patricia and
no highwayman and no red-
100 lipped landlord's daughter.

Seamus says a man in his
pub knew all the verses of the
highwayman poem. Seamus
has carried me the poem in
his head. He stands in the
middle of the ward leaning
on his mop and recites how
Bess warned the highwayman
by shooting herself dead with
110 a redcoat's musket and how
the highwayman returns for
revenge only to be shot down
by the redcoats.

> *Blood-red were his spurs*
> *in the golden noon; wine-*
> *red was his velvet coat,*
> *When they shot him down*
> *on the highway, Down like*
> *a dog on the highway,*
> 120 *And he lay in his blood on*
> *the highway, with a bunch*
> *of lace at his throat.*

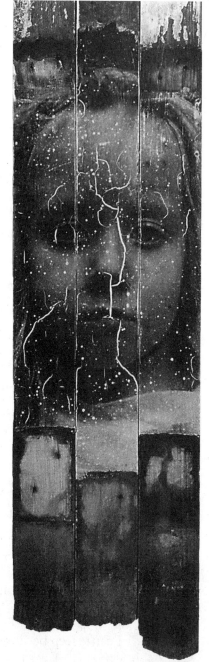

Courtesy of David Prifti

Seamus wipes his sleeve across his face and sniffles. He says,
"'Tis a very sad story and when I said it to my wife she cried all
evening. Now if you want to know any more poems, Frankie,
tell me and I'll get them from the pub and bring 'em back in my
head." A

Applying Your Skills

Typhoid Fever

LITERARY FOCUS: STYLE—DICTION, TONE, AND VOICE

DIRECTIONS: Pick one element of **style** (diction, sentence structure, tone, or voice) and write a short paragraph explaining how that element affected how you read "Typhoid Fever."

_____

_____

_____

_____

_____

READING FOCUS: EVALUATING WORD CHOICE

DIRECTIONS: Look at the author's **word choice** in the quotations below. Then decide what the author is saying about these characters based on the quotations.

Quotations	Evaluate Author's Word Choice
Sister Rita: "'Twould break your heart to think of what the English did to us, no pity at all for the little children . . . " (lines 60–62)	1.
Seamus: "Now if you want to know any more poems, Frankie, tell me and I'll get them from the pub and bring 'em back in my head." (lines 125–127)	2.

VOCABULARY REVIEW

DIRECTIONS: Write "Yes" after each sentence if the boldfaced vocabulary word is being used correctly. Write "No" if it is not being used correctly.

Word Box

pagan

privilege

1. When he got sick, Frank was sent to a **pagan** hospital. _____

2. Because he was caught laughing with Patricia instead of praying, Frank lost the **privilege** of having visitors. _____

Preparing to Read

from Into Thin Air
Based on the magazine article by Jon Krakauer

LITERARY FOCUS: STYLE

Remember that **style** is the particular way that an author uses language. For instance, one element of style is **sentence structure**—one writer may use mostly long, elaborate sentences, while another uses simple, direct ones. Another aspect of style is **mood**, or the atmosphere a writer creates—which can be joyful, gloomy, or humorous. As you read "Into Thin Air," pay attention to its mood and other elements that shape the author's style.

READING FOCUS: IDENTIFYING CAUSE AND EFFECT

A **cause** is *why* something happens. An **effect** is the *result* of something that has happened. A single effect may have several causes, and a single cause may lead to many effects. For example, everything that happens in the story you are about to read is connected by a series of causes and effects. As you read, look for the causes that lead to the disasters on Mount Everest and the effects of the climbers' decisions.

VOCABULARY

Look for these words and their context as you read the selection.

murderous (MUR DUHR UHS) *adj.:* extremely dangerous.

veteran (VEH TRUHN) *adj.:* experienced.

ascent (UH SEHNT) *n.:* the act of climbing; upward movement.

INTO THE MAGAZINE ARTICLE

Jon Krakauer, the journalist who wrote this true story, climbed Mount Everest and barely escaped with his life. Krakauer was part of an Everest expedition that ended in the mountain's worst tragedy. The day he reached the top, eight other climbers died on the mountain.

As Krakauer's account of his climb up Mount Everest begins, he is in the Death Zone, above 25,000 feet, where the air has so little oxygen that it is almost impossible to breathe. The lack of oxygen makes it difficult for climbers to think clearly and make good decisions.

SKILLS FOCUS

Literary Skills
Understand elements of style, including diction, sentence structure, imagery, figurative language, tone, and mood.

Reading Skills
Identify cause-and-effect relationships.

from INTO THIN AIR

Based on the magazine article by John Krakauer

Alan Kearney/Photographer's Choice/Getty Images

Standing on the top of Mount Everest, I stared dully at the huge curve of earth below. I knew that it was a spectacular sight, but I was too worn-out to care. I had not slept in fifty-seven hours and the oxygen in my tank was low. **A**

I took four quick photos of my climbing partners, then started down. After a few steps, I noticed clouds to the south. They looked no different from the harmless puffy clouds that rose from the valley every day. **B**

Later, people would ask why climbers had not paid attention
10   to the warning signs. I saw nothing that afternoon that suggested that a murderous storm was coming swiftly toward us.

After fifteen minutes of very careful shuffling along a seven-thousand-foot drop-off, I arrived at the notorious[1] Hillary Step, named after the first Westerner to climb the mountain. Thirty feet below, three climbers were pulling themselves up the rope, and there were twenty people waiting their turn.

---

1.   Someone or something that is **notorious** (NOH TAWR EE UHS) is well known because of something bad.

Adapted from *Into Thin Air* by Jon Krakauer. Copyright © 1997 by Jon Krakauer. Retold by Holt, Rinehart and Winston. Reproduced by permission of **Villard Books, a division of Random House, Inc**. and electronic format by permission of **John A. Ware Literary Agency**.

A   HERE'S HOW

Reading Focus

The author does not seem very excited that he has reached the top of Mount Everest. I think the **cause** of his lack of excitement is that he is very tired and low on oxygen.

B   HERE'S HOW

Literary Focus

I know this story ends with disaster, but the author has not gotten to that yet. So far the **mood** is fairly relaxed.

A YOUR TURN

A (YOUR TURN)

Reading Focus

What is the **effect** of Andy Harris accidentally releasing the last of the author's oxygen?

_____

_____

B (HERE'S HOW)

Language Coach

Sometimes I can figure out the meaning of an unfamiliar word by looking at **context clues**. For example, I am not sure what *mumbled* means in line 25. However, after I read the rest of the sentence, I think *mumbled* means "spoke quietly and unclearly."

C (YOUR TURN)

Literary Focus

As he recalls the events of the climb, the author uses some short sentences and some long ones. Why do you think he changes his **sentence structure** as he does?

_____

_____

D (YOUR TURN)

Reading Focus

What was the **cause** of Beck Weathers' poor vision at high altitudes?

_____

_____

Andy Harris, a guide with my team, came up behind me while I waited to go down. I asked him to turn off the valve[2] on my tank to save oxygen. Not meaning to, Harris opened the valve, and the

20 last of my oxygen was gone. Now I would have to climb down the most unprotected ground on the entire route without oxygen. **A**

Near the end of the group climbing past me were two of my teammates: guide Rob Hall and Yasuko Namba. Doug Hansen— my closest friend while we were on the mountain—also arrived. He mumbled something that I couldn't hear, shook my hand weakly, and continued slowly upward. **B**

It was after 2:30 when I made it down to the South Summit. By now the weather did not look so benign.[3] I grabbed a fresh oxygen tank, attached it to my breather,[4] and hurried down into

30 the gathering cloud.

Four hundred feet behind me, where the summit[5] was still in sunlight, my teammates were wasting time taking photos and giving high-fives. None of them suspected that on that day, every minute would count. **C**

When I reached the Balcony, about 4 P.M., I found Beck Weathers standing alone, shivering. Due to eye surgery, Weathers could not see at high altitudes. Hall had tried to send Weathers back down, but Weathers talked Hall into waiting to see if his vision[6] improved. If not, Weathers would have to wait at 27,500

40 feet for Hall and the group to return. **D**

I tried to convince Weathers to come with me, but he decided to wait.

By 5:30, the storm was now a full blizzard.[7] I was only two hundred feet above Camp Four, but I still had to climb down a bulge of rock-hard ice without a rope.

Suddenly, Harris stumbled out of the storm. His cheeks were coated with frost, one eye was frozen shut, and his speech

---

2. A **valve** (VALV) is a device that controls the flow of a gas, such as oxygen.
3. **Benign** (BIH NYN) means "mild; not harmful."
4. A **breather** (BREE THUHR) is a device for letting air out of a tank.
5. The **summit** (SUHM IHT) is the highest point.
6. **Vision** (VIHZH UHN) means "sense of sight."
7. A **blizzard** (BLIHZ UHRD) is a very cold, snowy storm.

was slurred. He desperately wanted to reach the tents and started scooting down the ice on his butt, facing forward. A second later he lost his grip and went rocketing down on his back.

Two hundred feet below, I could see Harris lying still. I was sure he'd broken at least a leg. Then, he stood up, waved, and stumbled toward camp. **E**

Twenty minutes later I was in my tent, the door zipped tight. I was safe. The others would be coming into camp soon. We'd climbed Mount Everest.

It would be many hours before I learned that everyone did not make it back to camp.

Hall and Hansen were still on the exposed summit ridge. Hall waited for over an hour for Hansen to reach the summit and return. Soon after they began their descent,[8] Hansen ran out of oxygen and collapsed.[9]

At 4:31 p.m., Hall radioed Base Camp to say that he and Hansen were above the Hillary Step and needed oxygen. Two full bottles were waiting for them at the South Summit, but Harris, in his oxygen-starved confusion, overheard the radio call and broke in to tell Hall that all the bottles at the South Summit were empty. Hall stayed with Hansen at the top of the Hillary Step. **F**

There was no further word from Hall until the middle of the night. He finally reached the South Summit after twelve hours—it should have taken half an hour—but could no longer walk. When asked how Hansen was doing, Hall replied, "Doug is gone."

Late the following day, Hall was connected by radio to his wife in New Zealand. After a few minutes of conversation, Hall told his wife, "I love you. Please don't worry too much," and signed off. **G**

These were the last words anyone heard him say. Twelve days later, Hall was found lying in a shallow ice-hollow, his upper body buried under a drift of snow.

Hutchison and a team of Sherpas, the local guides from Nepal, set out to find the bodies of our teammates Weathers

---

8. A **descent** (DIH SEHNT) is a going down; a trip down.
9. **Collapsed** (KUH LAPSD) means "fell down."

E QUICK CHECK

Why is Andy Harris in such a rush to get down the mountain?

_____

_____

F YOUR TURN

Reading Focus

Underline the sentence explaining what **caused** Hall to stay with Hansen at Hillary Step.

G LITERARY ANALYSIS

Why do you think Rob Hall told his wife not to worry? Explain your answer.

_____

_____

_____

_____

_____

_____

Reading Focus

What was the **effect** of Beck Weathers' severe frostbite?

_____

_____

B **HERE'S HOW**

Literary Focus

While the author's **mood** is sometimes relaxed, here it is serious again. This is because he is talking about the people who died that day on the mountain.

C **HERE'S HOW**

Vocabulary

I do not recognize the word *ascent*, but my dictionary defines it as "upward movement" or "the act of climbing." Both definitions seem reasonable, but the second one makes more sense for this sentence.

Galen Rowell/CORBIS

and Namba. Both were found barely alive, covered in thick ice. Hutchison asked Lhakpa Chhiri's advice. Lhakpa Chhiri, a veteran guide respected by everyone for his knowledge of the mountain, urged Hutchison to leave Weathers and Namba where they lay. Trying to rescue them would jeopardize[10] the lives of the other climbers. Hutchison decided that Chhiri was right.

Later that day, Beck Weathers lurched into camp, his horribly frostbitten right hand outstretched in a frozen salute,
90 looking like a mummy in a horror film. A month later, a team of Dallas surgeons would amputate[11] Weathers's dead right hand just below the wrist. **A**

Until I climbed in the Himalayas, I'd never seen death at close range. And there was so much of it: Eleven men and women lost their lives on Everest in May 1996. (After Krakauer wrote this article, a twelfth death was discovered.) **B**

Climbing mountains will never be safe. Famous mountain climbers—especially Everest climbers—have always been those who took great risks and got away with it. When given a chance
100 to reach the planet's highest point, people are quick to abandon caution completely. "Eventually," warns Tom Hornbein, thirty-three years after his ascent of Everest, "what happened this season is certain to happen again." **C**

---

10. **Jeopardize** (JEHP UHR DYZ) means "put in danger."
11. **Amputate** (AM PYUH TAYT) means "cut off a limb, such as an arm or a leg."

Applying Your Skills

from Into Thin Air

LITERARY FOCUS: STYLE

DIRECTIONS: Write a sentence or two commenting on the **mood** of each of the following excerpts in the chart below.

Text	This Passage's Mood
"After a few minutes of conversation, Hall told his wife, 'I love you. Please don't worry too much.'" (lines 74–75)	1.
"Climbing mountains will never be safe. Famous mountain climbers—especially Everest climbers—have always been those who take risks and got away with it." (lines 97–99)	2.

READING FOCUS: IDENTIFYING CAUSE AND EFFECT

DIRECTIONS: Complete the chart below by providing two **causes** for the problems that Krakauer's team encountered.

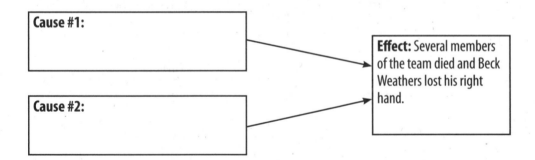

Cause #1:

Cause #2:

Effect: Several members of the team died and Beck Weathers lost his right hand.

VOCABULARY REVIEW

DIRECTIONS: Write the correct vocabulary words on the blanks to complete the following sentences.

Word Box

murderous

veteran

ascent

1. Everest is a dangerous mountain, even for _____ climbers.

2. During the team's _____ of Everest, the clouds seemed harmless.

3. As Krakauer left the summit, a _____ storm struck the mountain.

from 102 Minutes *and* And of Clay Are We Created

LITERARY FOCUS: THEMES ACROSS GENRES

Some experiences are universal. They apply to many different people, no matter where or when they lived. Writers throughout history have explored the experiences that are part of being human. They write about these shared experiences in a variety of **genres**, or types of literature. In nonfiction, their insights come across in the **main ideas**, or most important parts, of a text.

In fiction, writers use different **themes** to talk about a subject. The theme may not be stated outright. You have to pay attention to what the characters think, feel, say, and do to understand the central ideas of the text.

READING FOCUS: ANALYZING AN AUTHOR'S PURPOSE

Authors may have more than one **purpose**, or reason, for writing. They may write to inform, persuade, entertain, or move readers emotionally. An author's purpose affects the choices he or she makes about what to say and how to say it. It also affects his or her choice of genre.

As you read, you can make a chart like the one below to write down details from the two texts and what they suggest about the authors' purposes.

	Details	Purpose
102 Minutes		
And of Clay . . .		

SKILLS FOCUS

Literary Skills
Understand how genre relates to theme.

Reading Skills
Understand author's purpose.

VOCABULARY

paramedic (PAR UH MEHD IHK) *n.:* a person trained to do emergency medical work.

rubble (RUH BUHL) *n.:* fragments, especially from collapsed buildings.

trauma (TRAH MUH) *n.:* a very disturbing experience.

avalanche (A VUH LANCH) *n.:* a large amount of material moving downhill.

decomposing (DEE KUHM POH ZIHNG) *v.:* decaying; breaking down to become rotten.

from 102 MINUTES: THE UNTOLD STORY OF THE FIGHT TO SURVIVE INSIDE THE TWIN TOWERS

by Jim Dwyer and Kevin Flynn

> **BACKGROUND**
> On September 11, 2001, terrorists flew two airplanes into the Twin Towers of the World Trade Center in New York City. Both towers collapsed, killing or trapping many people. Reporters Jim Dwyer and Kevin Flynn interviewed survivors for their book. This selection tells what happened to two members of the Port Authority (a government commission that manages bridges, tunnels, airports, and other facilities of a port or city).

11:00 A.M. GROUND ZERO

Will Jimeno found himself buried but alive, pinned below the burning ground at the center of the trade center plaza. A load of concrete had fallen onto his lap, and a cinder-block wall rested on one of his feet. The oxygen tank strapped to his back also was wedged into rubble, fixing him in a semblance of a seated position, bent at a forty-five-degree angle. Of the four other Port Authority police officers who had been running with him through the concourse, pushing a cart full of rescue gear, only one, Sgt. John McLoughlin, was still alive. Two members of their group had been killed immediately by the collapse of the south tower. A third officer, Dominick Pezzulo, had managed to free himself and was picking at the rubble around Jimeno when the collapse of the north tower killed him. **A**

10

A QUICK CHECK

What has happened to Will Jimeno and John McLoughlin?

_____

_____

_____

_____

_____

_____

From "Epilogue" from *102 Minutes: The Untold Story of the Fight to Survive inside the Twin Towers* by Jim Dwyer and Kevin Flynn. Copyright © 2005 by Jim Dwyer and Kevin Flynn. Reproduced by permission of **Henry Holt** and **Company, LLC**.

Literary Focus

I know that this story is in the **genre** of nonfiction—it is a true story of survival. The men are "on their own" in line 23 because they are trapped and cannot see or hear anybody coming to rescue them. I think that survival and connections to other people are **main ideas** in this story.

© Yoni Brook/Corbis

Now Jimeno was slumped in the hole, talking occasionally with McLoughlin, who was even deeper in the heap than Jimeno. The two men had no view of each other.

"Can you see sky?" McLoughlin asked.

"No sky, but light," Jimeno replied.

The sergeant worked his radio. No one answered.

20   McLoughlin, who over the years had led elevator rescues at the trade center and rappelled[1] into the blind shafts, told Jimeno that the rescue operations would have to pull back for a day, until the scene was stable. They were on their own. A

All across the northeastern United States, people were essentially on their own, stepping into the first minutes of a new

---

1.   **rappelled** (RA PEHLD): descended a wall or shaft by using a rope to make a series of short drops.

epoch[2] without the protections of an old world order whose institutions and functions seemed to have turned instantly decrepit.[3] So a consideration of the events of September 11, 2001, could begin at any one of numerous spots across the globe, at

30 almost any moment over the preceding four decades: the end of the Cold War;[4] the collapse of the Soviet Union;[5] any hour of any year in the unfinished history of the Middle East; in the often empty and petty exercise of authority in the capital of the world's only superpower; at the boiling, nihilistic[6] springs of religious fundamentalism[7] that not only have endured but have thrived as forces in opposition to globalism, capitalism, modernism. **B** **C**

Those historic currents, and others, merged and crashed on the morning of September 11 at the two towers of the World Trade Center, and at the Pentagon, and in a field in Pennsylvania.

40 The particulars of the era that had just passed—the expectations of protection, the habits of defense, the sense of safety—seemed to have fossilized[8] from one breath to the next. What happened in New York City that morning was replicated through all the arms of government, differing only in details, duration, and cost.

IN OTHER WORDS On September 11, 2001, two New York Port Authority police officers, Will Jimeno and John McLoughlin, were buried alive after the collapse of the south tower of the World Trade Center. They had been on a rescue mission with three other officers, all of whom were killed in the collapse. Jimeno and McLoughlin could talk to each other, but Sgt. McLoughlin couldn't get an answer on his radio. They

---

2. **epoch** (EHP UHK): particular period of time or of history.
3. **decrepit** (DIH KREHP IHT): broken down; weakened.
4. **Cold War:** state of hostility and rivalry between the United States and the Soviet Union, as well as their allies, which began after World War II and ended by 1991.
5. **collapse of the Soviet Union:** The Soviet Union, established in 1922, was dissolved in 1991 after the republics that made up the union achieved independence.
6. **nihilistic** (NY UH LIHS TIHK): characterized by a destructive, violent rejection of established beliefs, such as those of religion and morality.
7. **religious fundamentalism:** religious movement or viewpoint that promotes a return to basic religious principles and the strict following of these principles.
8. **fossilized** (FAHS UH LYZD): become out-of-date.

B **LITERARY ANALYSIS**

What strong opinion are the authors expressing about possible causes of the September 11, 2001, terrorist attack?

_____

_____

_____

_____

_____

_____

_____

_____

C **VOCABULARY**

Word Study

Look at the last three words in line 36. The suffix –ism is used here to create nouns that refer to a school of thought. Write another word that has the suffix –ism.

_____

_____

from 102 Minutes **187**

Reading Focus

I think the **authors' purpose** for including details about Jimeno's family is to give me more information about Jimeno's life. Knowing that he has a family to live for makes his story even more moving, as I can feel the emotional pain of his situation.

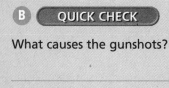

QUICK CHECK

What causes the gunshots?

_____

_____

_____

_____

_____

thought they were on their own. Other people in the north-eastern United States were feeling alone, too, and helpless. Whatever the causes of the terrorist attack, for many Americans their sense of safety and protection was gone in an instant.

An hour or so after the collapse, Will Jimeno, buried beneath the plaza, heard a voice coming through the same hole where the light was entering. The voice wanted to know if a particular person was down in the hole. Jimeno could not quite make out the name, but he was delighted by the sound of another human voice.

50   "No, but Jimeno and McLoughlin, PAPD are down here," he yelled.

The voice did not answer, but moved off, and they heard no more from him.

Balls of fire tumbled into their tidy space, a gust of wind or a draft steering them away, the fire spending itself before it could find another morsel of fuel. Jimeno, thirty-three years old, felt that death was near. His wife, Allison, and their four-year-old daughter, Bianca, would be sad, but proud, he thought. The Jimenos' second child was due at the end of November. So he prayed. **A**

60   Please, God, let me see my little unborn child.

Jimeno tried to make a bargain. He might die, but surely there was a way he could do something for this child.

Somehow in the future, he prayed, let me touch this baby.

Then shots rang out.

The fireballs had apparently heated up the gun of the late Dominick Pezzulo. The rounds pinged off pipes and concrete, erratic and unpredictable, until the last of the ammunition was gone. **B**

With his one free arm, Jimeno reached his gun belt for

70   something to dig with. He had graduated from the Port Authority Police Academy in January and was issued the standard police tools, but he already owned his own handcuffs—a pair made by Smith & Wesson, bought when he was a security guard in a store, arresting shoplifters. He scraped at the rubble with them, but the cuffs slipped out of his hands, and he could not find them again.

© John Labriola/AP Photo

IN OTHER WORDS About an hour after the collapse, Will Jimeno heard a voice. He yelled his own name and McLoughlin's, but he got no answer. Balls of fire blew into their space but went out because there was nothing to burn. Jimeno thought about his wife and daughter and the baby they were expecting in November. He prayed to see his little unborn child. Then shots rang out. The heat of the fires had set off the ammunition in the gun of one of the dead officers. Jimeno tried to dig at the rubble with his handcuffs, but they slipped out of his hand and were lost.

No one had heard from Chuck Sereika, and by midmorning, the messages had piled up on his telephone answering machine and in his e-mail. Can't believe it. Hope you're okay. Our hearts are with you.

80   Sereika woke up. He had slept through everything, not a whisper of trouble in his apartment in midtown Manhattan. The e-mails told him something awful had happened, then news on his computer spelled it out, and as he blinked into the new world, he heard the messages on his answering machine. His sister had called.

"I love you," she said. "I know you're down there helping."

Actually, he had been moping. A In his closet, he found a paramedic[9] sweatshirt and a badge he had not used for years. He had lost his paramedic license, let it lapse after he squandered too many days and nights carousing. He had gone into rehab

90 programs, slipped, then climbed back on the wagon. He had fought his way back to sobriety, but the paramedic work was behind him. B He still had the sweatshirt, though, and no one had taken the badge away. Maybe he could do some splints and bandages. He walked outside. Midtown Manhattan was teeming with people, a stream of humanity trooping in the middle of avenues, the subways shut down and scarcely a bus to be seen. The only way to move was on foot, and by the tens of thousands, people were walking north, or over to the river for ferries, or into Penn Station for a commuter train that would take them

100 east to Long Island or west to New Jersey.

Sereika walked a few blocks from his apartment to St. Luke's-Roosevelt Hospital Center. Then he hitched rides on ambulances going downtown.

IN OTHER WORDS Chuck Sereika slept through the attacks and only found out about them from his e-mails and news on his computer. His sister had left him a phone message, thinking he was helping at the World Trade Center. Although he had been a paramedic, he had lost his license. He had been in rehab more than once, but he was sober now. He decided he could still help, so he walked to a hospital and got rides on ambulances going to the scene.

Seven World Trade Center—a forty-seven-story building—collapsed at 5:20 that afternoon. The firefighters had decided to let the fire there burn itself out. There was no one inside. Against all that had happened, the loss of even such an enormous building seemed like a footnote.

---

9. **paramedic** (PAR UH MEHD IHK): of or relating to a person trained to provide emergency medical care.

David Karnes had arrived downtown not long after its

110 collapse, and as far as he could see, the searches were confined
entirely to the periphery of the complex, picking through the
rubble at the edges for signs of life. **C** Other structures were
now burning—the low-rise building at 4 World Trade Center was
shooting flames—and all hands were staying clear of the ruins of
the two towers and the plaza between them.

Karnes had started the morning in a business suit, working
as an accountant for Deloitte and Touche in Wilton, Connecticut.
After the attacks, he drove from Connecticut to Long Island and
went to a storage facility where he kept his Marine kit. His utility

120 trousers and jacket were freshly pressed, though his commitment
had ended months earlier. Trim as a whip, he slipped into them,
drove to a barber, and ordered a high and tight haircut. He
stopped at his church and asked for prayers with the pastor, then
with the top down on his new convertible, drove straight for
lower Manhattan.

He found the rescue workers in shock, depressed, doing
little by way of organized searches. Karnes spotted another
Marine, a man named Sergeant Thomas, no first name.

"Come on, Sergeant," Karnes said. "Let's take a walk."

130 Not another soul was around them. They swept across the
broken ground, yelling, "United States Marines. If you can hear
us, yell or tap."

No one answered. They moved forward, deeper into the
rubble. The fires roared at 4 World Trade Center. They plowed
across the jagged, fierce ground. **D**

Lost in thought, waiting for release, Will Jimeno listened to the
trade center complex ripping itself apart. He had gotten tired of
shouting at phantoms. He asked McLoughlin to put out a radio
message that Officer Jimeno wanted his newborn baby to be

140 named Olivia. The sergeant was in excruciating pain, his legs
crushed. There was nothing to do, Jimeno thought, except wait
until they sent out rescue parties in the morning. If they lived
that long.

C (HERE'S HOW)

Language Coach
I know that some words
have multiple meanings, or
several possible definitions.
The word *complex* can mean
"hard to understand." In line
111, though, *complex* means
"group of buildings that are
close together."

D (READING FOCUS)

What, do you think, is the
authors' **purpose** for writing
this selection? Has your guess
about the authors' purpose
changed since beginning the
selection? Why or why not?

_____

_____

_____

_____

_____

_____

A

YOUR TURN

Reading Focus

What might Jimeno and Karnes be feeling at this point? What do you think the authors' purpose was for choosing not to show the men's feelings directly?

_____

_____

_____

_____

_____

_____

B QUICK CHECK

How does Karnes get a message to the NYPD without leaving the site?

_____

_____

_____

_____

_____

_____

_____

Then came the voice.

"United States Marines. If you can hear us, yell or tap."

What? That was a person.

Jimeno shouted with every bit of strength he had.

"Right here! Jimeno and McLoughlin, PAPD! Here!"

"Keep yelling," Karnes said.

150   It took a few minutes, but Karnes found the hole.

"Don't leave," Jimeno pleaded.

"I'm not going anywhere," Karnes said. **A**

Karnes pulled out his cell phone and dialed 911, but the call did not go through. He tried again, without success. How could he get help, without leaving Jimeno and McLoughlin? Maybe the problem was with phone lines downtown, and he could find an electronic bridge via someone outside the city. He dialed his sister in a suburb of Pittsburgh and got through. She called the local police. They were able to reach the New York police. The

160   message had traveled 300 miles from the pile to Pennsylvania, then 300 miles back to police headquarters, but the NYPD finally learned that a few blocks away, two cops were buried in the middle of the pile, and a United States Marine was standing by to direct the rescuers. **B**

IN OTHER WORDS The collapse of a forty-seven-story building, Seven World Trade Center, didn't seem very shocking because so much else had happened. David Karnes was a former Marine who was now working as an accountant. When he heard about the attacks, he got his Marine uniform out of storage, got a short haircut, and went to his church and prayed with the pastor. Then he drove to Manhattan. He found another Marine at the World Trade Center, and they began to search the center of the area. Will Jimeno was tired of shouting; he was in terrible pain from his crushed legs and not sure he would live through the night. Then he heard Karnes's voice. Jimeno yelled until Karnes located him. Jimeno begged him not to leave, and Karnes said he wasn't going anywhere. His call to 911 didn't go through, so he called his

© Yoni Brook/Corbis

C **YOUR TURN**

Vocabulary

As Sereika climbs over the rocks and rubble, the text says he *stumbled*. Use context clues to help you define *stumbled*. You can use a dictionary to check your answer.

_____

_____

_____

_____

_____

_____

_____

sister in Pittsburgh. She called the police there, and they called the New York police. The NYPD learned that two cops were buried alive at the World Trade Center, and a United States Marine was there to show the rescuers the spot.

Chuck Sereika had been wandering the edge of that pile as evening approached, when he heard people yelling that someone had been found in the center of the place. Sereika set out, walking part of the way with a firefighter. They could see the flames roaring from the remains of 4 World Trade Center, an eight-story building. The fire-fighter peeled away. By himself, Sereika stumbled and climbed, until he found Dave Karnes standing alone. **C** From the surface, he could see nothing of Will Jimeno, but he could hear him. Sereika squeezed his way into a crevice, inching his way down the rubble, finally spotting Jimeno's hand.

"Hey," Sereika said.

"Don't leave me," Jimeno said.

Sereika felt for a pulse. A good, strong distal pulse,[10] a basic in emergency care.

170

---

10. **distal pulse:** *Distal* means "away from the center of the body." Here, *distal pulse* refers to the pulse in the wrist.

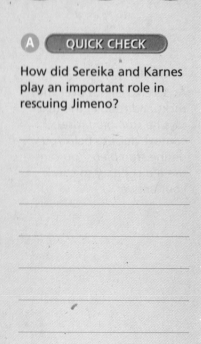

180   "Don't leave me," Jimeno said.

"We're not going to leave you," Sereika said. He pawed at the rubble and found Jimeno's gun, which he passed up to Karnes. Then he sent word for oxygen and an intravenous setup.[11] Two emergency service police officers, Scott Strauss and Paddy McGee, soon arrived, and Sereika handed rocks and rubble back to them. A fire-man, Tom Ascher, arrived with a hose to fight off the flames. They could hear McLoughlin calling out for help.

We will get there, they promised. **A**

IN OTHER WORDS Chuck Sereika was walking along the edge of a pile of rubble when he heard people shouting that someone had been found alive. Sereika stumbled and climbed until he found Dave Karnes standing alone. The former paramedic couldn't see Will Jimeno, but he could hear him. He squeezed into a crack in the rubble, and found Jimeno. Sereika felt a strong pulse in Jimeno's wrist. He passed Jimeno's gun to Karnes and called for oxygen and intravenous fluids. When two police officers arrived, Sereika began to clear rubble away from Jimeno, passing it back to the officers. A fireman arrived with a hose to fight off the flames. They could hear McLoughlin calling for help.

The basics of trauma care are simple: provide fluids and
190   oxygen. Simple—except that in the hole at the trade center, they could not take the next step in the classic formula: "load and go." First they had to extricate Jimeno, a highly delicate proposition.

Sereika could hear 4 World Trade Center groaning to its bones. To shift large pieces off Jimeno risked starting a new slide. There was room in the hole only for one person at a time, and Sereika was basically on top of him. It was not unlike working under the dash-board of a car, except the engine was on fire and the car was speeding and about to crash. The space was filled with smoke. Strauss and McGee were carefully moving

---

11. **intravenous setup:** equipment used to administer medicine or other substances directly into a vein.

200   the rubble, engineering on the fly, so that they could shift loads without bringing more debris down on themselves or on Jimeno and McLoughlin. Tools were passed from the street along a line of helpers. A handheld air chisel. Shears. When the Hurst jaws of life[12] tool arrived, the officers wanted to use it to lift one particularly heavy section, but they could not quite get solid footing on the rubble. Sereika, the lapsed paramedic, immediately sized up the problem and shimmed rubble into place for the machine to rest on. **B**

    The work inched forward, treacherous and hot and slow.

210   After four hours, at 11 P.M., Will Jimeno was freed. They loaded him into a basket, slid him up the path to the surface. That left only John McLoughlin, deeper still, but none of the group in and around the hole could go on. They called down a fresh team that would work until the morning before they finally pulled him out, not long before the last survivor from stairway B, Genelle Guzman, would also be reached.

    Aboveground, the men who had gone into the hole with Will Jimeno found they could barely walk. Smoke reeked from the hair on their heads, soot packed every pore on their skin.

220 Sereika stumbled up from the crevice in time to see Jimeno in his basket being passed along police officers and firefighters who had set up a line, scores of people deep, across the jagged, broken ground.

    He could not keep up with his patient. He could just about get himself to the sidewalk. He had worked for hours alongside the other men, first names only, and Sereika was employed by no official agency, no government body. Once they left the hole, the men lost track of each other. Just as people had come to work by themselves hours earlier, at the start of the day—an entire age

230 ago—now Chuck Sereika was starting for home on his own. His old paramedic shirt torn, he plodded north in the late-summer night, alone, scuffling down streets blanketed by the dust that had been the World Trade Center. **C** **D**

---

12. **Hurst jaws of life:** tool used to remove victims from collapsed concrete and steel structures.

B QUICK CHECK

What does Sereika do to help rescuers lift a heavy section of rubble?

_____

_____

_____

_____

C HERE'S HOW

Vocabulary

I do not know what the word *plodded* in line 231 means. Because Sereika is weak, tired, and alone, I think he must be walking very slowly. The dictionary defines *plodded* as "walked slowly," so my definition is correct.

_____

_____

_____

D LITERARY ANALYSIS

Why is Sereika "on his own" at the end of the selection?

_____

_____

_____

_____

IN OTHER WORDS Will Jimeno was trapped by large pieces of rubble, so former paramedic Chuck Sereika could not give Jimeno even basic trauma care. Rescuers worked very carefully as they dug Jimeno out of the rubble. If they moved the wrong piece, they could all be buried by a slide of heavy debris. A line of helpers passed tools to the rescuers from the street, and Sereika arranged pieces of rubble into a solid platform for an especially useful machine called the jaws of life. Jimeno was finally freed from the rubble at 11 P.M., after four hours of work by his rescuers. John McLoughlin, who was buried even deeper than Jimeno, was freed the next morning by a group of rescuers who had worked all night. The rescuers, including Sereika, were exhausted and covered in soot. After Sereika climbed out of the debris, he lost track of the other rescuers and headed for home alone.

AND OF CLAY ARE WE CREATED

Based on the short story by Isabel Allende

INTO THE SHORT STORY

On November 13, 1985, the Nevado del Ruiz volcano erupted in Colombia, in South America. The volcano resulted in deadly mudslides that killed more than 23,000 people. One thirteen-year-old girl, who was trapped in the mud, received a great deal of media attention, and many people learned about her death. Allende uses these facts as the basis for this work of fiction.

They discovered the girl's head sticking out of the mudpit, with her eyes wide open. Her name was Azucena, or Lily. In that place where so many had died, the little girl clinging to life became the symbol of the tragedy. **A** Television cameras transmitted the awful image of the head that seemed to be growing from the clay. Soon everyone recognized her and knew her name. And every time we saw her on the screen, right behind her was Rolf Carlé. He had gone there for work and never suspected that he would find a piece of his past, from
10 thirty years before.

Geologists had warned that the volcano was going to erupt. But people in the valley ignored them until a long roar announced the end of the world. Walls of snow broke loose, rolling in an avalanche of clay, stones, and water that buried the villages. **B**

The terrified people could see that houses, plazas, churches, cotton fields, and coffee forests had all disappeared. More than twenty thousand human beings and an unknown number of animals lay beneath the mud. Forests and rivers had also been swept away. **C**

"And of Clay Are We Created" adapted from *The Stories of Eva Luna* by Isabel Allende, translated by Margaret Sayers Peden. Copyright © 1989 by Isabel Allende; English translation copyright © 1991 by Macmillan Publishing Company. Retold by Holt, Rinehart and Winston. Reproduced by permission of **Scribner, an imprint of Simon & Schuster Adult Publishing Group** and electronic format by permission of **Agencia Literaria Carmen Balcells, S.A.**

A  **HERE'S HOW**

Vocabulary

A *symbol* is a thing that stands for something else. This must mean that, to the people who saw her on TV, Azucena represented the deaths and destruction caused by the eruption.

B **HERE'S HOW**

Reading Focus

I notice that the author begins by describing Azucena before she describes the volcano. I think this shows that her **purpose** is to make me feel for the girl, not simply to learn about the eruption.

C **QUICK CHECK**

What is the tragedy that happened?

_____

_____

When the narrator says she was sure Carlé "would be back the next day," it makes me think that he will not return so quickly. I think the **author's purpose** is to draw attention to how different this tragedy will be from others that Carlé has covered.

B **HERE'S HOW**

Vocabulary

I do not know what *quicksand* is. I can see that it is a combination of the words *quick* and *sand*. The next sentence says people will sink around Azucena, so I think *quicksand* is wet sand that sucks objects in.

C **YOUR TURN**

Vocabulary

By examining context clues, write a definition for *tensed*. Use a dictionary to check your answer.

_____

_____

© Corbis

20   When the station called before dawn, Rolf Carlé and I were together. I made coffee while he dressed in a hurry. He stuffed his gear in his green backpack, and we said goodbye. I had no idea of what was coming. I sipped my coffee and planned my long day without him. I was sure that he would be back the next day. **A**

He was one of the first to reach the scene. We watched Rolf Carlé on the television screen. He was up to his knees in muck and held a microphone in his hand. Lost children, wounded survivors, and dead bodies surrounded him. The story came to us in his calm voice. For years he had been a familiar newscaster. I was always

30 amazed at his calm in the face of danger and suffering. I believe that the camera lens had a strange effect on him. It seemed to allow him to watch events without participating in them. When I knew him better, I realized that this protected him from his own emotions.

Rolf Carlé was in on the story of Azucena from the beginning. The mud was like quicksand around her. Anyone trying to reach her was in danger of sinking. **B** Rolf threw down his backpack and waded into the mud. Into the microphone he said that it was cold and that one could smell the dead bodies.

"What's your name?" he asked the girl, and she told him

40 her flower name. "Don't move, Azucena," Rolf Carlé directed. He kept talking to her while he slowly moved forward through mud up to his waist.

Finally he was close enough to tie a rope under her arms. He told her that soon they would have her out. He signaled the others to pull, but as soon as the cord tensed, the girl screamed. **C** Her shoulders and arms appeared, but they could move her no farther. She was trapped. Someone suggested that her legs might be caught in the collapsed walls of her house, but she said that she was also held by the bodies of her brothers and sisters clinging to her legs.

50   "Don't worry, we'll get you out of here," Rolf promised. I loved him more than ever then.

During those first hours Rolf Carlé tried everything he could think of to rescue her. But nothing worked. The girl could not move, she barely could breathe, but she seemed to accept her fate. The reporter, on the other hand, was determined to save her and to stay close to her. He put a rubber tire under her arms to help her float in the mud. By radio, he sent a request for a pump to drain the mud. But he got a message that nothing could be sent until the next morning. **D**

60   "We can't wait that long!" Rolf Carlé shouted. Many more hours would go by before he accepted that time had stopped and reality had changed.

A doctor came to examine the girl, and said that her heart was strong. If she did not get too cold she could survive the night.

"Hang on, Azucena, we'll have the pump tomorrow," Rolf Carlé tried to comfort her.

"Don't leave me alone," she begged.

"No, of course I won't leave you." **E**

70   Someone brought him coffee. He helped the girl drink it, sip by sip. **F** She began telling him about her small life and about how things were before the volcano had erupted. She was thirteen. Rolf Carlé believed that everything would end well. To pass the hours he began to tell Azucena about his travels and adventures as a newshound. When he ran out of memories, he invented things to entertain her. From time to time she dozed, but he kept talking, so she would know that he was still there.

Many miles away, I watched Rolf Carlé and the girl on a television screen. I called all the important people in the city and

80   begged them for a pump. I got only vague promises. **G** Between

D QUICK CHECK

Why are Carlé and the other workers unable to get Azucena out of the mudpit?

_____

_____

_____

_____

E YOUR TURN

Reading Focus

The story is told mostly by the narrator. What is the **author's purpose** for including the dialogue between Carlé and Azucena here?

_____

_____

_____

F YOUR TURN

Language Coach

The word _drink_ has **multiple meanings** depending on whether it is used as a noun or a verb. Which part of speech is it in this sentence?

_____

G HERE'S HOW

Vocabulary

I am not sure what _vague_ means. I checked my dictionary, and it says "not clear" or "not definite."

A **HERE'S HOW**

Literary Focus

I think that the narrator feels connected to Carlé, but she is also separated by distance. This suggests that connections between people are important to the **theme** of this story. This is similar to the **main idea** of "102 Minutes," even though the two texts are different **genres** of literature.

B **YOUR TURN**

Vocabulary

Scarce means "occurring in small numbers." Is there enough food and water for the survivors and the rescue workers?

C **HERE'S HOW**

Vocabulary

I am not sure what the words *contaminated* and *decomposing* mean. I know from reading the sentence that these bodies can spread disease, so I think the words have something to do with disease. I checked my dictionary, and I was on the right track. If something is *contaminated*, it is "dirty or unfit for use." *Decomposing* means "breaking down to become rotten." So, the clay of the roads became unfit to use because the rotted bodies might spread disease to anyone who used the road.

calls I would run to the newsroom to monitor the satellite transmissions. The screen made the disaster seem small and emphasized the huge distance that separated me from Rolf Carlé. Still, I was there with him. The child's every suffering hurt me as it did him. I felt his frustration. **A**

I watched that hell on the first morning broadcast. Dead people and animals floated in new rivers formed from the melted snow. Above the mud rose the tops of trees and the bell towers of a church. Hundreds of soldiers and volunteers were clawing
90 through rubble searching for anyone who was still alive. Long rows of survivors waited for a cup of hot soup. Drinking water and food were scarce. **B** Most of the roads were impassable. To top it all, the clay contaminated by decomposing bodies threatened to spread disease. **C**

Azucena was shivering inside the tire that held her above the mud. She had become weak but she could still be heard when she spoke into a microphone. Rolf Carlé had started to grow a beard. He had dark circles beneath his eyes. Even from that distance I could sense his weariness. He had completely forgotten
100 the camera. He could not look at the girl through a lens any longer. In the morning, Rolf tried again to release the girl, but he did not dare use a tool for fear of injuring her. He fed Azucena a cup of cornmeal mush, but she vomited it up. A doctor said that

she had a fever, but he could not help her. A priest passed by and blessed her. By evening a gentle rain began to fall. **D**

"The sky is weeping," Azucena said. She, too, began to cry.

"Don't be afraid," Rolf begged. "You have to keep your strength up and be calm. Everything will be fine. I'll get you out."

Reporters returned to photograph Azucena and ask her

110 the same questions. She no longer answered. In the meantime, more television crews arrived. Azucena's face was beamed to millions of screens around the world. And all the while Rolf Carlé kept pleading for a pump. With improved transmission, I had the horrible sensation that Azucena and Rolf were by my side, separated from me by glass I could not break. I followed events hour by hour. I knew everything my love did to free the girl and stop her suffering. I overheard bits of what they said to each other. I was there when she taught Rolf to pray, and when he distracted her with the stories I had told him. **E**

120 On the second night, Rolf tried to sing Azucena to sleep with old Austrian folk songs he had learned from his mother. But she was beyond sleep. They spent most of the night talking. They were exhausted, hungry, and shaking with cold. That night the gates to Rolf Carlé's past began to open. The deepest and most secret layers of memory poured out. He could not tell it all to Azucena. She could not imagine Europe during the war. So he could not tell her about the afternoon the Russians had led them to the concentration camp to bury prisoners dead from starvation. Why should he describe to her the naked bodies piled like a

130 mountain of firewood? How could he tell this dying child about ovens and gallows? There was much he did not tell, but in those hours he relived for the first time all the things he had tried to forget.

Azucena's fear made Rolf confront his own. **F** There, beside that hellhole of mud, it was impossible for Rolf to flee from himself any longer. The terror he had lived as a boy suddenly invaded him. Like Azucena, he found himself trapped in a pit without escape. He was buried in life. Sorrow flooded through him. His father was punishing him once again. His

D LITERARY ANALYSIS

Carlé has "completely forgotten the camera." How does his relationship with Azucena change when he does not look at her "through a lens any longer"?

_____

_____

_____

E YOUR TURN

Literary Focus

What does this paragraph say about the **theme** of people being connected even while apart?

_____

_____

_____

_____

F HERE'S HOW

Literary Focus

I can tell that Carlé's interaction with Azucena is changing him. Even though the characters have each other, I think they are both alone with their thoughts. They have both experienced fear and tragedy, which are central **themes** of this story.

A **LITERARY ANALYSIS**

Allende writes that Carlé "was buried in the clay." As Carlé is not actually in the clay with Azucena, what does this statement mean?

_____

_____

_____

_____

B **YOUR TURN**

Reading Focus

What is the **author's purpose** for including this scene?

_____

_____

_____

140   father had locked him in a closet where Rolf had crouched for hours, trembling like a frightened animal. Wandering in his memories he found his sister Katharina, a sweet, retarded child who spent her life hiding from their father. With her, Rolf crawled beneath the dining room table and hid under the long white tablecloth. Katharina appeared before him, and at last he wept for her death and for the guilt of having deserted her. He understood then that all his adventures as a reporter were merely a way to keep his oldest fears away. He took risks to build his courage and train himself to conquer the memories that tormented

150   him. But he had come face to face with the moment of truth. He could not continue to escape his past. He was Azucena. He was buried in the clay. His terror was not a distant emotion. It was a claw sunk in his throat. He cried. **A**

     "Don't cry. I don't hurt anymore," Azucena said in the morning.

     "I'm not crying for you," Rolf Carlé smiled. "I'm crying for myself. I hurt all over."

     On the third day, the President visited the area. He asked to be taken to see Azucena, the girl the whole world had seen.

160   He waved to her. Microphones recorded his emotional voice as he told her that her courage was an example to the nation. Rolf Carlé interrupted to ask for a pump, and the President promised that he would get one. I saw Rolf kneeling beside the mudpit. On the evening news, he was still in the same position. I could tell that something had changed in him. I knew somehow that he had given in to grief. The girl had touched a part of him that he himself could not. Rolf had wanted to comfort her, but it was Azucena who had comforted him. **B**

     I recognized the moment when Rolf gave up the fight and

170   accepted the torture of watching the girl die. I was with them when she told him that no boy had ever loved her and that it was a pity to die without knowing love. Rolf assured her that he loved her more than he could ever love anyone. I watched as he leaned down to kiss her forehead. I felt how in that instant both were saved from despair, how they were freed from the clay, how

they rose above the vultures and helicopters, how together they flew above it all. How, finally, they were able to accept death. Rolf Carlé prayed in silence that she would die quickly, because such pain cannot be borne. **C**

180   By then I had gotten a pump. But that night, beneath the lens of a hundred cameras, Azucena gave up. Her eyes were still locked with the eyes of the friend who had sustained her to the end. Rolf Carlé removed the tire and closed her eyes. He held her to his chest for a few moments. Then he let her go. She sank slowly, a flower in the mud. **D**

You are back with me, but you are not the same man. I often go with you to the station and we watch the videos of Azucena again. You look for something you could have done to save her. Or maybe you study them to see yourself as if in a mirror. Your
190   cameras lie forgotten in a closet. You sit long hours staring at the mountains. Beside you, I wait for you to complete the voyage into yourself, for the old wounds to heal. I know that when you return from your nightmares, we shall again walk hand in hand, as before. **E**

C **YOUR TURN**

Literary Focus

What does the narrator mean when she says that Carlé and Azucena "were freed from the clay"? How does this relate to the **themes** of this story?

_____

_____

_____

_____

D **QUICK CHECK**

What has happened to Azucena in this paragraph?

_____

_____

E **HERE'S HOW**

Reading Focus

The story ends with the narrator speaking directly to Carlé. I think Allende's **purpose** for ending the story with this moment is to show that the narrator still feels close to Carlé, even though he has changed since the death of Azucena.

from 102 Minutes *and* And of Clay Are We Created

USE A COMPARISON CHART

Authors write about **themes** in order to explore human experiences. In "And of Clay Are We Created," Isabel Allende shows how a person can feel both connected to and distanced from another person at the same time.

DIRECTIONS: Think about the narrator's feelings for Carlé. Look for examples of how the narrator is both separated from Carlé and there with him as the events occur in the story. Record your examples in the chart below.

How the narrator is separated from Carlé	How the narrator is there with Carlé

Applying Your Skills

from 102 Minutes *and* And of Clay Are We Created

LITERARY FOCUS: THEMES ACROSS GENRES

DIRECTIONS: Answer the following questions in complete sentences.

1. Throughout "102 Minutes," the authors show that people are strangers and that they are alone. But they also show how many people were involved in the rescue. What **main idea** is suggested by these two points?

   _____

   _____

   _____

2. Many world religions and myths refer to people as being made from clay or dust and returning to the earth after they die. This suggests a universal **theme** that everyone shares a connection in life and in death. Why might Allende have titled the story "And of Clay Are We Created"?

   _____

   _____

   _____

READING FOCUS: ANALYZING AN AUTHOR'S PURPOSE

DIRECTIONS: Review the chart you started on the Preparing to Read page. What do you think are the authors' main **purposes** in writing these texts?

1. Main Purpose of "102 Minutes": _____

   _____

2. Main Purpose of "And of Clay": _____

   _____

Word Box

paramedic

rubble

trauma

avalanche

decomposing

VOCABULARY REVIEW

DIRECTIONS: Fill in the blanks with the correct word from the Word Box. Not all words will be used.

1. Many survivors of the terrorist attack experienced _____ after they were saved.

2. The firefighters searched through the _____ for survivors.

3. The _____ helped save many lives.

from The 9/11 Report: A Graphic Adaptation

By Sid Jacobson and Ernie Colón

INFORMATIONAL TEXT FOCUS: GENERATING RESEARCH QUESTIONS

When you do research, you ask questions and look for answers. Start by thinking of a subject and writing down what you already know about it. Then, ask questions about topics you want to know more about. Come up with questions that you can find answers to. Here are some tips for coming up with good questions:

- **Stay focused**. Do not write a long list of questions covering everything you could possibly ask about a general subject. Choose one **main idea**.

- **Do what reporters do**. Do not ask questions that can be answered with a *yes* or *no*. Reporters ask *5W-How?* **questions** that begin with *who*, *what*, *where*, *when*, *why*, and *how* that will lead to specific information.

- **Be realistic**. Ask questions that you think you can answer with the resources you have.

Into Action   Before you begin, create a **KWL chart** to help you focus your research. In the **K** column, list what you already know about the topic. In the **W** column, list the questions you have—what you want to learn. Once you have completed your research, you will fill out the **L** column with the information you have learned.

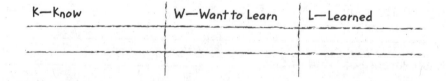

K—Know	W—Want to Learn	L—Learned

SKILLS FOCUS

Informational Text Skills
Generate relevant questions about readings on issues that can be researched.

VOCABULARY

Look for these words and their context as you read the following selection.

unprecedented (UHN PREHS UH DEHN TIHD) *adj.:* never done before; new.

integrated (IHN TUH GRAY TIHD) *v.* used as *adj.:* combined.

from THE 9/11 REPORT

By Sid Jacobson and Ernie Colón

INTO THE GRAPHIC ADAPTATION

On September 11, 2001, terrorists hijacked four planes. They flew two planes into the World Trade Center in New York City. In addition, one plane was crashed into the Pentagon in Washington, D.C. and another plane crashed in Pennsylvania. In December 2002, President George W. Bush created a 9/11 Commission to create a report on the attacks and to recommend how to prevent attacks in the future. The 9/11 Commission published its report in July 2004.

ABOUT THE 9/11 REPORT

From Text to Graphics

In 2006, fellow cartoonists Ernie Colón and Sid Jacobson decided to adapt *The 9/11 Report* into a graphic form.

"Our desire to adapt *The 9/11 Report* arose from the desire to render the complex accessible. After both of us struggled with the verbal labyrinth of the original report, we decided there must be a better way. Then it occurred to us . . . that visually adapting the information in the report—comics, the graphic medium—was the better way. We could tell the story graphically to make it more easily understood. . . . What was more, we could make it more informative, more available, and, to be frank, more likely to be read in its entirety." **A**

Tips for Reading Graphic Texts

When reading graphic texts, it's important to look at the images and read the accompanying text. Here are some tips for reading graphic texts:

- Read the panels as you would a printed page. Read from left to right and from the top of the page to the bottom.
- Read one panel at a time. First, read the text in the panel. Then, study the illustration.
- Look carefully at the faces of the characters. Think about what their facial expressions or body language tells you.
- Ask yourself, "What do the pictures add to the text?"

Terms to Know

Knowing the meanings of these abbreviations will help you understand the text.

FDNY: Fire Department of New York
WTC: World Trade Center
NYPD: New York Police Department
PAPD: Port Authority Police Department
The following excerpt from *The 9/11 Report* is from Chapter 9: "Heroism and Horror."

A **QUICK CHECK**

Why did Sid Jacobson and Ernie Colón decide to do a graphic adaptation of the 9/11 Report?

_____

_____

_____

_____

IN OTHER WORDS Cartoonists Ernie Colón and Sid Jacobson used The 9/11 Report to make a text with illustrations. When you read this selection, read the page from left to right and from top to bottom. Read one panel at a time. Read the text and look at the pictures. Think about what the pictures add to the writing.

Language Coach

A **prefix** is a group of letters added to the beginning of a word. I checked my dictionary, and a *precedent* is "something that has happened earlier." I know that the prefix *un-* means "not." The prefix *un-* changes the meaning of the word. *Unprecedented* must mean "never done before."

Vocabulary

I do not know what a *commissioner* is, but I know that ten people wrote a report. A *commissioner* must be someone who is a member of a government group that must make certain decisions.

Reading Focus

The ten commissioners had to do research to write their report. Some good **research questions** for the commissioners could have been: How did the 9/11 attacks happen? How can we prevent attacks in the future?

What is the 9/11 Commission?

_____

_____

_____

IN OTHER WORDS The attack on September 11, 2001, was unlike anything the United States had ever experienced. How did the attack happen? How can we stop something like it from happening again? Ten people were chosen to answer these questions. They shared the information they collected on July 22, 2004.

From *The 9/11 Report: A Graphic Adaptation* by Sid Jacobson and Ernie Colón Copyright © by Castlebridge Enterprises, Inc. Reproduced by permission of **Hill and Wang, a division of Farrar, Strauss and Giroux, LLC.**

Emergency Response at the Pentagon

IF IT HAD HAPPENED ON ANY OTHER DAY, THE DISASTER AT THE PENTAGON WOULD BE REMEMBERED AS A SINGULAR CHALLENGE AND AN EXTRAORDINARY NATIONAL STORY.
BUT THE CALAMITY AT THE WORLD TRADE CENTER THAT SAME MORNING, WHICH INSTANTLY IMPERILED TENS OF THOUSANDS, MADE THE TWO EXPERIENCES NOT COMPARABLE.
NEVERTHELESS, THERE ARE LESSONS IN THE RESPONSE AT THE PENTAGON.

E

METRO ENTRANCE

AT 9:37, THE WEST WALL OF THE PENTAGON WAS HIT BY HIJACKED AMERICAN FLIGHT 77...

RIVER ENTRANCE

...KILLING ALL 64 PEOPLE ABOARD AS WELL AS 125 PEOPLE INSIDE THE PENTAGON.

MALL ENTRANCE

LOCAL, STATE, AND FEDERAL AGENCIES IMMEDIATELY RESPONDED AND WERE EFFECTIVE.

THE INHERENT COMPLICATIONS OF RESPONSE ACROSS JURISDICTIONS WERE OVERCOME BECAUSE OF THE INCIDENT COMMAND SYSTEM, A MANAGEMENT STRUCTURE FOR EMERGENCY RESPONSE THAT WAS IN PLACE IN THE NATIONAL CAPITAL REGION.

F

SEVERAL FACTORS DISTINGUISH THIS RESPONSE FROM THAT IN NEW YORK. THIS WAS A SINGLE INCIDENT AND IT WAS NOT 1,000 FEET ABOVE THE GROUND.
THE INCIDENT SITE WAS RELATIVELY EASY TO SECURE, AND THERE WERE NO OTHER BUILDINGS IN THE AREA.

G

YET THERE WERE SIGNIFICANT PROBLEMS WITH SELF-DISPATCHING AND COMMUNICATIONS, ECHOING THOSE EXPERIENCES IN NEW YORK.

IN OTHER WORDS The same morning that the World Trade Center was attacked, a hijacked airplane hit the Pentagon, the headquarters of the U.S. Department of Defense in Washington, D.C. We can learn from the rescue response at the Pentagon. A command system made it easier for different teams of rescue workers to communicate. The site was also easier to manage than the towers in New York.

E YOUR TURN

Vocabulary

Is a *calamity* a good or bad thing? How do you know?

_____

_____

F YOUR TURN

Reading Focus

What **questions** do you have about the incident command system? Where might you look to find more information on the incident command system?

_____

_____

_____

_____

_____

_____

G QUICK CHECK

What were some of the major differences between the response at the Pentagon and the response in New York?

_____

_____

_____

_____

_____

_____

Analysis

IN NEW YORK, THE FDNY, NYPD, THE PORT AUTHORITY, WTC EMPLOYEES, AND THE WTC OCCUPANTS THEMSELVES DID THEIR BEST TO COPE WITH AN UNIMAGINABLE CATASTROPHE FOR WHICH THEY WERE UNPREPARED IN TERMS OF TRAINING AND MIND-SET.

IT HAS BEEN ESTIMATED THAT BETWEEN 16,400 AND 18,800 CIVILIANS WERE IN THE WTC AS OF 8:46 ON SEPTEMBER 11. AT MOST, 2,152 INDIVIDUALS DIED AT THE WTC COMPLEX WHO WERE NOT RESCUE WORKERS OR ON THE TWO PLANES.

OUT OF THIS NUMBER, 1,942 WERE AT OR ABOVE **A** THE IMPACT ZONES. THIS DATA STRONGLY SUPPORTS THAT THE EVACUATION WAS A SUCCESS FOR CIVILIANS BELOW THE IMPACT.

THE EVACUATION WAS AIDED BY CHANGES MADE BY THE PORT AUTHORITY IN RESPONSE TO THE 1993 BOMBING, REDUCING EVACUATION TIME FROM MORE THAN FOUR HOURS TO UNDER AN HOUR ON SEPTEMBER 11.

THE CIVILIANS AT OR ABOVE THE IMPACT ZONE HAD THE SMALLEST HOPE OF SURVIVAL. THEIR ONLY HOPE WAS A SWIFT AIR RESCUE, BUT THIS WAS IMPOSSIBLE.

WTC 2   WTC 1

78TH 84TH FLOORS   94TH 98TH FLOORS

THE WTC LACKED ANY PLAN FOR EVACUATION OF THE UPPER FLOORS IN THE EVENT ALL STAIRWELLS WERE IMPASSABLE.

WE'VE GOT TO GET OUT OF HERE!

THE "FIRST" RESPONDERS ON 9/11 WERE PRIVATE-SECTOR CIVILIANS. BECAUSE 85% OF OUR NATION'S INFRASTRUCTURE IS CONTROLLED BY THE PRIVATE SECTOR, CIVILIANS ARE LIKELY TO BE THE FIRST RESPONDERS IN ANY FUTURE CATASTROPHE. THEREFORE, THE COMMISSION MAKES THE FOLLOWING CONCLUSIONS.

NO DECISION HAS BEEN CRITIZED MORE THAN THAT OF BUILDING PERSONNEL NOT TO EVACUATE THE SOUTH TOWER AFTER THE NORTH WAS HIT.

LESS UNDERSTANDABLE TO THE COMMISSION WAS THE INSTRUCTION TO SOME CIVILIANS WHO HAD REACHED THE LOBBY TO RETURN TO THEIR OFFICES! **B**

NYPD 911 OPERATORS AND FDNY DISPATCH WERE NOT ADEQUATELY INTEGRATED AND GAVE OUT WRONG DIRECTIONS.

ONE LESSON IS THE NEED TO INTEGRATE THEM INTO THE RESPONSE SYSTEM AND INVOLVE THEM IN PROVIDING UP-TO-DATE ASSISTANCE AND INFORMATION.

INDIVIDUALS SHOULD KNOW THE EXACT LOCATION OF EVERY STAIRWELL AND HAVE ACCESS AT ALL TIMES TO FLASHLIGHTS.

SORRY, THIS IS RESERVED FOR FIRE TRUCKS ONLY.

LADDER 2 FIRE

THOUGH MAYOR GIULIANI'S EMERGENCY DIRECTIVE OF JULY 2001 WAS FOLLOWED TO SOME DEGREE...

...IT IS CLEAR THAT THE RESPONSE LACKED THE KIND OF INTEGRATED COMMUNICATION AND UNIFIED COMMAND CONTEMPLATED IN THE DIRECTIVE.

A   QUICK CHECK

According to the report, how many people died who were at or below the impact zones?

_____

_____

B   YOUR TURN

Reading Focus

What **questions** do you have about the instruction this man is giving?

_____

_____

_____

IN OTHER WORDS When the World Trade Center was attacked, many different groups worked to rescue people trapped in the buildings. But they were not prepared to save people. There were not clear instructions for what to do. Communication among rescuers was not as easy or effective as at the Pentagon.

210   *from* **The 9/11 Report**

IN OTHER WORDS For a rescue effort to be effective, groups of rescue workers must be able to communicate among each other and with other groups. This did not happen on 9/11. Groups did not share information. In order to prepare for the next attack, we must work to improve communication, especially for the first rescue workers that enter a site.

C **QUICK CHECK**

How does this graphic of the NYPD officer support the claim that the NYPD experienced fewer communications issues?

_____

_____

_____

_____

D **HERE'S HOW**

Vocabulary

I do not know what *optimal* means. Because the plan "falls short of *optimal* response," I think *optimal* means "good." The dictionary defines it as "best or most favorable," so I understood the word correctly.

E **HERE'S HOW**

Reading Focus

I still have **questions** about The 9/11 Report. I can use the Internet to look up the original report, or I can look in the library for articles written about the report to find out more information.

Skills Practice

from The 9/11 Report

USE A *5W-HOW?* CHART

Reporters use the **5W-How? questions** when they are writing a news story. These questions begin with the words: *who, what, where, when, why* and *how.*

DIRECTIONS: Think about the information that you have just read about the tragic events of September 11, 2001. In the chart below, write a question for each *5W-How?* box that you still have after reading the selection.

Who	
What	
Where	
When	
Why	
How	

Applying Your Skills

from The 9/11 Report

INFORMATIONAL TEXT FOCUS: GENERATING RESEARCH QUESTIONS

DIRECTIONS: Circle the correct answer to each multiple-choice question.

1. Which of the following **research questions** is *not* related to the issues in this selection?

   A. Who were the hijackers involved in the 9/11 attacks?

   B. How has communication between groups of workers gotten better since the 9/11 report?

   C. Why was the Pentagon site easier for rescuers to work at than the World Trade Center site?

   D. Why was there chaos and confusion at the rescue sites of the Pentagon and the World Trade Center?

2. Which sentence best states the **main idea** of the selection?

   A. The first responders were mostly civilians.

   B. The NYPD was the most successful department at the World Trade Center.

   C. Civilians and emergency workers need to be better prepared for terrorist attacks in the future.

   D. There were fewer communications problems at the Pentagon than at the World Trade Center.

DIRECTIONS: Review the KWL chart you filled in as you read. Then write a brief paragraph telling what you learned.

_____

_____

_____

_____

_____

Word Box

unprecedented

integrated

VOCABULARY REVIEW

DIRECTIONS: Fill in the blanks with the correct words from the Word Box.

1. The nature of the 9/11 attack was _____; Americans had never seen anything like it before.

2. The rescue workers presented an _____ effort that combined all of their resources and skills.

Skills Review

Collection 5

VOCABULARY REVIEW

DIRECTIONS: Use a dictionary or a thesaurus to find a synonym for each vocabulary word below. Remember that a synonym is a word with nearly the same meaning as another word. Then, write a sentence using each vocabulary word. Include context clues to make the meaning of the vocabulary word clear.

EXAMPLE:

struggle: <u>fight</u>   <u>The wrestlers struggled to overpower each other.</u>

1. rubble: _____

_____

_____

2. veteran: _____

_____

_____

3. privilege: _____

_____

_____

4. decomposing: _____

_____

_____

5. integrated: _____

_____

_____

6. component: _____

_____

_____

Skills Review

Collection 5

LANGUAGE COACH: MULTIPLE-MEANING WORDS

DIRECTIONS: Many words in the English language have **multiple meanings** that depend on how the word is used in a sentence. Each of the words below has more than one definition. Write two sentences for each word, using each definition correctly.

1. *complex n.:* a group of similar buildings on the same site.

_____

complex adj.: complicated.

_____

2. *crane n.:* a large machine for moving heavy objects.

_____

crane n.: a tall, long-necked bird.

_____

3. *pin n.:* a small piece of metal for attaching things.

_____

pin v.: to hold someone down so he or she is unable to move.

_____

WRITING ACTIVITY

At the end of "And of Clay Are We Created," Carlé is left completing a voyage that teaches him about himself. Write a paragraph in which you identify what you think this voyage is and how it will affect Carlé. Support your explanation with one or two examples from the selection.

_____

_____

_____

_____

_____

_____

Persuasion

9th November, 2002, Crook, P.J./Private Collection/
The Bridgeman Art Library International

Literary and Academic Vocabulary for Collection 6

LITERARY VOCABULARY

credibility (KREH DIH BIHL UH TEE) *n.:* believability.

An author's credibility depends on who he or she is and what information is included in the text.

evidence (EHV UH DIHNS) *n.:* proof.

I agreed with the author's argument because she included evidence from a variety of believable sources.

logical appeals (LAHJ IH KUHL UH PEELS) *n.:* arguments that speak to reason and common sense and are supported by evidence.

The writer made a logical appeal to his readers by interviewing an expert in the field of dog training.

emotional appeals (EE MOH SHUHN UHL UH PEELS) *n.:* arguments that make the reader feel a certain way.

The writer made an emotional appeal by stating that his favorite candidate would make sure the readers' families were protected.

ACADEMIC VOCABULARY

challenge (CHAL UHNJ) *v.:* call to a contest or fight; dare.

The tennis player challenged her opponent to a match.

debate (DIH BAYT) *n.:* an argument or discussion.

Martin Luther King, Jr. was part of a national debate on racial equality.

demonstrate (DEHM UHN STRAYT) *v.:* show or prove by using evidence.

The teacher will demonstrate how to write a bibliography.

evident (EHV UH DUHNT) *adj.:* easy to see; obvious.

It is evident that the politician is a good persuasive speaker.

There Comes a Time When People Get Tired *and* Eulogy for Martin Luther King, Jr.

LITERARY FOCUS: PERSUASION—APPEALS TO EMOTION

When writers try to **persuade**, or convince, you of something, they sometimes appeal to your emotions rather than your logic. This means that they are making an **emotional appeal**. An emotional appeal results when a writer tries to affect the way his or her readers feel. Writers may want you to feel sympathy or anger. They may use **loaded words** (words with strong emotional connections, called **connotations**) to sway you to their point of view. Writers may also use **anecdotes**, or brief stories, to connect with readers emotionally.

For example, suppose that a writer wants his readers to vote for a certain political candidate. Instead of using facts to back up this appeal, the writer may talk about how the candidate cares about readers' families. This is an example of an emotional appeal.

READING FOCUS: SUMMARIZING

When you read a speech, you can **summarize** the most important ideas to help you keep track of the speaker's message. To summarize, find the main idea and its supporting details. Then, try to simplify the main idea into a statement about the writer's argument.

As you read, you can track the main idea and supporting details in a chart like this one:

Main Idea:	Supporting Details:

SKILLS FOCUS

Literary Skills
Understand persuasive techniques; understand logical and emotional appeals.

Reading Skills
Summarize as a strategy for comprehension.

VOCABULARY

intimidated (IHN TIHM UH DAY TUHD) *n.:* frightened.

eulogy (YOO LUH JEE) *n.:* a speech praising someone who has died.

dedicated (DEH DIH KAY TEHD) *v.:* worked toward a goal.

THERE COMES A TIME WHEN PEOPLE GET TIRED

Based on the speech by Dr. Martin Luther King, Jr.

INTO THE SPEECH

During the 1950s and 1960s, many people helped bring about change in America by joining the Civil Rights Movement. This was led by a group of people who fought for all people to share the same rights and to be equal. There were protests, demonstrations in the streets, and speeches that supported equality between all races. Dr. Martin Luther King, Jr. was an important leader of this movement. He delivered the following speech on December 5, 1955, in Montgomery, Alabama.

My friends, we are here this evening for serious business. We are here first and foremost because we are American citizens. We are also here because of our belief that democracy is the greatest form of government on earth. **A**

10   But we are here in a specific sense because of the bus situation in Montgomery. We are here because we are determined to get the situation corrected. For many years now, Negroes have suffered crippling fear on buses in our community. **B** On many occasions, Negroes have been

© Don Cravens/Time & Life Pictures/Getty Images

A HERE'S HOW

Literary Focus

I can tell that Dr. King is trying to make an **emotional appeal** in this paragraph. He addresses his audience as his "friends" and appeals to their belief in the power of democracy.

B HERE'S HOW

Vocabulary

The dictionary says that *crippling* means "making disabled." In this context, I think Dr. King means that African Americans are often frightened about riding on the buses.

Adapted from "There Comes a Time When People Get Tired" (Address to First Montgomery Improvement Association [MIA] Mass Meeting, at Holt Street Baptist Church, December 5, 1955, Montgomery, Alabama) by Martin Luther King, Jr. Copyright © 1963 by Martin Luther King, Jr.; copyright renewed © 1991 by Coretta Scott King. Retold by Holt, Rinehart and Winston. Reproduced by permission of **The Estate of Martin Luther King, Jr., c/o Writers House as agent for the proprietor, New York, NY.**

Reading Focus

I can write a **summary** of the bus problem Dr. King describes: The bus system in America is unfair because black riders are intimidated, humiliated, and forced to sit in sections separate from white riders.

B (**QUICK CHECK**)

Who was Rosa Parks, and why does Dr. King include her in his speech?

_____

_____

_____

C (**YOUR TURN**)

Vocabulary

Think about whether or not Dr. King supports using violence. Read the paragraph carefully and use his position on violence to help define *advocating* in line 37. Use a dictionary to check your answer.

_____

_____

© Don Cravens/Time & Life Pictures/Getty Images

intimidated and humiliated and oppressed only because they

20 were Negroes.

Just the other day, one of the finest citizens in Montgomery was taken from a bus and carried to jail and arrested because she refused to give her seat to a white person. Now the press would have us believe that she refused to leave a reserved section for Negroes but there is no reserved section. The law has never been clear about that. **A**

Mrs. Rosa Parks is a fine person. Since this had to happen, I'm happy that it happened to a person like Mrs. Parks, for nobody can doubt her character. Nobody can doubt her

30 Christian commitment. And just because she refused to get up, she was arrested.

And you know, my friends, there comes a time when people get tired of being trampled. There comes a time when people get tired of being humiliated, where they experience despair. There comes a time. **B**

We are here this evening because we are tired now. And I want to say that we are not here advocating violence. The only weapon that we have in our hands is the weapon of protest. That's all. **C**

40   The great glory of American democracy is the right to protest for right. My friends, there will be nobody among us who will defy the Constitution. We are only here because of our wish to see right exist. My friends, we're going to work with determination to gain justice on the buses in this city.

    And we are not wrong. If we are wrong, the Supreme Court of this nation is wrong. If we are wrong, the Constitution of the United States is wrong. If we are wrong, God Almighty is wrong. If we are wrong, justice is a lie and love has no meaning. And we are determined here in Montgomery to work and fight until
50 justice runs down like water and righteousness like a mighty stream. **D**

    We must stick together. If we are united we can get many of the things that we desire and we deserve. Don't let anybody frighten you. We are not afraid of what we are doing because we are doing it within the law. We have been oppressed for so long, and we are tired. And now we are reaching out for freedom and justice and equality.

    I say to you, my friends, that we must keep God at the front of our minds. But I want to tell you this evening that it is not
60 enough for us to talk about love. Standing beside love is always justice, and we are only using the tools of justice, the tools of education and lawmaking. **E**

    And as we prepare ourselves for what lies ahead, let us go out with the determination that we are going to stick together. Right here in Montgomery, when the history books are written in the future, somebody will have to say, "There lived a race of people, a black people, a people who had the moral courage to stand up for their rights. And they gave a new meaning to history and civilization." We're going to do that. God grant that we will
70 do it before it is too late. **F**

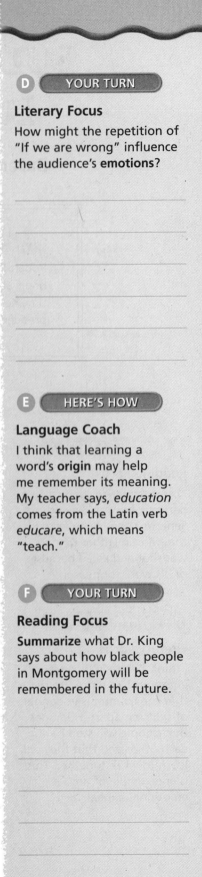

D   YOUR TURN

Literary Focus

How might the repetition of "If we are wrong" influence the audience's **emotions**?

_____

_____

_____

_____

_____

E   HERE'S HOW

Language Coach

I think that learning a word's **origin** may help me remember its meaning. My teacher says, *education* comes from the Latin verb *educare*, which means "teach."

F   YOUR TURN

Reading Focus

Summarize what Dr. King says about how black people in Montgomery will be remembered in the future.

_____

_____

_____

_____

_____

EULOGY FOR MARTIN LUTHER KING, JR.

Based on the speech by Robert F. Kennedy

> **INTO THE SPEECH**
> Robert F. Kennedy gave this eulogy, or tribute speech, several
> hours after Martin Luther King, Jr. was shot and killed. At the
> time Kennedy was a senator who was campaigning to be elected
> president in 1968. He and King fought for racial equality.

A **HERE'S HOW**

Reading Focus

I can **summarize** the first two
paragraphs of this speech:
Senator Kennedy believes
that Martin Luther King, Jr.
was shot and killed because
of his work for peace.

B **HERE'S HOW**

Literary Focus

I think Kennedy discusses
emotions like hatred to show
that the country is in danger
of splitting apart. He hopes
that people will stop hating
each other and that they will
learn to work together. This
is an example of an
emotional appeal.

I have bad news for people who love peace all over the world.
Martin Luther King was shot and killed tonight.

Martin Luther King dedicated his life to love and justice for
his fellow human beings. He died because of that effort. **A**

At this difficult time for the United States, it is a good idea
to ask what kind of a nation we are and what direction we want
to move in. For those of you who are black, you can be filled with
bitterness, with hatred, and a desire for revenge. We can move
in that direction as a country. We can split apart. Black people
10   can live only with black people and white people only with white
people. We can all be filled with hatred toward one another.

Or we can try, as Martin Luther King did, to understand,
and to replace that violence with an effort to understand with
love. **B**

For those of you who are tempted to be filled with hatred
and distrust against all white people, I can only say that I feel in
my own heart the same kind of feeling. I am a white man, and a
member of my family was killed by another white man. But we
have to try to get past these difficult times.

20   What we need in the United States is not division, hatred,
violence or lawlessness. We need love and wisdom. We need a

© Flip Schulke/Corbis

feeling of justice toward those who still suffer within our country, whether they are white or black. **C**

So I shall ask you tonight to say a prayer for the family of Martin Luther King. More importantly, say a prayer for our country, which all of us love.

We can do well in this country, but we will have difficult times too. We've had difficult times in the past. We will have difficult times in the future. This is not the end of violence or 30 lawlessness. **D**

But most white people and black people in this country want to live together. They want to improve the quality of our life, and they want justice for everyone. **E**

Let us dedicate ourselves to that, and say a prayer for our country and for our people. **F**

C YOUR TURN

Literary Focus

Kennedy talks about **emotions** here, not facts. How do these emotions make the paragraph more **persuasive**?

_____

_____

_____

D HERE'S HOW

Vocabulary

I know that the suffix _–less_ means "without," so _lawlessness_ must be the state of being without laws.

E QUICK CHECK

What does Kennedy want to see happen after Dr. King's death?

_____

_____

F YOUR TURN

Reading Focus

In your own words, **summarize** the main points in Kennedy's speech.

_____

_____

_____

_____

_____

There Comes a Time When People Get Tired *and* Eulogy for Martin Luther King, Jr.

USE AN ORGANIZATION CHART

DIRECTIONS: Complete the organization charts below by determining the main idea of each reading and supplying two supporting details. Organizing information in this manner can be helpful when **summarizing** a reading.

There Comes a Time When People Get Tired
Main Idea:
Supporting Details:

Eulogy for Martin Luther King, Jr.
Main Idea:
Supporting Details:

Applying Your Skills

There Comes a Time When People Get Tired *and* Eulogy for Martin Luther King, Jr.

LITERARY FOCUS: PERSUASION–APPEALS TO EMOTION

DIRECTIONS: Both Robert Kennedy and Dr. Martin Luther King, Jr. use **emotional appeals** in their speeches. On the lines below, list one example of an emotional appeal from each speech.

1. "There Comes a Time:" _____

_____

2. "Eulogy:" _____

_____

3. How did these two speeches make you feel? What emotions did they stir up as you read them? Write your answers below.

_____

_____

_____

READING FOCUS: SUMMARIZING

DIRECTIONS: On the previous page, you filled in organization charts with the main ideas and supporting details of both speeches. Now, choose *one* of the speeches and **summarize** it on the lines below.

_____

_____

_____

_____

Word Box

intimidated

eulogy

dedicated

VOCABULARY REVIEW

DIRECTIONS: Fill in the blanks with the correct words from the Word Box. Not all words will be used.

1. A _____ is a speech given in honor of someone who has died.

2. Dr. King was _____ to the cause of equality in America.

from Cesar's Way *and* Pack of Lies

LITERARY FOCUS: ARGUMENTS: PRO AND CON

In an argument, an author must present a claim, or opinion. An author may use a **logical appeal**, in which he supports his opinion with evidence, such as facts, numbers, examples, and experts' opinions. He may also use an **emotional appeal**, in which he uses words or stories to make the reader feel a certain way. An author may use a certain **tone**, or attitude, to sway a reader's feelings. When you read an author's claim, you need to decide whether or not the argument is **credible**, or believable.

READING FOCUS: QUESTIONING

Asking **questions** as you read persuasive writing will help you spell out the main points of the author's argument. Important questions draw attention to the strong and weak points of the argument. When you understand the strengths and weaknesses of the author's claim, you can evaluate whether you agree or disagree.

Record your questions as you read the following selections. You can do this by making a chart like the one below. If you learn the answer to a question as you read, write it down. You should also indicate if you need more information to answer a question.

from Cesar's Way and Pack of Lies		
Questions	**Answers**	**More Information Needed**
Is there proof that dogs have a "pack instinct"?		

Literary Skills
Understand argument.

Reading Skills
Question the text.

VOCABULARY

primal (PRY MUHL) *adj.:* first in importance; essential.

submissive (SUHB MIHS IHV) *adj.:* obedient; under another's control.

discipline (DIH SIH PLIHN) *n.:* controlled behavior.

from CESAR'S WAY

by Cesar Millan

> ### INTO THE EXCERPT
> Cesar Millan is an expert on dog behavior. He began hosting the television series *The Dog Whisperer* in 2004. He also wrote a book with Melissa Jo Peltier called *Cesar's Way: The Natural, Everyday Guide to Understanding and Correcting Common Dog Problems*. In the book, he explains how to train dogs and shows how people can correct their dogs' bad behavior.

A dog's pack is his life force. **(A)** The pack instinct is his primal instinct. His status in the pack is his self, his identity. The pack is all important to a dog because if anything threatens the pack's harmony, it threatens each individual dog's harmony. If something threatens the pack's survival, it threatens the very survival of every dog in it. The need to keep the pack stable and running smoothly is a powerful motivating force in every dog— even in a pampered poodle that has never met another dog or left the confines of your backyard. Why? It's deeply ingrained in
10 his brain. Evolution and Mother Nature took care of that.

It's vital for you to understand that your dog views all his interactions with other dogs, with you, and even with other animals in your household in the "pack" context. Humans—in fact, all primates—are pack animals, too. In fact, dog packs are really not so different from the human equivalent of packs. We call our packs families. Clubs. Football teams. Churches. Corporations. Governments. Sure, we think of our social groups as infinitely more complicated than dogs' groups, but are they really all that different? When you break it down, the basics
20 are the same: every one of the "packs" I've mentioned has a

(A) ┤ HERE'S HOW ├

Vocabulary
I know that a *pack* can be a container or a group of items. Here, I think it means a group of dogs. The dictionary defines a *pack* as "a group of animals that live and hunt together," so I am correct.

"Power of the Pack" from *Cesar's Way* by Cesar Millan and Melissa Jo Peltier. Copyright © 2006 by Cesar Millan and Melissa Jo Peltier. Reproduced by permission of **Crown Publishers, a division of Random House, Inc.** and electronic format by permission of **Trident Media Group, LLC.**

Literary Focus

I know that the author is trying to make me understand how dog packs work. I think he is using a **logical appeal**. He compares dog packs to human "packs" that are familiar to me. I believe the comparison, and I think that this argument is **credible**, or believable.

HERE'S HOW

Reading Focus

I know that it is good to ask **questions** while I read to help identify strengths and weaknesses of the writer's argument. One question I have is: How effective is this philosophy of dog training? I will read on to learn more.

QUICK CHECK

What reason does the author give for why dogs seem to eat even when they are not hungry?

_____

_____

_____

_____

hierarchy,[1] or it doesn't work. There is a father or mother, a chairman, a quarterback, a minister, a CEO, a president. Then there are varying levels of status for the people under him or her. That's how a pack of canines[2] works, too.

The concept of pack and pack leader is directly related to the way in which dogs interact with us when we bring them into our homes. **A** **B**

IN OTHER WORDS Dogs instinctively recognize that being part of a group, or a "pack," is very important. Humans also organize themselves in packs—families, teams, and so forth. A pet dog views its owners as its pack. Dog owners must understand the pack mentality.

The Natural Pack

If you study a wolf pack in the wild, you'll observe a natural rhythm to its days and nights. First, the animals in the pack
30 walk, sometimes up to ten hours a day, to find food and water. Then they eat. If they kill a deer, the pack leader gets the biggest piece, but everyone cooperates in sharing the rest. They'll eat until the entire deer is gone—not just because they don't have Saran Wrap in the wild, but because they don't know when there's going to be another deer again. What they eat today may have to hold them for a long time. That's where the expression "wolfing down" food comes from, and you'll see it in your own dog's behavior much of the time. Wolves don't necessarily eat just when they're hungry; they eat when the food is there. Their
40 bodies are designed to conserve. It's the root of your own dog's often seemingly insatiable appetite. **C**

Only after wolves and wild dogs have finished their daily work do they play. That's when they celebrate. And in nature, they usually go to sleep exhausted. Not once, while watching

---

1. A **hierarchy** (HY UH RAHR KEE) is a structure in which the members of a group are ranked based on ability or status.
2. **Canines** (KAY NYNZ) are members of the family of mammals that includes dogs, wolves, and foxes.

the dogs on my grandfather's farm, did I ever see a sleeping dog having nightmares, the way domestic dogs in America do. Their ears would twitch, their eyes would move, but there was no whimpering or whining or moaning. They were so completely worn out from their day's work and play that they slept
50 peacefully, every night. **D**

Every pack has its rituals. These include traveling, working for food and water, eating, playing, resting, and mating. Most important, the pack always has a pack leader. The rest of the animals are followers. Within the pack, the animals fall into their own order of status, usually determined by that animal's inborn energy level. **E** The leader determines—and enforces—the rules and boundaries by which the members will live.

A puppy's first pack leader is his mother. From birth, puppies learn how to be cooperative members of a pack oriented
60 society. At about three or four months, after they're weaned, they fall into the regular pack structure, and take their cues from the pack leader, not their mother. In packs of wolves and wild dogs, the leader is often a male, because the hormone[3] testosterone— present in male puppies from the time they are very small— seems to be a cue to dominance[4] behaviors. **F**

---

3. **hormone** (HAWR MOHN): substance produced by the body that affects an organ or other tissues.
4. **Dominance** is the state of having the most power.

© Max Morse/Reuters/Corbis

D YOUR TURN

Vocabulary

Use context clues to write a definition of the word *domestic*. Check your answer against a dictionary definition.

_____

_____

_____

E QUICK CHECK

What quality determines each member's status, or rank, in a pack?

_____

_____

_____

F YOUR TURN

Reading Focus

Answer this **question**: Why are pack leaders in the wild usually males?

_____

_____

_____

from **Cesar's Way**   229

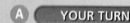

A · YOUR TURN

Literary Focus

Based on your own experience, does the information presented in this paragraph seem **credible**?

_____

_____

_____

_____

IN OTHER WORDS Wolves and wild dogs do everything working together in packs. Wild dogs play together only after the day's work is done. Every pack also has a leader, which is usually the member with the highest natural energy level. In the wild, pack leaders tend to be males. Puppies initially treat their mothers as leaders, but they grow to recognize the true pack leaders.

Though hormones are part of what makes a pack leader, energy plays an even greater role. When humans live in households with more than one dog, the dominant dog can be either male or female. The gender doesn't matter, only the inborn

70 energy level, and who establishes dominance. In many packs, there is an "alpha couple," a male and female pair who seem to run things between them. **A**

In the wild, pack leaders are born, not made. They don't take classes to become leaders; they don't fill out applications and go on interviews. Leaders develop early and they show their dominant qualities quite young. It's that all-important energy we discussed earlier that separates the pack leader from the follower. A pack leader must be born with high or very high energy. The energy must also be dominant energy, as well as calm-assertive[5] energy.

80 Medium- and low-energy dogs do not make natural pack leaders. Most dogs—like most humans—are born to be followers, not leaders. Being a pack leader isn't only about dominance, it's also about responsibility. Think about our own species, and the percentage of people who would like to have the power and perks of the president, or the money and goodies of a Bill Gates.[6] Then tell those people that the trade-off is that they will have to work around the clock, 24–7, almost never see their families, and rarely take weekends off. Tell them they'll be financially responsible for thousands of people, or responsible for the national security of hundreds of

90 millions of people. How many people would choose those leadership roles after being presented with such daunting realities?

---

5. **Calm-assertive** means "relaxed but confident and in control."
6. **Bill Gates** is the cofounder of the giant computer company Microsoft and one of the wealthiest people in the world.

I believe most people would choose comfortable but simpler lives over great power and wealth—if they truly understood the work and sacrifice that leadership costs. **B**

Similarly, in a dog's world, the pack leader has the responsibility for the survival of all the pack members. The leader leads the pack to food and water. He decides when to hunt; decides who eats, how much, and when; decides when to rest and when to sleep and when to play. The leader sets all the regulations and structures that the other pack members must live by. A pack leader has to have total confidence and know what he's doing. And just as in the human world, most dogs are born to follow rather than do all the work it takes to maintain the position of pack leader. Life is easier and less stressful for them when they live within the rules, boundaries, and limitations that the pack leader has set for them. . . . **C**

IN OTHER WORDS In households with more than one dog, gender does not matter in determining the pack leader. In the wild, some animals are just natural leaders. For both dogs and humans, leaders must not only be dominant but responsible as well. They must often make sacrifices to ensure that their packs are well off.

To Lead or to Follow?

To dogs, there are only two positions in a relationship: leader and follower. Dominant and submissive. **D** It's either black or white. There is no in-between in their world. When a dog lives with a human, in order for the human to be able to control the dog's behavior, she must make the commitment to take on the role of pack leader, 100 percent of the time. It's that simple. . . .

A dog will usually accept a human as its pack leader if that human projects the correct calm-assertive energy, sets solid rules, boundaries, and limitations, and acts responsibly in the cause of the pack's survival. **E** This doesn't mean that we can't still be uniquely human pack leaders. Just as dogs shouldn't have to give up what's unique about them to live with us, we shouldn't have to give up what's so special about being human. We are, for

100

110

B **YOUR TURN**

Literary Focus

In this paragraph, is the writer making a **logical** or an **emotional** appeal to make his point about responsibility? Explain your answer.

_____

_____

_____

C **LITERARY ANALYSIS**

Do you agree that most humans are born to follow? Why or why not?

_____

_____

_____

D **HERE'S HOW**

Language Coach

My teacher says that the **prefix** _sub–_ comes from the Latin word for "under." For instance, the adjective _submissive_ means "under another's control."

E **QUICK CHECK**

What traits must a human have for a dog to acknowledge them as its pack leader?

_____

_____

Literary Focus

How would you describe the writer's **tone**, or attitude, in this paragraph? Does his tone here make his **argument** more convincing?

_____

_____

_____

_____

_____

_____

_____

_____

120 instance, the only pack leaders who are going to love the dogs in the way we humans define love. Their canine pack leader will not buy them squeaky toys or throw birthday parties for them. Their canine pack leader won't directly reward their good behavior. He won't turn around and say, "Gee, guys, thanks for following me ten miles." It's expected that they do that! A mother dog won't say, "You know, you pups have behaved so well today. Let's go to the beach!" In their natural world, the reward is in the process. (That's a concept we humans could sometimes do well to remember.) For a dog there's a reward in simply fitting in with the pack and helping to ensure its survival. Cooperation automatically results

130 in the primal rewards of food, water, play, and sleep. Rewarding our dogs with treats and the things that they love is one way we can bond with them and reinforce good behavior. But if we don't project strong leadership energy before we give rewards, we're never going to have a truly functional "pack." A

IN OTHER WORDS Because dogs see themselves as either leaders or followers, it is important for dog owners to establish themselves as the leaders. Dogs will recognize their owners as pack leaders if the owners are both calm and assertive. Good owners can still show love and affection for their dogs, but it is important to project strong leadership first.

Who's Top Dog in Your House?

Once my clients start to grasp the concept of the pack and the pack leader, they usually ask me, "How can I tell who's the pack leader in my house?" The answer is very simple: who controls the dynamics of your relationship?

There are dozens and dozens of different ways in which your
140 dog will tell you, loud and clear, who's the dominant one between the two of you. If he jumps on you when you come home from work in the evening, he's not just happy to see you. He is the pack leader. If you open the door to go for a walk and he exits ahead of you, it's not just because he loves his walks so much. He is the pack leader. If he barks at you and then you feed him, it's not

"cute." He is the pack leader. If you are sleeping and he wakes you up at five in the morning pawing you to say "Let me out; I gotta pee," then he's showing you even before the sun comes up who's running the house. Whenever he makes you do anything, he is the pack leader. Simple as that. **B**

Most of the time dogs are the pack leaders of the human world because the human will say, "Isn't that adorable? He's trying to tell me something." There it is, that old Lassie syndrome again, "What's that, Lassie? Gramps fell down the well?"[7] Yes, in this case, human, your dog is trying to tell you something—he's trying to remind you that he is the leader and you are his follower. **C**

So, when you wake up on your own terms, you are the pack leader. When you open the door on own your terms, you are the pack leader. When you exit the house ahead of your dog, you are the pack leader. When you are the one who makes the decisions in the household, then you are the pack leader. And I'm not talking about 80 percent of the time. I'm talking about 100 percent of the time. If you give only 80 percent leadership, your dog will give you 80 percent following. And the other 20 percent of the time he will run the show. If you give your dog any opportunity for him to lead you, he will take it. **D**

IN OTHER WORDS If a dog controls its owner, then the dog is the pack leader of that household. For instance, if an owner feeds his dog when it barks, then the dog is in control. Most pet dogs are pack leaders because owners view such behavior as "cute." But if owners want obedient dogs, they must be in control 100 percent of the time.

Leading Is a Full-time Job

Dogs need leadership, from the day they're born to the day they die. They instinctively need to know what their position is in regard to us. Usually owners have a position for their dogs

---

7. **Lassie syndrome . . . the well:** In a much-loved TV show that aired from 1954 until the early 1970s, Lassie, a collie dog, helped rescue people. The character originally appeared in a 1938 short story, and over the years she has been the subject of books, movies, and a second TV series.

B **YOUR TURN**

Literary Focus
Discuss the ways in which the author uses **emotional appeals** in this paragraph.

_____

_____

_____

_____

_____

C **YOUR TURN**

Language Coach
The **prefix** _re–_ usually means "back" or "again." How does this prefix factor into the definition of the word _remind_? What does _remind_ mean?

_____

_____

_____

D **YOUR TURN**

Reading Focus
What **questions** do you have for the writer at this point in his argument?

_____

_____

_____

_____

Vocabulary

At first I was confused by the phrase "runs roughshod over." My teacher explained that this is just an expression that means "treats harshly."

What point is Millan making by discussing Jada Pinkett Smith?

_____

_____

_____

_____

_____

_____

_____

170 in their hearts but not in their "packs." That's when the dogs take over. They take advantage of a human who loves them but offers no leadership. Dogs don't reason. They don't think, "Gee, it's so great that this person loves me. It makes me feel 180 so good, I'll never attack another dog again." You

© Alan Weissman

can't say to a dog like you'd say to a child, "Unless you behave, you're not going to the dog park tomorrow." A dog can't make that connection. Any show of leadership you give dogs must be given at the moment of the behavior that needs correction. **A**

In your household, anybody can be a pack leader. In fact, it is vital that all the humans in the house be the dog's pack leader—from the smallest infant to the oldest adult. Male or female. Everybody must get with the program. I go to many households 190 where the dog respects one person, but runs roughshod over the rest of the family. **B** This can be another recipe for disaster. In my family, I am the dogs' pack leader, but so are my wife and two sons. Andre and Calvin can walk through my pack dogs at the Dog Psychology Center without the dogs so much as blinking an eye. The boys learned pack leadership from watching me, but all children can be taught how to assert leadership with animals.

Pack leadership doesn't hinge on size or weight or gender or age. Jada Pinkett Smith weighs maybe 110 pounds soaking wet, but she was able to handle four Rottweilers at once even better than 200 her husband was. Will Smith[8] was good with the dogs and they respected him, but Jada really put in the time and energy needed to be a strong pack leader. She's gone with me to the beach and the mountains, where I take the pack out for off-leash walks. **C**

8. **Jada Pinkett Smith** and **Will Smith** are well-known actors who are married to each other.

Leading a dog on a walk—as evidenced by the dogs who live with the homeless—is the best way to establish pack leadership. It's a primal activity that creates and cements those pack leader–follower bonds. As simple as it sounds, it's one of the keys to creating stability in the mind of your dog.

In dogs that are trained for specific jobs, the pack leader doesn't even need to be out in front. In Siberian husky dogsled teams, though the human pack leader is at the back of the sled, it's she who is running the sled. Dogs who live with handicapped people—people in wheelchairs, the blind, people with special needs—often have to take the physical lead in some situations. But the person they are helping is always the one in control. It's a beautiful thing to watch a service dog who lives with a handicapped person. Often, the two seem to have a kind of supernatural connection between them—a sixth sense. They are so in tune with each other that the dog can often sense what that person needs before being given a command. That's the kind of bond dogs in packs have with one another. Their communication is unspoken, and it comes from the security they have within the pack structure. **D**

With the proper calm-assertive energy, pack leadership, and discipline, you, too, can have this sort of deep connection with your dog. In order to accomplish this, however, it's important to be aware of the things you may be inadvertently doing that are contributing to your dog's problems. **E**

IN OTHER WORDS All human members of a household, even young children, should act as the pack leaders of their pet dogs. Even when dogs work to help people (such as dogs that assist blind people), the owners still must establish themselves as the leaders. Owners can have beautiful relationships with their dogs, but first it is necessary to have the right attitude and act as the pack leader.

210

220

D YOUR TURN

Language Coach
Define *unspoken*. If necessary, check a dictionary. Considering this definition, what do you think the **prefix** *un–* means?

_____

_____

_____

E YOUR TURN

Literary Focus
Now that you have finished reading the selection, evaluate the **credibility** of the writer's arguments based on the kinds of evidence he offered. Is this author credible? Why or why not?

_____

_____

_____

_____

_____

_____

_____

_____

PACK OF LIES

Based on the article by Mark Derr

INTO THE ARTICLE

Mark Derr is the author of two books about dogs. He wrote this article for the newspaper *The New York Times* because he disagrees with Cesar Millan's methods for training dogs. Cesar Millan is a popular dog trainer and television figure, and Derr presents a different perspective of how to best train dogs.

A **HERE'S HOW**

Vocabulary

I do not know what *devoted* means. The dictionary says it is an adjective meaning "very loving or loyal." People that follow Millan's teachings must really believe in what he says.

B **QUICK CHECK**

What does Derr think is wrong with Millan's views on training dogs?

_____

_____

_____

_____

Cesar Millan has taken the world of canine behavior by storm. He has the top-rated program, "Dog Whisperer," on the National Geographic Channel, a best-selling book and a devoted following.

Millan's view of dogs' social structure is too simple. He has used this idea to make a one-size-fits-all approach to dog training. In Mr. Millan's world, humans' failure to be the "pack leader" and dominate the dog completely causes dog behavior problems. **B**

10 Mr. Millan's training methods include finger jabs, choke collars, extended sessions on a treadmill and what is called flooding, or overwhelming the animal with the thing it fears. These methods place Mr. Millan in a long tradition of punishment-based dog trainers.

Mr. Millan's show brings his ideas into millions of homes each week. He is charming, but his methods threaten 40 years of learning about dog behavior. For 40 years, trainers have developed reward-based training programs. The trainers see each dog as an individual. They try to understand what motivates it, what frightens it and what its talents and limits are. They build

20 on strengths and deal with weaknesses. These trainers often work wonders with their dogs, but it takes time.

Mr. Millan supposedly delivers fast results. His mantra is "exercise, discipline, affection." For him, discipline means "rules." There are almost no rewards or praise. Animals are corrected and forced to submit, even if doing so makes them panic. **C** **D**

Mr. Millan bases his methods on a simplistic understanding of the dog's "natural" pack, controlled by a dominant alpha animal. **E** Among pet owners, he says, that leader is the human. Millan believes that behavior problems in dogs arise when an owner fails to dominate the dog.

Women are the worst offenders in this world. In one DVD, Mr. Millan explains that a "woman always applies affection before discipline. Man applies discipline then affection. All animals follow dominant leaders; they don't follow lovable leaders," he says. Mr. Millan's outdated sexist ideas deserve to be laughed at.

The idea that an "alpha pack leader" dominates all other pack members comes from studies of captive wolf packs. It doesn't apply to the social structure of natural packs.

L. David Mech is one of the world's leading wolf experts. "In a typical wolf pack," wrote Dr. Mech in 1999, "dominance contests with other wolves are rare, if they exist at all." That's very different from what Mr. Millan says dogs need. **F**

Unlike their wolf ancestors, dogs live among humans. They have been bred to live that way. Studies show that they are attentive to people, and that most are eager to please.

But sometimes the relationship goes very wrong, and it is time to call on a professional. Aggressive behavior is a problem for more than 20 percent of the nation's 65 million dogs. Mr. Millan treats this by forcing the dog to exercise on a treadmill. He also shows his authority by rolling the dog on its back. That technique was once believed to be a good way to establish dominance. We now know that it is a good way to get bitten. In fact, many experts believe that it actually makes dogs more aggressive.

More important, aggression often has underlying medical causes. Some dogs bite because they are in pain. Some have inherited behavior problems. Vets have found that many

30

40

50

C **HERE'S HOW**

Reading Focus

Millan says he includes affection when training dogs. I can ask the **question**: how does Millan show dogs affection after they have been disciplined?

D **YOUR TURN**

Reading Focus

Write one **question** about Derr's description of Millan's method of training dogs.

_____

_____

_____

E **YOUR TURN**

Vocabulary

What do you think *simplistic* means? Use a dictionary to check your definition.

_____

_____

F **HERE'S HOW**

Literary Focus

I know that Derr includes this quotation from Mech to make his argument more **credible**. Mech is a wolf expert, so I believe his view that wolves do not fight with other wolves for dominance. This is an example of a **logical argument**.

aggressive dogs suffer from low levels of serotonin. They have had successfully treated such dogs with antidepressant drugs like Prozac.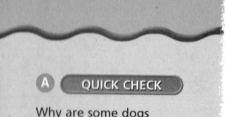

Mr. Millan's quick fix might make for good television. It might even produce lasting results in some cases. But it goes against what professional animal trainers have learned about

60 normal and abnormal behavior in dogs. **B** **C**

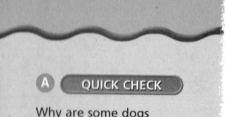

A QUICK CHECK

Why are some dogs aggressive?

_____

_____

_____

B YOUR TURN

Literary Focus

How does Derr try to show that Millan's approach to dog training is not **credible**, or believable?

_____

_____

_____

_____

C YOUR TURN

Language Coach

The **prefix** *ab-* means "not" or "away from." Knowing this, what do you think the word *abnormal* means?

_____

_____

Applying Your Skills

from Cesar's Way *and* Pack of Lies

LITERARY FOCUS: ARGUMENTS: PRO AND CON

DIRECTIONS: Review and think about the **arguments** and claims that each author makes. Answer the following questions in complete sentences.

1. According to Millan, what purpose does a pack serve for wolves and wild dogs?

   _____

   _____

   _____

   _____

2. Which of Millan's methods for training dogs does Derr disagree with? Why?

   _____

   _____

   _____

   _____

READING FOCUS: QUESTIONING

DIRECTIONS: Now that you have read both arguments, answer the following **question**: Is there proof that dogs have a "pack instinct"?

_____

_____

_____

_____

_____

VOCABULARY REVIEW

DIRECTIONS: Fill in the blanks with the correct words from the Word Box. Not all words will be used.

Word Box

primal

submissive

discipline

1. Millan believes in enforcing _____ when training dogs.

2. Derr and Millan have different views on how to make a dog be _____ to its owner.

Skills Review

Collection 6

VOCABULARY REVIEW

DIRECTIONS: Match each vocabulary word with its definition. Write the correct letters on the blanks.

_____ 1. challenge
_____ 2. submissive
_____ 3. demonstrate
_____ 4. debate
_____ 5. eulogy
_____ 6. evident
_____ 7. discipline
_____ 8. intimidated

a. controlled behavior
b. dare
c. show
d. obvious; easy to understand
e. obedient
f. discussion of opposing arguments
g. frightened
h. speech praising someone who has died

DIRECTIONS: Write three separate sentences on the lines below. In each sentence, correctly use one or more of the words above.

1. _____

_____

2. _____

_____

3. _____

_____

Skills Review

Collection 6

DIRECTIONS: Circle the **prefix** of each word listed below. Then write a definition for each word. If necessary, check a dictionary.

1. antisocial

   _____

   _____

2. detach

   _____

   _____

3. uninterested

   _____

   _____

4. submarine

   _____

   _____

5. hyperactive

   _____

   _____

ORAL LANGUAGE ACTIVITY

DIRECTIONS: Imagine that your class just got a puppy. Now you have to decide how to train it. In a small group, work together to prepare a short **argument**. The goal of your group's argument is to persuade your classmates to train the dog using either Cesar Millan's approach or Mark Derr's approach. Present your argument to the rest of the class.

Collection

7

Poetry

© Eduardo Munoz/Sicardi Gallery, Texas

Literary and Academic Vocabulary for Collection 7

LITERARY VOCABULARY

imagery (IHM MUHJ REE) *n.:* language that appeals to our five senses and creates a picture in our minds.

Because of the imagery that the writer used, I could imagine exactly what the old mansion looked like.

sonnet (SAH NUHT) *n.:* a fourteen-line poem with a certain structure.

William Shakespeare's "Shall I Compare Thee to a Summer's Day?" is an example of a sonnet.

metaphor (MEH TUH FAWR) a comparison between two things that are not alike.

A metaphor is like a simile, but does not use the words "like" or "as" to compare two things.

ACADEMIC VOCABULARY

transform (TRANS FAWRM) *v.:* change.

A poem can transform ordinary objects into unusual images.

literal (LIHT UHR UHL) *adj.:* the usual meaning of a word.

A literal interpretation of a metaphor may not always make sense.

evoke (IH VOHK) *v.:* bring out; call forth.

For some people, the grandmother's condition in the poem may evoke sadness.

complement (KAHM PLUH MUHNT) *v.:* complete; fullfill a lack of any kind.

The title and introduction complement the poem.

Same Song

By Pat Mora

LITERARY FOCUS: IMAGERY AND ALLUSION

Imagery is language that appeals to the five senses—sight, hearing, touch, taste, and smell. An image can help you "see" a literary character, object, or scene in your mind. For example, an author may write that a character is eating a red, crunchy apple. Can you picture that scene in your mind from those words?

An **allusion** is an indirect reference. Allusions may be about literature, history, myth, religion, politics, sports, science, or the arts. In this poem, the writer makes an allusion to a fairy tale. Instead of telling you directly about the fairy tale, the writer gives you hints that remind you of the fairy tale. When you recognize an allusion, it will form a picture in your mind that helps you understand the poem.

READING FOCUS: VISUALIZING

Poetry often has strong images that make you think about people, scenes, or objects differently than you ever have before. When you **visualize** an image, you see it in your mind. Take the time to visualize the images in a poem. Experience the smells, sounds, tastes, and textures of the writing. It will make your reading more interesting and enjoyable.

VOCABULARY

strokes (STROHKS) *v.:* moves across a surface.

expanding (EHKS PAHN DIHNG) *v.:* becoming larger.

INTO THE POEM

As you read the following poem, think about the fairy tale "Snow White." In that story, an evil queen wants to be more beautiful than her stepdaughter, Snow White. The queen has a magic mirror that she asks, "Mirror, mirror on the wall, who's the fairest of them all?" The mirror replies that Snow White is the most beautiful. The queen becomes very angry that Snow White is more beautiful than she is. "Same Song" is based on a similar theme as the fairy tale "Snow White." Read on to find out what that theme is.

SKILLS FOCUS

Literary Skills
Understand imagery; understand allusion.

Reading Skills
Use visualization as a strategy for comprehension.

SAME SONG

By Pat Mora

© Elizabeth Barakah Hodges/SuperStock

While my sixteen-year-old son sleeps,

my twelve-year-old daughter

stumbles into the bathroom at six a.m. **A**

plugs in the curling iron

5 squeezes into faded jeans

curls her hair carefully

strokes Aztec Blue shadow on her eyelids

smoothes Frosted Mauve blusher on her cheeks

outlines her mouth in Neon Pink **B**

10 peers into the mirror, mirror on the wall

frowns at her face, her eyes, her skin,

not fair. **C**

IN OTHER WORDS My son is sixteen. My daughter is
twelve. My daughter gets dressed early in the morning, while
my son is still sleeping. My daughter puts on jeans, curls her

"Same Song" from *Borders* by Pat Mora. Copyright © 1986 by Pat Mora. Published by **Arte Público Press-University of Houston, Houston, TX**. Reproduced by permission of the publisher.

A HERE'S HOW

Vocabulary

I am not sure what *stumbles* means. I know that the daughter is going into the bathroom, so *stumbles* could be another word for "walks." I looked it up in my dictionary and *stumbles* means "trips repeatedly." I was right that the daughter is walking to the bathroom, but she *stumbles* because it is six a.m. and she is tired.

B HERE'S HOW

Reading Focus

I notice that the poet starts each line here with a different verb. These words help me **visualize** what the daughter is doing. I can picture her as she *squeezes* into tight pants and *smoothes* make-up on her face.

C HERE'S HOW

Literary Focus

This line sounds very familiar. I have heard it in the fairy tale "Snow White." Snow White's evil stepmother asks her mirror, "Mirror, mirror on the wall, who's the fairest of them all?" I understand that Mora is making an **allusion** to the fairy tale.

A HERE'S HOW

Language Coach

Biceps and *triceps* are different muscles in the arm. Both words have Latin **roots**. *Bi-* means "two," and *tri-* means "three." *Biceps* means "two-headed muscle" because the muscle joins the bone in two places.

B YOUR TURN

Reading Focus

How does Mora help you **visualize** the son's workout? Circle key words that help you picture what he is doing.

C YOUR TURN

Literary Focus

What **allusion** does Mora repeat in the end of the poem? Why do you think she uses this allusion in the poem?

_____

_____

_____

_____

_____

_____

_____

_____

hair, and does her make up. She looks in the mirror and is not happy with what she sees.

> At night this daughter
> stumbles off to bed at nine
> 15 eyes half-shut while my son
> jogs a mile in the cold dark
> then lifts weights in the garage
> curls and bench presses
> expanding biceps, triceps, pectorals, **A**
> 20 one-handed push-ups, one hundred sit-ups **B**
> peers into that mirror, mirror and frowns too. **C**
>
> *for Libbes*

IN OTHER WORDS At night, when my daughter is asleep, my son goes running and lifts weights. He looks in the mirror and is not happy with what he sees, either.

Applying Your Skills

Same Song

LITERARY FOCUS: IMAGERY AND ALLUSION

DIRECTIONS: Review the poem and answer the following question.

In this poem, the writer alludes to a fairy tale. What image does this **allusion** bring to your mind? Explain how the girl and boy in the poem can be compared to the queen in "Snow White."

_____

_____

_____

_____

READING FOCUS: VISUALIZING

DIRECTIONS: What images does Pat Mora use in this poem to help you **visualize** the characters? Find two images from the poem and write them below. Then explain what each image shows about the characters and their actions.

1. Image: _____

What it shows: _____

_____

_____

_____

2. Image: _____

What it shows: _____

_____

_____

_____

VOCABULARY REVIEW

DIRECTIONS: Fill in the blank with the correct word from the Word Box.

Word Box

strokes

expanding

1. By lifting weights, the son is working on _____ his muscles.

Shall I Compare Thee to a Summer's Day?

By William Shakespeare

LITERARY FOCUS: SONNET

William Shakespeare published 154 sonnets during his lifetime. All **Shakespearean**, or **English**, **sonnets** have a set form. The Shakespearean sonnet is 14 lines long. The sonnet begins with three four-line units that rhyme, called **quatrains**. The sonnet always ends with two lines that rhyme, called a **couplet**. Each quatrain makes a point or gives an example, and the final couplet sums everything up.

READING FOCUS: READING A POEM

While **reading a poem**, pay attention to its punctuation. Punctuation marks will tell you where sentences—and complete thoughts—begin and end. Rearrange inverted sentences, phrases, and words in your mind by placing subjects, verbs, and complements in the traditional order. Finally, **paraphrase** each line, or restate it in your own words, to ensure that you understand the entire poem.

VOCABULARY

Look for these words and their context as you read the selection.

temperate (TEHM PUHR IHT) *adj.:* not too hot or cold; mild; moderate in behavior.

complexion (KUHM PLEHK SHUHN) *n.:* appearance of the skin, especially the face.

INTO THE SONNET

William Shakespeare had already written many famous plays when his sonnets were published in 1609—apparently without his permission. No one knows when he wrote the sonnets or if the speakers in the poems are real people, imagined characters, or Shakespeare himself. In Shakespeare's day, every gentleman was expected to write sonnets in praise of his loved one. Writing a sonnet was seen as a challenge, a kind of game.

SKILLS FOCUS

Literary Skills
Understand the characteristics of sonnets.

Reading Skills
Read a poem.

SHALL I COMPARE THEE TO A SUMMER'S DAY?

By William Shakespeare

Shall I compare thee to a summer's day?
Thou art more lovely and more temperate.
Rough winds do shake the darling buds of May,
And summer's lease[1] hath all too short a date. **A**

5 Sometime too hot the eye of heaven shines,
And often is his gold complexion dimmed; **B**
And every fair from fair sometime declines,
By chance, or nature's changing course, untrimmed;[2]
But thy eternal summer shall not fade, **C**

10 Nor lose possession of that fair thou ow'st,[3]
Nor shall Death brag[4] thou wand'rest in his shade,
When in eternal lines to time thou grow'st:

  So long as men can breathe or eyes can see,
  So long lives this, and this gives life to thee. **D**

IN OTHER WORDS Should I compare you to a summer day? You are lovelier and more reliable. Summer can be disturbed by strong winds, and summer is too short. During the summer, sometimes the sun is too hot. The sun is also frequently covered by clouds. And every feature of something beautiful eventually withers away—due to bad luck or uncontrollable changes; but your beauty will never fade; you will never lose your beautiful features. Not even Death can stop your beauty, because it will continue to grow in this poem, which will last forever. As long as men live and read, this poem will give life to you—making you eternal.

---

1. **Lease** (LEES) means "a fixed period of time."
2. **Untrimmed** means "without trimmings (decorations)."
3. **Thou ow'st** is the same as saying "you own."
4. **Brag** means "boast."

A   **HERE'S HOW**

Literary Focus

In the first **quatrain** the speaker is comparing someone to a summer day. I will keep reading to see how this comparison develops.

B   **HERE'S HOW**

Reading Focus

While **reading a poem**, I know to pause fully at periods and slightly at other punctuation marks. Here, I will pause briefly for the semi-colon.

C   **HERE'S HOW**

Reading Focus

I can **paraphrase** here: I think "thy eternal summer shall not fade" means "your beauty will last forever."

D   **QUICK CHECK**

Who do you think this poem's speaker is addressing?

_____

_____

Shall I Compare Thee to a Summer's Day?

USE A PARAPHRASING TABLE

DIRECTIONS: Complete the exercise below by **paraphrasing** the selected lines from "Shall I Compare Thee to a Summer's Day?"

Original Text	Paraphrase
"Shall I compare thee to a summer's day? / Thou art move lovely and more temperate." (lines 1–2)	**1.**
"And every fair from fair sometime declines, / By chance, or nature's changing course, untrimmed;" (lines 7–8)	**2.**
"So long as men can breathe or eyes can see, / So long lives this, and gives life to thee." (lines 13–14)	**3.**

Applying Your Skills

Shall I Compare Thee to a Summer's Day?

LITERARY FOCUS: SONNET

DIRECTIONS: What message is delivered in the final **couplet** of this sonnet? Write a short paragraph discussing the poem's couplet and how the three preceding **quatrains** support its message.

_____

_____

_____

_____

_____

_____

READING FOCUS: READING A POEM

DIRECTIONS: Read the poem again and then answer the following questions.

1. Remember that a poem's punctuation can help you find where complete thoughts begin and end. How many complete sentences are there in this poem? _____

2. Try reading the poem aloud. Does this improve your understanding of it? Explain your answer.

_____

_____

_____

_____

VOCABULARY REVIEW

DIRECTIONS: Write "Yes" after each sentence if the boldfaced vocabulary word is being used correctly. Write "No" if it is not being used correctly.

1. The dog had a **temperate** personality—he was always barking and whining! _____

2. Great poetry is **complexion**; it lasts forever. _____

since feeling is first

By E.E. Cummings

LITERARY FOCUS: METAPHOR

A **metaphor** is a comparison between two things that are not alike. A metaphor is like a simile, but it does not use the words *like* or *as* to make the comparison. Instead, a metaphor usually states or suggests that something *is* something else. In this poem, the poet uses metaphors that have to do with writing to talk about two lovers.

READING FOCUS: ANALYZING WORD CHOICE

Poets choose their **words** very carefully. Even words that are similar can have slightly different meanings that affect the meaning of the poem. When a poet chooses a certain word for a metaphor, he or she chooses it for the thoughts and images that have to do with that word. This makes the meaning of the metaphor stronger. Analyzing the poet's choice of words helps you to better understand comparisons in a poem. The chart below provides an example of the associations a word can carry.

Word	Makes Me Think Of
"fool"	silly, giggling

VOCABULARY

syntax (SIHN TAKS) *n.:* sentence structure.

gesture (JEHS CHUHR) *n.:* a movement, usually by part of the body.

parenthesis (PUH REHN THUH SIHS) *n.:* a curved line that sets off words or phrases in a sentence.

INTO THE POEM

In his poetry, E.E. Cummings liked to use lowercase letters. Cummings put his words in different spaces across the page, and sometimes did not even use spaces between words. He used his own style of punctuation. Even though this can make his poems challenging, the themes are familiar. As you read the following poem, think about two lovers and how they feel about being separated.

SINCE FEELING IS FIRST

By E.E. Cummings

A ❘ HERE'S HOW

Vocabulary

I am confused about what is going on in the opening lines of the poem. I know that *syntax* means "sentence structure." I think the poet is saying that emotions are important, so anyone who only cares about *syntax*, or things in the brain rather than the heart, will never really be in love.

B ❘ YOUR TURN

Vocabulary

Re-read this stanza and think about what eyelids do to come up with a definition for *flutter*. Use a dictionary to check your definition.

since feeling is first
who pays any attention
to the syntax of things
will never wholly kiss you;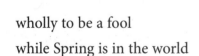

5 wholly to be a fool
while Spring is in the world

my blood approves,
and kisses are a better fate
than wisdom
10 lady i swear by all flowers. Don't cry
—the best gesture of my brain is less than
your eyelids' flutter which says **B**

"since feeling is first" from *Complete Poems, 1904–1962* by E. E. Cummings, edited by George J. Firmage. Copyright 1926, 1954, © 1991 by the Trustees for the E. E. Cummings Trust; copyright © 1985 by George James Firmage. Reproduced by permission of **Liveright Publishing Corporation**.

To understand the **metaphor** "life's not a paragraph," I need to think about what a paragraph is like. Paragraphs show divisions between thoughts on a page. I think the poet is saying that each life is not its own separate section. Life is not a paragraph because it is not easy to define or understand.

B **HERE'S HOW**

Language Coach

The word *parenthesis* is more commonly used in its **plural** form, *parentheses*. Most plurals are formed by adding –*s* or –*es* to words.

C **YOUR TURN**

Reading Focus

Parenthesis can have three meanings: 1) "a punctuation mark"; 2) "a word or phase that adds a comment to a full sentence"; or 3) "an interruption." Analyze the poet's **word choice** in the last line of the poem. Which meaning of *parenthesis* best fits the context of the poem? Why?

we are for each other:then

laugh,leaning back in my arms

15 for life's not a paragraph **A**

And death I think is no parenthesis **B** **C**

IN OTHER WORDS People pay attention to what they feel. Anyone who only cares about being intellectual will never be truly in love. I would rather be a fool and be able to kiss you than be smart and not have you. Anything I think of is less important than your love. We will always be together.

Applying Your Skills

since feeling is first

LITERARY FOCUS: METAPHOR

DIRECTIONS: Re-read the poem and review the definition of **metaphor**. Then answer the following question.

1. E.E. Cummings uses metaphors to write about his feelings on love and death. Choose a metaphor from the poem. Explain what is being compared in the metaphor. What does this metaphor say about the lovers in the poem?

   _____

   _____

   _____

   _____

READING FOCUS: ANALYZING WORD CHOICE

DIRECTIONS: Think about the **words** used in this poem. Complete the exercise below by describing what the selected words made you think of while reading the poem.

Word	Makes Me Think Of
1. fate	
2. flower	

VOCABULARY REVIEW

DIRECTIONS: Fill in the blanks with the correct words from the Word Box. Not all words will be used.

Word Box

syntax

gesture

parenthesis

1. The man made a _____ with his hand that suggested he was happy with either choice.

2. The sentence had complicated _____, which made it difficult to understand.

We Real Cool

By Gwendolyn Brooks

LITERARY FOCUS: SOUND EFFECTS

When you read a poem, pay attention to the way words sound. Poets make music with the sounds of words. **Alliteration** is the repetition of the same or similar consonant sounds. These sounds are usually at the beginning of words that are close together. The tongue twister "Peter Piper picked a peck of pickled peppers" has alliteration throughout. **Onomatopoeia** (ON OH MAHT OH PEE YAH) is the use of a word, such as *buzz*, whose sound is like its meaning. Rhythm, rhyme, repetition, alliteration, and onomatopoeia all give a poem its sound effects.

READING FOCUS: READING ALOUD

Read "We Real Cool" **aloud**. Listen carefully for the sound effects Gwendolyn Brooks creates. Think about how the sounds add to the overall meaning of the poem. As you read, fill in a chart like the one below with examples of sound effects in "We Real Cool." Write phrases from the poem and then identify the type of sound effect.

Phrase	Sound Effect
1. lurk late	**1.** alliteration
2.	**2.**
3.	**3.**

VOCABULARY

lurk (LUHRK) *v.*: stay hidden while waiting for someone or something.

strike (STRYK) *v.*: deliver a blow; hit.

SKILLS FOCUS

Literary Skills
Understand rhyme, rhythm, meter, onomatopoeia, and alliteration.

Reading Skills
Read aloud.

INTO THE POEM

Gwendolyn Brooks was born in Kansas but wrote a lot about African Americans in Chicago. Much of her writing follows the speech and rhythm of people in Chicago. Brooks wrote "We Real Cool" after seeing some youths playing pool at a neighborhood pool hall during the school day. In 1966, the Broadside Press of Detroit published "We Real Cool" on a poster. This kind of poster is also called a broadside. As you read "We Real Cool," think about who the "We" are and how they feel.

WE REAL COOL

The Pool Players Seven At The Golden Shovel

By Gwendolyn Brooks

We real cool. We

Left school. We

Lurk late. We **A**

Strike straight. We

5   Sing sin. We

Thin gin. We

Jazz June. We

Die soon. **B** **C**

IN OTHER WORDS   We are cool. We dropped out of
school. We are pool players. We hang out after dark. We sing,
we drink alcohol, we play jazz music, and we die young.

© The Granger Collection, NY

A **HERE'S HOW**

Literary Focus

When I read the poem, I can
hear different **sound effects**.
Left, *lurk*, and *late* all start
with the letter "l." I can hear
the repetition of the "l"
sound as I read. This must be
an example of **alliteration**.

B **LITERARY ANALYSIS**

Remember that Brooks wrote
this poem after seeing young
students skipping school
to go play pool. The last
sentence: "We / Die soon" is
a powerful way to end the
poem. What do you think
the poet's message is in this
poem? Explain your answer.

_____

_____

_____

_____

C **YOUR TURN**

Reading Focus

Read the poem **aloud**. Draw
an arrow connecting each set
of words that rhyme.

"We Real Cool" from *Blacks* by Gwendolyn Brooks. Copyright © 1991 by Gwendolyn Brooks.
Published by Third World Press, Chicago, 1991. Reproduced by permission of **Brooks Permissions**.

We Real Cool

USE A SOUND EFFECTS CHART

DIRECTIONS: Review the chart you were told to make on the Preparing to Read page. Fill in the chart below with your phrases and the type of **sound effect** those phrases create. Then, fill in the third column of the chart with what you feel is the meaning for each phrase that you listed.

Phrase	Sound Effect	Meaning
1. lurk late	alliteration	Hang out after curfew
2.		
3.		

Applying Your Skills

We Real Cool

LITERARY FOCUS: SOUND EFFECTS

DIRECTIONS: Re-read the poem and circle the examples of **alliteration**. Think about how the poem sounds aloud and how it would be different without the alliteration. In the space below, explain how alliteration affects the poem.

_____

_____

_____

_____

_____

_____

READING FOCUS: READING ALOUD

DIRECTIONS: Review the chart you filled in on the Skills Practice page. Now, **read the poem aloud** again. This time, replace the poet's phrases with the meanings you listed for each word or phrase. Which choice of words adds more to the poem? How do the words that Gwendolyn Brooks uses affect the poem?

_____

_____

_____

_____

_____

VOCABULARY REVIEW

DIRECTIONS: Fill in the blanks with the correct words from the Word Box.

Word Box
lurk
strike

1. The store owner did not want anyone to _____ outside.

2. When playing pool, you have to _____ each ball in the right spot.

Skills Review

Collection 7

VOCABULARY REVIEW

DIRECTIONS: Fill in the blanks with the correct words from the Word Box. Not all words will be used.

Word Box

transform
syntax
complexion
gesture
parenthesis
lurk
expanding
literal
strike
temperate

1. In boxing, you must physically _____ your opponent.

2. I hope my _____ clears up before our class pictures are taken.

3. The baseball coach made a hand _____ to let the pitcher know what kind of pitch to throw.

4. The teacher marked up my essay because the _____ was incorrect.

5. In horror movies, the monsters always _____ in the darkness and the shadows.

6. The league is really _____; this year there are five more teams than last year.

7. A great writer can _____ an everyday event and make it sound great.

Now, choose two words from the Word Box that were not used in the above activity. Write a complete sentence using those words.

8. _____

_____

9. _____

_____

Skills Review

Collection 7

LANGUAGE COACH: WORD ROOTS

DIRECTIONS: As you have learned, many English words have Latin **roots**. Look at the Latin words below. What English words do you think came from each Latin root? Write the English word derived from each Latin root on the correct blank line.

1. insania _____

2. absorbeo _____

3. medius _____

4. redemptor _____

5. relaxo _____

6. studio _____

7. monstrum _____

ORAL LANGUAGE ACTIVITY

DIRECTIONS: Choose one of the poems you read in this collection. Read the poem to yourself to become familiar with the words and the punctuation. Then, with a partner, practice reading the poem **aloud**. Give one another tips on how to improve your reading. Once you feel like you have your poem down, get up and read it in front of the class!

Elements of Drama

Museo Nazionale del Bargello, Florence, Italy/
Eric Lessing/Art Resource, NY

Literary and Academic Vocabulary Collection 8

LITERARY VOCABULARY

drama (DRAH MUH) *n.:* a story that is enacted in real space and time by live actors for a live audience.

William Shakespeare is the world's most famous writer of drama.

tragedy (TRAH JUH DEE) *n.:* a play ending in sorrow or regret.

The play Julius Caesar *is an example of a famous tragedy because the main character is killed.*

dialogue (DY UH LAWG) *n.:* conversations between characters onstage.

Listening closely to the dialogue in a play is important in order to learn about the characters.

ACADEMIC VOCABULARY

highlight (HY LYT) *v.:* make a subject or idea stand out so people will pay attention.

The evil actions of the villain in a play may sometimes highlight the good qualities of the hero.

predominant (PREE DOM UH NUHNT) *adj.:* more powerful, common, or noticeable than others.

Rock 'n Roll is the predominant musical genre on my favorite radio station.

principal (PRIHN SUH PUHL) *adj.:* most important.

Conflict is the principal element in a tragedy.

criteria (KRY TIHR EE UH) *n.:* rules or standards for making a judgment; test.

Theater reviewers have many criteria about what makes a good play.

from The Tragedy of Julius Caesar

By William Shakespeare

LITERARY FOCUS: TRAGEDY

Shakespeare tells us in the title of his play that *Julius Caesar* is a tragedy. A **tragedy** is a play, novel, or other narrative that involves serious and important events and ends unhappily for the main character. Shakespeare's tragedies share these characteristics:

- The main character is often high ranking and dignified, not an ordinary man or woman.

- The main character has a **tragic flaw**—a defect in character or judgment—that directly causes the character's downfall.

- The play ends unhappily, and the main character dies.

READING FOCUS: READING A PLAY

Reading Shakespeare's plays can be difficult. You must not only read the lines but also *between* the lines. Use the characters' words and actions to **make inferences**, or educated guesses, about what the characters are really thinking and feeling. For instance, Cassius usually acts nicely toward Caesar but secretly hates him. Look for clues that reveal the characters' true motives. **Reading a play aloud** will give you a better understanding of the characters' relationships. Finally, **paraphrasing** (or restating the text in your own words) can help you comprehend difficult passages. One example of paraphrasing Shakespeare's difficult language is provided below.

Literary Skills
Understand characteristics of tragedy including complication, dramatic irony, turning point, suspense, and climax.

Reading Skills
Read dramas; read Shakespeare; make inferences; read aloud and paraphrase.

Original Text	Paraphrase
"If my name were liable to fear, / I do not know the man I should avoid / So soon as that spare Cassius. He reads much, He is a great observer, and he looks / Quite through the deeds of men."	If I feared any men, I would fear Cassius the most. He is intelligent and insightful. He can look through men's actions to determine their true feelings and motives.

from THE TRAGEDY OF JULIUS CAESAR ACT I, SCENE 2; ACT III, SCENE 2

By William Shakespeare

INTO THE PLAY

At the time this story takes place, Rome has been a republic, with elected leaders, for 450 years. However, some Romans worry that Julius Caesar, a successful general, is becoming too powerful. Caesar has conquered many lands for the Roman Republic, has gained much popularity with the Roman plebeians (commoners), and has been made dictator. Some elected officials want to get rid of Caesar before the plebeians try to make him king. Act I, Scene 2 opens with a ceremonial footrace. Caesar instructs Antony, an athletic young man running in the race, to touch his wife, Calphurnia, as he passes. Caesar believes that if Calphurnia is touched by Antony during the race, she will finally be able to have children.

ACT I, SCENE 2

Scene 2. *A public place.*

Enter CAESAR, ANTONY (*dressed for the race*), CALPHURNIA, PORTIA, DECIUS, CICERO, BRUTUS, CASSIUS, CASCA, *a* SOOTHSAYER;[1] *after them,* MARULLUS *and* FLAVIUS **A**

Caesar.

Calphurnia!

Casca.   Peace, ho! Caesar speaks.

Caesar.   Calphurnia!

Calphurnia. Here, my lord.

Caesar.

Stand you directly in Antonius' way

When he doth run his course. Antonius!

A (HERE'S HOW)

Literary Focus

My teacher told me about the main characters in this **tragedy**. Caesar is a general and the dictator of Rome. Calphurnia is his wife. Antony and Brutus are Caesar's friends. Brutus is suspicious about Caesar's desire for more power. Cassius and Casca are plotting against Caesar.

---

1. A **soothsayer** is a person who foretells the future.

Literary Focus

In lines 1–7, I see that Caesar is a character with great power. (This is one of the elements of a **tragedy**.) When Caesar speaks, everyone is quiet and listens. When he talks to Calphurnia and to Antony, they reply immediately.

B (QUICK CHECK)

What do lines 7–13 tell you about the character of Antony?

_____

_____

_____

_____

_____

_____

C (QUICK CHECK)

What is a soothsayer? Do you think Caesar should take his warning seriously?

_____

_____

_____

_____

_____

_____

_____

Antony. Caesar, my lord? **A**

Caesar.

    Forget not in your speed, Antonius,

    To touch Calphurnia; for our elders say

10   The barren, touchèd in this holy chase,

    Shake off their sterile curse.[2]

Antony.   I shall remember:

    When Caesar says "Do this," it is performed. **B**

Caesar.

    Set on, and leave no ceremony out.

Soothsayer. Caesar!

Caesar. Ha! Who calls?

Casca.

    Bid every noise be still; peace yet again!

Caesar.

    Who is it in the press[3] that calls on me?

    I hear a tongue, shriller than all the music,

20   Cry "Caesar." Speak; Caesar is turned to hear.

Soothsayer.

    Beware the ides of March.[4]

Caesar.   What man is that?

Brutus.

    A soothsayer bids you beware the ides of March. **C**

IN OTHER WORDS A crowd has gathered to watch a ceremonial race. A voice calls out to Caesar from the crowd. It is a fortuneteller telling Caesar to beware the ides of March.

Caesar.

    Set him before me; let me see his face.

Cassius.

    Fellow, come from the throng; look upon Caesar.

---

2. **sterile curse:** at the Lupercal festival, runners raced around a hill. Romans believed that women who stood in the path of the runners would soon become pregnant.

3. Here, **press** means "crowd."

4. **ides** (YDZ) **of March:** March 15.

Caesar.

What say'st thou to me now? Speak once again.

Soothsayer.

Beware the ides of March.

Caesar.

He is a dreamer, let us leave him. Pass. **D**

>   [*Sennet.*[5] *Exeunt all except* BRUTUS *and* CASSIUS.]

Cassius.

Will you go see the order of the course?

30 **Brutus.** Not I.

Cassius. I pray you do. **E**

Brutus.

I am not gamesome: I do lack some part

Of that quick spirit that is in Antony.

Let me not hinder, Cassius, your desires;

I'll leave you.

Cassius.

Brutus, I do observe you now of late;

I have not from your eyes that gentleness

And show of love as I was wont to have;

You bear too stubborn and too strange a hand[6]

40 Over your friend that loves you.

Brutus.   Cassius,

Be not deceived: if I have veiled my look,

I turn the trouble of my countenance

Merely[7] upon myself. **F**   Vexèd I am

Of late with passions of some difference,[8]

Conceptions only proper to myself,

Which give some soil,[9] perhaps, to my behaviors;

But let not therefore my good friends be grieved

(Among which number, Cassius, be you one)

---

5. **Sennet** (SEHN IHT): flourish, or fanfare of trumpets announcing a ceremonial entrance or exit.

6. **You . . . hand:** Cassius is comparing Brutus's treatment of him to the way a trainer treats a horse.

7. Here, **merely** means "wholly."

8. **Passions of some difference** are conflicting feelings or emotions.

9. **Give some soil** means "stain or mar."

D   (HERE'S HOW)

Reading Focus

I can **paraphrase**, or restate in my own words, Caesar's response to the soothsayer. Caesar tells him: I do not take this warning seriously. You can leave me now.

E   (HERE'S HOW)

Vocabulary

The word *pray* can mean "ask for" or "speak to God." Based on its context here, I think *pray* means "ask for."

F   (HERE'S HOW)

Vocabulary

Brutus says that he *veiled* his look. I know that a *veil* is a piece of fabric worn over the face. It hides the face. I think Brutus is saying that his expression was like a *veil* that hid what was going on in his mind.

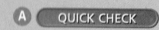

A **QUICK CHECK**

In lines 41–52, how does Brutus respond to Cassius?

_____

_____

_____

_____

_____

_____

B **HERE'S HOW**

Reading Focus

Lines 53–58 are a little confusing, so I will **paraphrase** them. First, Cassius asks Brutus if he can see himself. Brutus answers that a man can only see a reflection of himself—he cannot see himself exactly as others do.

50   Nor construe[10] any further my neglect

Than that poor Brutus, with himself at war,

Forgets the shows of love to other men. Ⓐ

IN OTHER WORDS   Caesar orders the fortuneteller to come forward and speak. However, Caesar does not take the warning seriously. The group heads off to the race, leaving Brutus and Cassius behind. Cassius says that Brutus, his friend, seems cold and unfriendly lately. Brutus explains that he simply has a lot on his mind.

Cassius.

Then, Brutus, I have much mistook your passion,[11]

By means whereof this breast of mine hath buried

Thoughts of great value, worthy cogitations.[12]

Tell me, good Brutus, can you see your face?

Brutus.

No, Cassius; for the eye sees not itself

But by reflection, by some other things. Ⓑ

___

10. **Construe** (KUHN STROO) means "interpret."
11. Here, **passion** is feeling.
12. **Worthy cogitations** (KOJ UH TAY SHUHNZ) are reflections of great value.

© Suzanne Worthington/Royal Shakespeare Company

Cassius.

'Tis just:[13]

60   And it is very much lamented, Brutus,

That you have no such mirrors as will turn

Your hidden worthiness into your eye,

That you might see your shadow.[14] I have heard

Where many of the best respect[15] in Rome

(Except immortal Caesar), speaking of Brutus,

And groaning underneath this age's yoke,

Have wished that noble Brutus had his eyes. **C**

Brutus.

Into what dangers would you lead me, Cassius,

That you would have me seek into myself

70   For that which is not in me?

Cassius.

Therefore, good Brutus, be prepared to hear;

And since you know you cannot see yourself

So well as by reflection, I, your glass[16]

Will modestly discover to yourself

That of yourself which you yet know not of.

And be not jealous on[17] me, gentle Brutus:

Were I a common laughter,[18] or did use

To stale with ordinary oaths my love

To every new protester,[19] if you know

80   That I do fawn on men and hug them hard,

And after scandal them;[20] or if you know

That I profess myself in banqueting

To all the rout,[21] then hold me dangerous.

---

13. Here, **just** means "true."
14. Here, Brutus's **shadow** is a reflection (of what others think of him).
15. Here, **respect** means "reputation."
16. Here, **glass** is a mirror.
17. **Jealous on** means "suspicious of."
18. **Common laughter** means "butt of a joke; object of mockery."
19. **To stale . . . new protestor:** In other words, if he swore to love everyone who came along.
20. Here, **scandal them** means "ruin them by gossip."
21. Here, **rout** (ROWT) are common people.

C   QUICK CHECK

What is Cassius telling Brutus in lines 59–67?

_____

_____

_____

_____

_____

_____

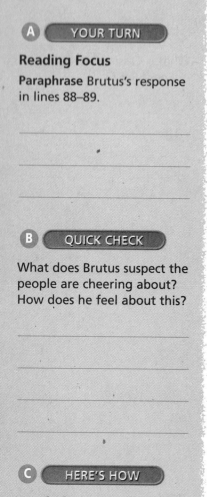

Reading Focus

Paraphrase Brutus's response in lines 88–89.

_____

_____

_____

B QUICK CHECK

What does Brutus suspect the people are cheering about? How does he feel about this?

_____

_____

_____

C HERE'S HOW

Vocabulary

I looked up the word *aught* in a dictionary and found out that it means "anything." When I substitute "anything" for *aught*, Brutus's speech keeps the same meaning.

IN OTHER WORDS Cassius begins to flatter Brutus, suggesting that many in Rome consider him Caesar's equal. He says he wishes that Brutus could see himself as others see him. Brutus asks why Cassius is urging such dangerous ideas. Cassius tries to persuade Brutus to trust him.

[*Flourish*[22] *and shout.*]

Brutus.

What means this shouting? I do fear the people

Choose Caesar for their king.

Cassius. Ay, do you fear it?

Then must I think you would not have it so.

Brutus.

I would not, Cassius, yet I love him well.

But wherefore do you hold me here so long? **A**

90 What is it that you would impart to me?

If it be aught toward the general good,

Set honor in one eye and death i' th' other,

And I will look on both indifferently;[23]

For let the gods so speed me, as I love

The name of honor more than I fear death. **B C**

Cassius.

I know that virtue to be in you, Brutus,

As well as I do know your outward favor.[24]

Well, honor is the subject of my story.

I cannot tell what you and other men

100 Think of this life, but for my single self,

I had as lief[25] not be, as live to be

In awe of such a thing as I myself.

I was born free as Caesar; so were you:

We both have fed as well, and we can both

Endure the winter's cold as well as he:

For once, upon a raw and gusty day,

---

22. **Flourish** (FLUR ihsh) is the brief, elaborate music of trumpets.
23. Here, **indifferently** means "impartially; fairly."
24. **Outward favor** is appearance.
25. **As lief** (LEEF) means "just as soon."

The troubled Tiber chafing with[26] her shores,

Caesar said to me "Dar'st thou, Cassius, now

Leap in with me into this angry flood,

110 And swim to yonder point?" Upon the word,

Accout'red as I was, I plungèd in

And bade him follow: so indeed he did.

The torrent roared, and we did buffet it

With lusty sinews, throwing it aside

And stemming it with hearts of controversy.[27]

IN OTHER WORDS Offstage, there is the sound of trumpets and shouting. Brutus fears that the noise means the people are making Julius Caesar king. (Rome is a republic and has no king.) Brutus says that he is loyal to Caesar, but would not want him to be king. He asks Cassius what he wants. Cassius replies that in Rome all free men are equal citizens, Caesar included.

But ere we could arrive the point proposed,

Caesar cried "Help me, Cassius, or I sink!"

I, as Aeneas,[28] our great ancestor,

Did from the flames of Troy upon his shoulder

120 The old Anchises bear, so from the waves of Tiber

Did I the tired Caesar. **D** And this man

Is now become a god, and Cassius is

A wretched creature, and must bend his body

If Caesar carelessly but nod on him. **E**

He had a fever when he was in Spain,

And when the fit was on him, I did mark

How he did shake; 'tis true, this god did shake.

His coward lips did from their color fly,

---

26. **Chafing** (CHAYF IHNG) **with** means "raging against." (The river was rough with waves and currents.)

27. Here, **hearts of controversy** (KON TRUH VUR SEE) are hearts full of aggressive feelings, or fighting spirit.

28. **Aeneas** (IH NEE UHS): legendary forefather of the Roman people who, in Virgil's *Aeneid*, fled from the burning city of Troy carrying his old father on his back. (In many accounts of the legend, Romulus and Remus were descendants of Aeneas.)

D YOUR TURN

Vocabulary

The word *bear* can mean "a big, shaggy animal," "carry," or "move to the side." Which meaning do you think *bear* has in line 120? Explain your answer.

_____

_____

_____

_____

E HERE'S HOW

Literary Focus

Cassius tells of an instance in which Caesar challenged him to a swimming contest, but ultimately, Cassius had to save Caesar from drowning. I think Caesar's **tragic flaw** may be that he is too proud or too cocky.

A **QUICK CHECK**

What story does Cassius tell about Caesar in lines 125–134?

_____

_____

_____

_____

B **YOUR TURN**

Reading Focus

What **inferences** can you make about Cassius based on these lines and his two earlier stories about Caesar?

_____

_____

_____

_____

_____

_____

_____

_____

And that same eye whose bend doth awe the world

130   Did lose his luster; I did hear him groan;

Ay, and that tongue of his, that bade the Romans

Mark him and write his speeches in their books,

Alas, it cried, "Give me some drink, Titinius,"

As a sick girl. **A** Ye gods! It doth amaze me,

A man of such a feeble temper should

So get the start of the majestic world,

And bear the palm[29] alone.

[*Shout. Flourish.*]

    Brutus. Another general shout?

    I do believe that these applauses are

140   For some new honors that are heaped on Caesar.

Cassius.

    Why, man, he doth bestride the narrow world

    Like a Colossus,[30] and we petty men

    Walk under his huge legs and peep about

    To find ourselves dishonorable graves.

    Men at some time are masters of their fates:

    The fault, dear Brutus, is not in our stars,[31]

    But in ourselves, that we are underlings. **B**

IN OTHER WORDS Cassius tells two stories about his days in the army under Caesar. Both stories show Caesar as weak. Caesar, he says, is no better a man than he is; in fact, he is less of one. Why should Caesar be like a god, while he and Brutus seem small and unimportant? Why should they allow Caesar to have power over them?

---

29. **bear the palm:** hold the palm branch, an award given to a victorious general.
30. **Colossus** (KUH LOS UHS): huge statue of Helios that was said to straddle the entrance to the harbor at Rhodes, an island in the Aegean Sea. The statue, so huge that ships passed under its legs, was one of the Seven Wonders of the Ancient World. It was destroyed by an earthquake in 224 B.C.
31. **stars:** Elizabethans believed that one's life was governed by the stars or constellation one was born under.

Brutus and Caesar: what should be in that "Caesar"?

Why should that name be sounded more than yours?

150 Write them together, yours is as fair a name;

Sound them, it doth become the mouth as well;

Weigh them, it is as heavy; conjure with 'em,

"Brutus" will start a spirit as soon as "Caesar."

Now, in the names of all the gods at once,

Upon what meat doth this our Caesar feed,

That he is grown so great? Age, thou art shamed!

Rome, thou hast lost the breed of noble bloods!

When went there by an age, since the great flood,[32]

But it was famed with more than with one man?

160 When could they say (till now) that talked of Rome,

That her wide walks encompassed but one man?

Now is it Rome indeed, and room[33] enough,

When there is in it but one only man.

O, you and I have heard our fathers say,

There was a Brutus once that would have brooked[34]

Th' eternal devil to keep his state in Rome

As easily as a king.[35]

Brutus.

That you do love me, I am nothing jealous;

What you would work me to, I have some aim;[36]

170 How I have thought of this, and of these times,

I shall recount hereafter. For this present,

I would not so (with love I might entreat you)

Be any further moved. What you have said

I will consider; C what you have to say

I will with patience hear, and find a time

---

32. **the great flood:** flood sent by Zeus to drown all the wicked people on Earth. Only the faithful couple Deucalion and Pyrrha were saved.

33. **Rome . . . room:** a pun; both words were pronounced "room" in Shakespeare's day.

34. Here, **brooked** means "put up with."

35. **Th' eternal . . . king:** This refers to the ancestor of Brutus who, in the sixth century B.C., helped to expel the last king from Rome and set up the Republic.

36. Here, **aim** means "idea."

C **HERE'S HOW**

Language Coach

Shakespeare's language can be hard to understand. I believe Shakespeare is using inverted word order when Brutus says, "What you have said / I will consider." In modern English, I would probably say, "I will consider what you have said."

Literary Focus

I know that one element of a **tragedy** is the death of the main character. I am beginning to think that Cassius and Brutus may plot to kill Caesar.

Reading Focus

Paraphrase Cassius' response in lines 182–184.

_____

_____

_____

_____

Vocabulary

Based on its context, write a definition for the word *pluck* in line 186. If necessary, check a dictionary.

_____

_____

Both meet[37] to hear and answer such high things. **A**

Till then, my noble friend, chew upon this:

Brutus had rather be a villager

Than to repute himself a son of Rome

180   Under these hard conditions as this time

Is like to lay upon us.

Cassius.   I am glad

That my weak words have struck but thus much show

Of fire from Brutus. **B**

IN OTHER WORDS Cassius says there is no reason that Brutus should not be as great as Caesar. He reminds Brutus of his ancestor, who helped get rid of the last king of Rome and make their nation a republic. Brutus replies that he trusts Cassius's friendship. He has some idea of what Cassius wants him to do, but he is not ready to give an answer. He will think about what Cassius has said.

[*Enter* CAESAR *and his* TRAIN.]

Brutus.

The games are done, and Caesar is returning.

Cassius.

As they pass by, pluck Casca by the sleeve,

And he will (after his sour fashion) tell you

What hath proceeded worthy note today. **C**

Brutus.

I will do so. But look you, Cassius,

190   The angry spot doth glow on Caesar's brow,

And all the rest look like a chidden[38] train:

Calphurnia's cheek is pale, and Cicero[39]

Looks with such ferret[40] and such fiery eyes

As we have seen him in the Capitol,

Being crossed in conference by some senators.

---

37. Here, **meet** means "appropriate."
38. Here, **chidden** (CHIHD UHN) means "rebuked; corrected."
39. **Cicero** was a great speaker who supported the Republic.
40. Here, a **ferret** is a weasel-like animal, usually considered crafty.

Cassius.

> Casca will tell us what the matter is.

Caesar. Antonius.

Antony. Caesar?

Caesar.

> Let me have men about me that are fat,
200 Sleek-headed men, and such as sleep a-nights.
> Yond Cassius has a lean and hungry look;
> He thinks too much: such men are dangerous. **D**

Antony.

> Fear him not, Caesar, he's not dangerous;
> He is a noble Roman, and well given.[41]

Caesar.

> Would he were fatter! But I fear him not.
> Yet if my name were liable to fear,
> I do not know the man I should avoid
> So soon as that spare Cassius. **E** He reads much,
> He is a great observer, and he looks
210 Quite through the deeds of men.[42] He loves no plays,
> As thou dost, Antony; he hears no music;
> Seldom he smiles, and smiles in such a sort[43]
> As if he mocked himself, and scorned his spirit
> That could be moved to smile at anything.
> Such men as he be never at heart's ease
> Whiles they behold a greater than themselves,
> And therefore are they very dangerous.
> I rather tell thee what is to be feared
> Than what I fear; for always I am Caesar.
220 Come on my right hand, for this ear is deaf,
> And tell me truly what thou think'st of him.

> > [*Sennet. Exeunt* CAESAR *and his* TRAIN.]

---

41. Well given means "well disposed to support Caesar."
42. he looks . . . of men: In other words, he looks through what men do to search out their feelings and motives.
43. Here, **sort** means "manner."

Sidebar:

D **HERE'S HOW**

Reading Focus

I will pause and **paraphrase** lines 199–202: Caesar says he does not trust men such as Cassius who are ambitious and dissatisfied. Caesar would rather be surrounded by men who are content with what they have.

E **LITERARY ANALYSIS**

What does Caesar say about fear in lines 205–208? What does this tell you about Caesar's personality?

_____

_____

_____

_____

_____

_____

_____

IN OTHER WORDS Caesar and the others return. Cassius suggests that Brutus take Casca aside and find out what has been happening. Brutus notices that neither Caesar nor his followers look happy.

Caesar sees the two men, and tells Antony that Cassius is ambitious and dissatisfied, and therefore dangerous. Antony tells him not to be afraid—Cassius is a loyal supporter. Caesar says that he is not afraid of anyone, but if he were to be afraid, he would fear Cassius.

Casca.

You pulled me by the cloak; would you speak with me?

Brutus.

Ay, Casca; tell us what hath chanced today,

That Caesar looks so sad.[44]

Casca.

Why, you were with him, were you not?

Brutus.

I should not then ask Casca what had chanced.

Casca. Why, there was a crown offered him; and being offered him, he put it by[45] with the back of his hand, thus; and then the people fell a-shouting.

230 **Brutus.** What was the second noise for?

Casca. Why, for that too.

Cassius.

They shouted thrice; what was the last cry for?

Casca. Why, for that too.

Brutus. Was the crown offered him thrice?

Casca. Ay, marry,[46] was't, and he put it by thrice, every time gentler than other; and at every putting-by mine honest neighbors shouted. A

Cassius.

Who offered him the crown?

---

44. Here, **sad** means "serious."
45. **Put it by** means "pushed it aside."
46. Here, **marry** refers to a mild oath meaning "by the Virgin Mary."

Casca. Why, Antony.

Brutus.

240   Tell us the manner of it, gentle Casca. **B**

B (**HERE'S HOW**)

Language Coach
In **Shakespeare's Language,**
gentle means "kind."

IN OTHER WORDS Brutus stops Casca and asks what made Caesar look so unhappy. Casca explains that Antony offered Caesar a crown in front of the crowd three times, and Caesar refused it three times. The shouts they heard were the crowd cheering Caesar's refusal to be king.

Casca. I can as well be hanged as tell the manner of it:
it was mere foolery; I did not mark it. I saw Mark
Antony offer him a crown—yet 'twas not a crown
neither, 'twas one of these coronets[47]—and, as I told
you, he put it by once; but for all that, to my thinking,
he would fain[48] have had it. Then he offered it to him
again; then he put it by again; but to my thinking, he
was very loath to lay his fingers off it. And then he

---

47. **Coronets** (KAWR UH NEHTZ) are small crowns.
48. **Fain** (FAYN) means "happily."

B QUICK CHECK

What do we learn about Casca in lines 255–257?

_____

_____

_____

_____

_____

250 offered it the third time. He put it the third time by; and still as he refused it, the rabblement hooted, and clapped their chopt[49] hands, and threw up their sweaty nightcaps,[50] and uttered such a deal of stinking breath because Caesar refused the crown, that it had, almost, choked Caesar; for he swounded[51] and fell down at it. **A** And for mine own part, I durst not laugh, for fear of opening my lips and receiving the bad air. **B**

Cassius.

But, soft,[52] I pray you; what, did Caesar swound?

Casca. He fell down in the market place, and foamed
260 at mouth, and was speechless.

Brutus.

'Tis very like he hath the falling-sickness.[53]

Cassius.

No, Caesar hath it not; but you, and I,
And honest Casca, we have the falling-sickness.

Casca. I know not what you mean by that, but I am sure Caesar fell down. If the tag-rag people[54] did not clap him and hiss him, according as he pleased and displeased them, as they use to do the players in the theater, I am no true man.

Brutus.

What said he when he came unto himself?

270 **Casca.** Marry, before he fell down, when he perceived the common herd was glad he refused the crown, he plucked me ope[55] his doublet[56] and offered them his

---

49. **Chopt** means "chapped (raw and rough from hard work and the weather)."
50. **nightcaps:** Casca is mockingly referring to the hats of the workingmen.
51. **Swounded** (SWOON DIHD) means "swooned or fainted."
52. Here, **soft** means "wait a minute."
53. **falling-sickness:** old term for the disease we now call epilepsy, which is marked by seizures and momentary loss of consciousness.
54. Here, **tag-rag people** is a contemptuous reference to the commoners in the crowd.
55. **Plucked me ope** means "plucked open."
56. A **doublet** is a close-fitting jacket.

throat to cut. An[57] I had been a man of any
occupation,[58] if I would not have taken him at a
word, I would I might go to hell among the rogues.
And so he fell. When he came to himself again, he
said, if he had done or said anything amiss, he desired
their worships to think it was his infirmity. Three or
four wenches,[59] where I stood, cried "Alas, good

280
soul!" and forgave him with all their hearts; but
there's no heed to be taken of them; if Caesar had
stabbed their mothers, they would have done no less. **C**

Brutus.

And after that, he came thus sad away?

IN OTHER WORDS Casca says that Caesar really wanted
to be king, and hoped that the people would urge him to
accept the crown. When they failed to react the way he
hoped, he ripped open his shirt and offered to die for the
people. Then he fell down in a fit.

Casca. Ay.

Cassius.

Did Cicero say anything?

Casca. Ay, he spoke Greek.

Cassius. To what effect?

Casca. Nay, an I tell you that, I'll ne'er look you i' th'
face again. But those that understood him smiled at

290
one another and shook their heads; but for mine own
part, it was Greek to me. I could tell you more news
too: Marullus and Flavius, for pulling scarfs off
Caesar's images, are put to silence.[60] Fare you well.
There was more foolery yet, if I could remember it.

Cassius. Will you sup with me tonight, Casca?

---

57. Here, **an** means "if."
58. Here, a **man of any occupation** is a working man.
59. Here, **wenches** are girls or young women.
60. **Put to silence** means "silenced, perhaps being dismissed from their
positions as tribunes or by being exiled."

C YOUR TURN

Reading Focus
Paraphrase what Casca
says about Caesar in lines
276–282.

_____

_____

_____

_____

_____

_____

_____

_____

_____

_____

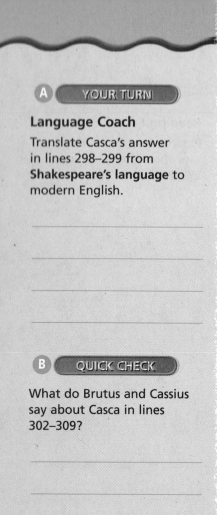

A YOUR TURN

Language Coach

Translate Casca's answer in lines 298–299 from **Shakespeare's language** to modern English.

_____

_____

_____

_____

B QUICK CHECK

What do Brutus and Cassius say about Casca in lines 302–309?

_____

_____

_____

_____

_____

_____

_____

Casca. No, I am promised forth.[61]

Cassius. Will you dine with me tomorrow?

Casca. Ay, if I be alive, and your mind hold, and your

　　dinner worth the eating. **A**

300 **Cassius.** Good; I will expect you.

Casca. Do so. Farewell, both.　　　　　[_Exit._]

Brutus.

　　What a blunt fellow is this grown to be!

　　He was quick mettle[62] when he went to school.

Cassius.

　　So is he now in execution

　　Of any bold or noble enterprise,

　　However he puts on this tardy form.[63]

　　This rudeness[64] is a sauce to his good wit,[65]

　　Which gives men stomach to disgest[66] his words

　　With better appetite. **B**

IN OTHER WORDS Cassius asks how Cicero reacted to all this. Casca says Cicero made a comment in Greek, so he did not understand it. He also says that two opponents of Caesar have been silenced. Cassius invites Casca to dinner, and Casca agrees to come the next day. Then Casca leaves, and Cassius tells Brutus that Casca acts so rude to disguise his sharp intelligence.

Brutus.

310　　And so it is. For this time I will leave you.

　　Tomorrow, if you please to speak with me,

　　I will come home to you; or if you will,

　　Come home to me, and I will wait for you.

---

61. Here, **forth** means "elsewhere" (he has other plans).
62. **Quick mettle** means "lively of disposition."
63. **Tardy form** is a sluggish appearance.
64. Here, **rudeness** is a rough manner.
65. **Wit** is intelligence.
66. Here, **disgest** is the same as "digest."

Cassius.

I will do so. Till then, think of the world.[67]

[*Exit* BRUTUS.]

Well, Brutus, thou art noble; yet I see

Thy honorable mettle may be wrought

From that it is disposed;[68] therefore it is meet

That noble minds keep ever with their likes;

For who so firm that cannot be seduced? **C**

320 Caesar doth bear me hard,[69] but he loves Brutus.

If I were Brutus now and he were Cassius,

He should not humor[70] me. I will this night,

In several hands,[71] in at his windows throw,

As if they came from several citizens,

Writings, all tending to the great opinion

That Rome holds of his name; wherein obscurely

Caesar's ambition shall be glancèd at.[72]

And after this, let Caesar seat him sure;[73]

For we will shake him, or worse days endure. **D**   [*Exit.*]

IN OTHER WORDS Brutus says he and Cassius will continue their talk the day. He leaves. Alone Cassius says he will send Brutus anonymous notes in several different handwritings, flattering Brutus further, and hinting that other Romans see Caesar as too ambitious.

WHAT HAPPENS NEXT *In the final scene of Act I, Cicero and Casca meet on a stormy night. Casca tells Cicero of supernatural events. When Cicero leaves, Cassius arrives. He interprets the strange events as divine warnings that Caesar will destroy the Republic. Cassius wants Casca to help him oppose Caesar. When Cinna agrees to the plot, Cassius urges him to*

---

67. Here, **the world** refers to the state of affairs in Rome.
68. **Thy honorable . . . disposed:** In other words, he may be persuaded against his better nature to join the conspirators.
69. **Bear me hard** means "has a grudge (hard feelings) against me."
70. Here, **humor** means "influence by flattery."
71. Here, **hands** are varieties of handwriting.
72. Here, **glancèd at** means "touched on."
73. **Seat him sure** means "make his position secure."

C QUICK CHECK

In lines 315–319, what does Cassius say about Brutus?

_____

_____

_____

D LITERARY ANALYSIS

How does Cassius figure to convince Brutus to go along with his plan? What does this say about Cassius's character?

_____

_____

_____

_____

_____

_____

_____

_____

Vocabulary

I wondered about the word *pulpit* in the stage directions. My teacher explained that when the play is presented on stage, the *pulpit* is a semicircular raised platform with steps leading up to it. This means that the audience can see Brutus over the heads of the crowd of plebeians.

persuade Brutus to join them. The three conspirators—Casca, Cassius, and Cinna—agree to meet with other men to advance their cause.

In Act II, Brutus decides Caesar should be killed. Though he is a close personal friend of Caesar, he feels the Roman people will be treated very badly as Caesar's power grows. The conspirators—Cassius, Casca, Cinna, now joined by Decius, Metellus Cimber, and Trebonius—meet with Brutus and agree to exclude Cicero from the conspiracy. Cassius argues that Mark Antony should be killed along with Caesar. Brutus reasons that this is unnecessary.

Bad omens continue to warn of coming danger. Caesar's wife and close advisors feel he will put himself at risk by attending that morning's Senate session. But Decius, one of the conspirators, finally convinces Caesar not to stay home. Caesar decides to go to the Capitol.

At the beginning of Act III, a man hands Caesar a note warning of the plot against him, but Caesar refuses to read it. Caesar enters the Capitol. Trebonious takes Antony aside so he will not interfere. The conspirators surround Caesar and suddenly, from behind, Casca stabs him. Caesar falls and dies. Antony flees, and then comes back to pay tribute to his fallen friend. Antony pretends to make peace with the murderers and asks to speak at Caesar's funeral. In private, Antony speaks to Caesar's corpse, asking forgiveness for having been gentle with his killers. A servant enters and announces that Octavius Caesar, Caesar's adopted son and heir, is coming to Rome. The servant and Antony exit, carrying Caesar's body.

ACT III, SCENE 2

Scene 2. *The Forum*

Enter BRUTUS *and goes into the pulpit, and* CASSIUS, *with the* PLEBEIANS.[74] **A**

Plebeians.

We will be satisfied! Let us be satisfied!

---

74. Here, **plebeians** (PLIH BEE UHNZ) are the common people.

Brutus.

Then follow me, and give me audience, friends.

Cassius, go you into the other street

And part the numbers.

Those that will hear me speak, let 'em stay here;

Those that will follow Cassius, go with him;

And public reasons shall be renderèd

Of Caesar's death. **B**

First Plebeian.   I will hear Brutus speak.

Second Plebeian.

10   I will hear Cassius, and compare their reasons,

When severally we hear them renderèd.

[*Exit* CASSIUS, *with some of the* PLEBEIANS.]

Third Plebeian.

The noble Brutus is ascended. Silence!

Brutus. Be patient till the last.

Romans, countrymen, and lovers[75], hear me for my

cause, and be silent, that you may hear. Believe me

for mine honor, and have respect to mine honor, that

you may believe. Censure[76] me in your wisdom, and

awake your senses,[77] that you may the better judge.

If there be any in this assembly, any dear friend of

20   Caesar's, to him I say that Brutus' love to Caesar

was no less than his. If then that friend demand why

Brutus rose against Caesar, this is my answer: Not

that I loved Caesar less, but that I loved Rome more.

Had you rather Caesar were living, and die all slaves,

than that Caesar were dead, to live all free men? As

Caesar loved me, I weep for him; as he was fortunate,

I rejoice at it; as he was valiant, I honor him; but, as

he was ambitious, I slew him. There is tears, for his

love; joy, for his fortune; honor, for his valor; and

30   death, for his ambition. **C** Who is here so base, that

---

75. Here, **lovers** are those who love Rome.
76. Here, **censure** (SEHN SHUHR) means "judge."
77. Here, **senses** are reasoning powers.

B **HERE'S HOW**

Language Coach

I did not know why there is a mark over the last *e* in *renderèd* in line 7. My teacher explained that in **Shakespeare's language** the mark means that *ed* is pronounced. Usually *rendered* is pronounced REHN DUHRD. With the mark over the last *e*, the pronunciation is REHN DUHR EHD.

C **YOUR TURN**

Reading Focus

What **inferences** can you draw from Brutus's speech? Why did he kill Caesar?

_____

_____

_____

_____

_____

_____

_____

_____

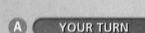
would be a bondman?[78] If any, speak; for him have I offended. Who is here so rude,[79] that would not be a Roman? If any, speak; for him have I offended. Who is here so vile, that will not love his country? If any, speak; for him have I offended. I pause for a reply.

All. None, Brutus, none!

Brutus.

Then none have I offended. I have done no more to Caesar than you shall do to Brutus. The question

40 of his death is enrolled[80] in the Capitol; his glory not extenuated,[81] wherein he was worthy, nor his offenses enforced,[82] for which he suffered death.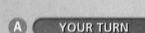

[_Enter_ MARK ANTONY, _with Caesar's body._]

Here comes his body, mourned by Mark Antony, who, though he had no hand in his death, shall receive the benefit of his dying, a place in the commonwealth, as which of you shall not? With this I depart, that, as I slew my best lover for the good of Rome, I have the same dagger for myself, when it shall please my country to need my death.

50 **All.** Live, Brutus! Live, live!

First Plebeian.

Bring him with triumph home unto his house.

Second Plebeian.

Give him a statue with his ancestors.

Third Plebeian.

Let him be Caesar.

Fourth Plebeian. Caesar's better parts[83]

Shall be crowned in Brutus.

---

78. A **bondman** was a slave.
79. Here, **rude** means "rough and uncivilized."
80. In other words, there is a record of the reasons he was killed.
81. Here, **extenuated** (EHK STEHN yu ay TEHD) means "lessened."
82. Here, **enforced** (EHN FOHRST) means "exaggerated."
83. Here, **better parts** are better qualities.

First Plebeian.

We'll bring him to his house with shouts and clamors. **B**

Brutus. My countrymen—

Second Plebeian.   Peace! Silence! Brutus speaks.

First Plebeian. Peace, ho!

Brutus.

60   Good countrymen, let me depart alone,

And, for my sake, stay here with Antony.

Do grace to Caesar's corpse, and grace his speech[84]

Tending to Caesar's glories, which Mark Antony

By our permission, is allowed to make.

I do entreat you, not a man depart,

Save I alone, till Antony have spoke. [*Exit.*] **C**

First Plebeian.

Stay, ho! And let us hear Mark Antony.

Third Plebeian.

Let him go up into the public chair;[85]

We'll hear him. Noble Antony, go up.

Antony.

70   For Brutus' sake, I am beholding to you.

Fourth Plebeian.

What does he say of Brutus?

Third Plebeian.   He says, for Brutus' sake,

He finds himself beholding to us all.

Fourth Plebeian.

'Twere best he speak no harm of Brutus here!

First Plebeian.

This Caesar was a tyrant.

Third Plebeian.   Nay, that's certain.

We are blest that Rome is rid of him.

Second Plebeian.

Peace! Let us hear what Antony can say.

Antony.

You gentle Romans—

---

84. Here, **grace his speech** means "listen respectfully to Antony's funeral oration."

85. Here, a **public chair** is a pulpit or Rostrum.

Vocabulary

What do you think the word *clamors* means? Write a definition below. Circle the other word in that line with a similar meaning.

_____

_____

_____

C   HERE'S HOW

Vocabulary

I think that the word *entreat* means "beg" or "ask," because Brutus wants everyone to stay and listen to Antony's speech. When I use *beg* or *ask* in place of *entreat*, the meaning of the sentence stays the same.

Reading Focus

Paraphrase the opening two lines of Antony's speech.

_____

_____

_____

_____

80   **All.**   Peace, ho! Let us hear him.

Antony.

Friends, Romans, countrymen, lend me your ears;

I come to bury Caesar, not to praise him. **A**

IN OTHER WORDS Brutus leaves, and Antony is ready to speak. The crowd has turned entirely against Caesar and in favor of Brutus. Antony faces a hostile crowd. He has promised Brutus to say nothing against Caesar's killers. He promises the crowd that he does not intend to praise Caesar.

The evil that men do lives after them,

The good is oft interrèd with their bones;

So let it be with Caesar. The noble Brutus

Hath told you Caesar was ambitious.

If it were so, it was a grievous fault,

And grievously hath Caesar answered[86] it.

Here, under leave of Brutus and the rest

90   (For Brutus is an honorable man,

So are they all, all honorable men),

Come I to speak in Caesar's funeral.

He was my friend, faithful and just to me;

But Brutus says he was ambitious,

And Brutus is an honorable man.

He hath brought many captives home to Rome,

Whose ransoms did the general coffers[87] fill;

Did this in Caesar seem ambitious?

When that the poor have cried, Caesar hath wept;

100   Ambition should be made of sterner stuff.

Yet Brutus says he was ambitious;

And Brutus is an honorable man.

You all did see that on the Lupercal

I thrice presented him a kingly crown,

Which he did thrice refuse. Was this ambition?

---

86. Here, **answered** means "paid the penalty for."
87. Here, **general coffers** (KAWF UHRZ) are public funds.

Yet Brutus says he was ambitious;

And sure he is an honorable man. **B**

I speak not to disprove what Brutus spoke,

But here I am to speak what I do know.

110 You all did love him once, not without cause;

What cause withholds you then to mourn for him?

O judgment, thou art fled to brutish beasts,

And men have lost their reason! Bear with me;

My heart is in the coffin there with Caesar,

And I must pause till it come back to me.

First Plebeian.

Methinks there is much reason in his sayings.

Second Plebeian.

If thou consider rightly of the matter,

Caesar has had great wrong.

Third Plebeian. Has he, masters?

120 I fear there will a worse come in his place.

Fourth Plebeian.

Marked ye his words? He would not take the crown, **C**

B **LITERARY ANALYSIS**

Why do you think Antony repeats the phrase "Brutus is an honorable man" so many times? What does he really want the crowd to believe about Brutus?

_____

_____

_____

_____

C **QUICK CHECK**

Underline words on this page that show that the plebeians are changing how they think about Brutus.

from **The Tragedy of Julius Caesar Act III, Scene 2** **287**

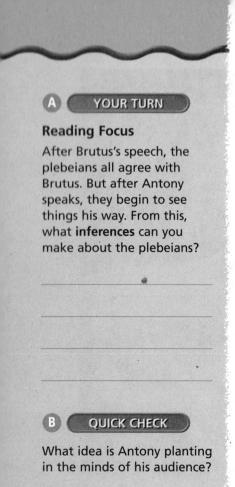

Therefore 'tis certain he was not ambitious. **A**

First Plebeian.

If it be found so, some will dear abide it.[88]

Second Plebeian.

Poor soul, his eyes are red as fire with weeping.

Third Plebeian.

There's not a nobler man in Rome than Antony.

Fourth Plebeian.

Now mark him, he begins again to speak.

IN OTHER WORDS Antony's speech is filled with irony—saying one thing but meaning the opposite. For example, he says that Brutus and the other assassins are honorable men, though he certainly believes the opposite. While pretending to agree with Brutus, Antony questions whether Caesar's actions were really overly ambitious. Antony reminds the crowd of all the good Caesar did for Rome. He scolds the people for forgetting their love for Caesar so quickly. The crowd, easily persuaded, turns again in favor of Caesar and Antony.

Antony.

But yesterday the word of Caesar might

Have stood against the world; now lies he there,

And none so poor to[89] do him reverence.

130　O masters! If I were disposed to stir

Your hearts and minds to mutiny and rage,

I should do Brutus wrong and Cassius wrong,

Who, you all know, are honorable men. **B**

I will not do them wrong; I rather choose

To wrong the dead, to wrong myself and you,

Than I will wrong such honorable men.

But here's a parchment with the seal of Caesar;

I found it in his closet; 'tis his will.

Let but the commons hear this testament,

---

88. Here, **dear abide it** means "pay dearly for it."
89. Here, **so poor to** means "so low in rank as to."

140   Which, pardon me, I do not mean to read,

And they would go and kiss dead Caesar's wounds,

And dip their napkins[90] in his sacred blood;

Yea, beg a hair of him for memory,

And dying, mention it within their wills,

Bequeathing it as a rich legacy

Unto their issue.[91]

Fourth Plebeian.

We'll hear the will; read it, Mark Antony.

All. The will, the will! We will hear Caesar's will! **C**

IN OTHER WORDS   Antony says he would never want to stir up the crowd against the "honorable" Cassius and Brutus. He brings out Caesar's will. However, he says that he will not read it, because it would make their grief over Caesar's death even more unbearable. Antony tells the crowd they are Caesar's heirs. Naturally, the crowd insists on hearing what is in Caesar's will.

Antony.

Have patience, gentle friends, I must not read it.

150   It is not meet you know how Caesar loved you. **D**

You are not wood, you are not stones, but men;

And being men, hearing the will of Caesar,

It will inflame you, it will make you mad.

'Tis good you know not that you are his heirs;

For if you should, O, what would come of it?

Fourth Plebeian.

Read the will! We'll hear it, Antony!

You shall read us the will, Caesar's will!

Antony.

Will you be patient? Will you stay awhile?

I have o'ershot myself[92] to tell you of it.

160   I fear I wrong the honorable men

---

90. Here, **napkins** are handkerchiefs.
91. Here, **issue** means "children; heirs."
92. **O'ershot myself** means "gone farther than I intended."

C   **YOUR TURN**

Reading Focus

How does Antony convince the crowd that he should read Caesar's will? What can you **infer** about Antony's personality from this?

_____

_____

_____

_____

_____

D   **YOUR TURN**

Vocabulary

The word *meet* can mean "come together," "fitting and proper," or "a gathering." Which meaning does it have here?

_____

_____

A YOUR TURN

Literary Focus

How do you think the **tragedy** will end for Cassius and Brutus? Explain your answer.

_____

_____

_____

_____

_____

_____

_____

_____

Whose daggers have stabbed Caesar; I do fear it.

Fourth Plebeian.

They were traitors. Honorable men!

All. The will! The testament!

Second Plebeian. They were villains, murderers! The

will! Read the will! **A**

Antony.

You will compel me then to read the will?

Then make a ring about the corpse of Caesar,

And let me show you him that made the will.

Shall I descend? And will you give me leave?

170   **All.** Come down.

Second Plebeian. Descend.

[ANTONY *comes down.*]

Third Plebeian. You shall have leave.

Fourth Plebeian. A ring! Stand round.

First Plebeian.

Stand from the hearse, stand from the body!

Second Plebeian.

Room for Antony, most noble Antony!

Antony.

Nay, press not so upon me; stand far off.

All. Stand back! Room! Bear back.

Antony.

If you have tears, prepare to shed them now.

You all do know this mantle; I remember

180   The first time ever Caesar put it on:

'Twas on a summer's evening, in his tent,

That day he overcame the Nervii.[93]

Look, in this place ran Cassius' dagger through;

See what a rent the envious[94] Casca made;

Through this the well-belovèd Brutus stabbed,

And as he plucked his cursèd steel away,

Mark how the blood of Caesar followed it,

---

93. **Nervii:** one of the tribes conquered by Caesar, in 57 B.C.
94. Here, **envious** (EHN VEE UHS) means "spiteful."

As rushing out of doors, to be resolved

If Brutus so unkindly knocked, or no;

190   For Brutus, as you know, was Caesar's angel. **B**

IN OTHER WORDS Antony pretends to be reluctant to read the will, saying that he does not want to do wrong to Caesar's "honorable" killers. The crowd shouts out that the assassins are traitors and villains. Antony comes down off his platform and stands by Caesar's body. He tells the crowd to gather around, directing the crowd to make a circle around the body. Antony then shows them Caesar's torn, bloody cloak and describes the stabbing.

Judge, O you gods, how dearly Caesar loved him! **C**

This was the most unkindest cut of all;

For when the noble Caesar saw him stab,

Ingratitude, more strong than traitors' arms,

Quite vanquished him. Then burst his mighty heart;

And, in his mantle muffling up his face,

Even at the base of Pompey's statue[95]

(Which all the while ran blood) great Caesar fell.

O, what a fall was there, my countrymen!

200   Then I, and you, and all of us fell down,

Whilst bloody treason flourished over us.

O, now you weep, and I perceive you feel

The dint[96] of pity; these are gracious drops.

Kind souls, what weep you when you but behold

Our Caesar's vesture[97] wounded? Look you here,

Here is himself, marred as you see with traitors.

First Plebeian. O piteous spectacle!

Second Plebeian. O noble Caesar!

Third Plebeian. O woeful day!

210   **Fourth Plebeian.** O traitors, villains!

First Plebeian. O most bloody sight!

---

95. statue: pronounced in three syllables for meter's sake.
96. Here, **dint** means "stroke."
97. Here, **vesture** is clothing.

B YOUR TURN

Reading Focus
How would you deliver Antony's speech if you were **reading the play aloud**? Explain your answer.

_____

_____

_____

_____

_____

C YOUR TURN

Reading Focus
Paraphrase line 191 of Antony's speech.

_____

_____

_____

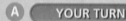

Second Plebeian. We will be revenged.

All. Revenge! About! Seek! Burn! Fire! Kill! Slay! Let not a traitor live! **A**

Antony. Stay, countrymen.

First Plebeian. Peace there! Hear the noble Antony.

Second Plebeian. We'll hear him, we'll follow him, we'll die with him!

Antony.

Good friends, sweet friends, let me not stir you up

220 To such a sudden flood of mutiny.

They that have done this deed are honorable.

What private griefs[98] they have, alas, I know not,

That made them do it. They are wise and honorable,

And will, no doubt, with reasons answer you.

I come not, friends, to steal away your hearts;

I am no orator, as Brutus is;

But (as you know me all) a plain blunt man

That love my friend, and that they know full well

That gave me public leave to speak of him.

230 For I have neither writ, nor words, nor worth,

Action, nor utterance, nor the power of speech

To stir men's blood; I only speak right on.

I tell you that which you yourselves do know,

Show you sweet Caesar's wounds, poor poor dumb mouths, **B**

And bid them speak for me. But were I Brutus,

And Brutus Antony, there were an Antony

Would ruffle up your spirits, and put a tongue

In every wound of Caesar that would move

240 The stones of Rome to rise and mutiny. **C**

All.

We'll mutiny.

First Plebeian. We'll burn the house of Brutus.

Third Plebeian.

Away, then! Come, seek the conspirators.

---

98. Here, **griefs** means "grievances."

IN OTHER WORDS Antony says that what really killed Caesar was not the daggers, but Caesar's sorrow at being betrayed by his beloved Brutus. In a stirring speech, Antony says that when Caesar fell, all Rome fell to the traitors that plotted against him. The crowd shouts for revenge against Caesar's killers. Antony claims to be a simple, plainspoken man—not a skilled speechmaker, like Brutus.

Antony.

Yet hear me, countrymen. Yet hear me speak.

All.

Peace, ho! Hear Antony, most noble Antony!

Antony.

Why, friends, you go to do you know not what:

Wherein hath Caesar thus deserved your loves?

Alas, you know not; I must tell you then:

You have forgot the will I told you of. **D**

All.

250   Most true, the will! Let's stay and hear the will.

Antony.

Here is the will, and under Caesar's seal.

To every Roman citizen he gives,

To every several⁹⁹ man, seventy-five drachmas.¹⁰⁰

Second Plebeian.

Most noble Caesar! We'll revenge his death!

Third Plebeian. O royal Caesar!

Antony. Hear me with patience.

All. Peace, ho!

Antony.

Moreover, he hath left you all his walks,

His private arbors, and new-planted orchards,

260   On this side Tiber; he hath left them you,

And to your heirs forever: common pleasures,¹⁰¹

D **YOUR TURN**

Reading Focus

Paraphrase Antony's words in lines 246–249.

_____

_____

_____

_____

---

99. Here, **several** means "individual."

100. **drachmas** (DRAK MUHZ): silver coins (Greek currency).

101. Here, **common pleasures** are public recreation areas.

To walk abroad and recreate yourselves.

Here was a Caesar! When comes such another?

IN OTHER WORDS The crowd is eager to rush off and punish the assassins. Antony tells them to wait, and he finally reads Caesar's will. The will states that Caesar has divided his fortune among the people of Rome. Each citizen is to receive seventy-five silver coins. In addition, Caesar has left his land as a public park for the people of Rome to enjoy.

First Plebeian.

Never, never! Come, away, away!

We'll burn his body in the holy place,

And with the brands fire the traitors' houses. **A**

Take up the body.

Second Plebeian. Go fetch fire.

Third Plebeian. Pluck down benches.

270   **Fourth Plebeian.** Pluck down forms, windows,[102]

anything!

[*Exeunt* PLEBEIANS *with the body.*]

Antony.

Now let it work: Mischief, thou art afoot,

Take thou what course thou wilt.

[*Enter* SERVANT.]

How now, fellow?

Servant.

Sir, Octavius is already come to Rome.

Antony. Where is he?

Servant.

He and Lepidus are at Caesar's house.

Antony.

And thither will I straight to visit him;

He comes upon a wish. Fortune is merry,

280   And in this mood will give us anything. **B**

---

102. Here, **forms, windows** are long benches and shutters.

Servant.

I heard him say, Brutus and Cassius

Are rid[103] like madmen through the gates of Rome.

Antony.

Belike[104] they had some notice of the people,

How I had moved them. Bring me to Octavius. **C**

[*Exeunt.*]

C **YOUR TURN**

Reading Focus
Paraphrase Antony's final
lines in this scene.

_____

_____

_____

IN OTHER WORDS Now the mob rushes off to set fire to the houses of Caesar's killers. Antony is satisfied that he has accomplished what he set out to do. A servant enters and tells Antony that Octavius, Caesar's nephew and adopted son, has arrived in Rome. Octavius brings the news that Brutus and Cassius have fled. Antony goes to visit Octavius.

FINAL SUMMARY *In Act IV, Antony, Octavius, and Lepidus form the Second Triumvirate and meet in Rome. They make plans to fight against the armies being organized by Brutus and Cassius.*

Brutus and Cassius argue over ambition and honor, but make amends. They agree to march toward Philippi to meet the advancing armies of Octavius and Antony. That night, Caesar's ghost appears to Brutus. The ghost calls itself "thy evil spirit" and says they will meet again at Philippi.

In Act V, Brutus and Cassius meet Octavius and Antony at Philippi. The opposing generals argue bitterly. In battle, Cassius mistakenly believes the enemy has won. Instead of surrendering, he kills himself. When Titinius and Massala discover Cassius dead, Titinius kills himself with Cassius's sword. Brutus and the others find the bodies of Cassius and Titinius, pay their respects, and then prepare for battle. Antony sends his soldiers to search for Brutus. Brutus and his forces are weary from battle. Brutus tells his men it is time for him to die. As Strato holds his sword, Brutus runs onto it, killing himself. When they capture Brutus's army, Antony,

---

103. **Are rid** means "have ridden."
104. **Belike** means "probably."

Octavius, Messala, Lucilius, and others come upon the leader's corpse. Antony delivers a brief speech over the body of Brutus, stating that while others killed Caesar out of personal envy, Brutus acted in what he felt were the best interests of the Roman people. As the battle ends, Octavius promises a proper funeral for Brutus. Octavius and his friends celebrate their victory.

Applying Your Skills

from The Tragedy of Julius Caesar

LITERARY FOCUS: TRAGEDY

DIRECTIONS: Complete the chart below by describing the **tragic flaws** of Caesar and Brutus. Provide one example from the text of each character's tragic flaw. Then, discuss how that flaw contributed to his downfall.

Caesar	Brutus
Tragic flaw:	Tragic flaw:
Example from text:	Example from text:
How this tragic flaw caused his fall:	How this tragic flaw caused his fall:

READING FOCUS: READING A PLAY

DIRECTIONS: Paraphrase the following quote from Antony in Act I, Scene 2. Then, write a brief paragraph discussing the significance of the quote. Was Antony's statement of Cassius correct? Why was this an important moment in the play?

Antony: "Fear him [Cassius] not, Caesar, he's not dangerous;

He is a noble Roman, and well given." (lines 204–205)

_____

_____

_____

_____

A Big-Name Brutus in a Caldron of Chaos

Based on the theater review from *The New York Times*

by Ben Brantley

INFORMATIONAL TEXT FOCUS: EVALUATING AN ARGUMENT

How do you decide what books to read or which movies to see? Some writers write reviews to share their opinions on books, plays, or movies. These writers, or reviewers, must also explain why they have those opinions. Reviewers often share their credentials, or qualifications that make their opinions worth reading. What does the author of a movie or theater review want to convince you to think and do? Use the following tips to find a reviewer's **intent**, or purpose.

- Judge the writer's standards for quality. For example, what parts of a performance make it "great"?

- What is the evidence? This could include the reviewer's judgments, opinions, or facts. The reviewer might talk about different parts of the play, book, or movie, like the plot and the characters.

- How much evidence does the reviewer give? A convincing opinion has many details to support it.

Create a chart like the one below to help you evaluate the reviewer's opinion of the play.

Argument → Criteria → Evidence

VOCABULARY

assassinating (A SAS IHN AY TIHNG) *v.:* murdering an important person by a secret attack.

interaction (IHN TUHR AK SHUHN) the influence or effect of people or things on one another.

intense (IHN TEHNS) *adj.:* performed with great energy.

INTO THE THEATER REVIEW

In 2005, *Julius Caesar* was performed on Broadway in New York City. The following review is about that production of the play.

SKILLS FOCUS

Informational Text Skills
Evaluate author's argument.

A BIG-NAME BRUTUS IN A CALDRON OF CHAOS

Based on the theater review by Ben Brantley

from *The New York Times*, 2005

In the Belasco Theater's production of Shakespeare's "Julius Caesar," actors drip blood and recite speeches, but they have no believable emotions. Even movie star Denzel Washington can't save the play. **A**

Mr. Washington, who has won two Academy Awards, is the reason people want to see this show. He is playing Brutus, the most important part. Mr. Washington does not embarrass himself. But he can't help getting lost in this mixed-up production.

10 This is too bad, since Mr. Washington seems like a good choice to play Brutus. In many of his performances, Mr. Washington has a serious, unsettled air. **B** Casting him as "poor Brutus, with himself at war," seems obvious.

In several scenes, Mr. Washington shines. Such moments, however, usually happen when there is no interaction with other characters. When Brutus thinks about assassinating Caesar, Mr. Washington is filled with the uneasiness of a good man who is struggling with himself.

He has the tired, open face of someone filled with doubt. 20 That quality comes through in the speech Brutus makes after Caesar has been killed. You can see why people like Brutus. You can also see why he will soon be replaced by the more confident Mark Antony.

This Brutus, however, seems insecure, not bothered by moral questions. Mr. Washington's voice is often rushed and soft. His Brutus does not seem able to guide other characters. **C**

A (HERE'S HOW)

Reading Focus

It seems like the reviewer does not believe the actor's emotions. He says the main star "can't save the play," so I know he thinks the production is bad. I think the reviewer's **intent** will be to convince his readers that the play is not worth seeing. I will read on to look for the evidence the reviewer gives for this argument.

B (HERE'S HOW)

Language Coach

Unsettled combines the word part *un-* with the word *settled*. I know that *un-* is a **prefix** that means "not," so *unsettled* must mean "not settled," or "uneasy."

C (YOUR TURN)

Language Coach

The **prefix** *in-* gives a word its opposite meaning. Find the word in this paragraph with the prefix *in-* and write what the word means. Use a dictionary to check your answer.

_____

_____

A

HERE'S HOW

Reading Focus

This review gives the opinion that the actors "seem to come from different planets." This means one standard for quality is that the actors work together. I will read on to **evaluate** the author's opinion.

B

YOUR TURN

Reading Focus

A convincing **argument** has evidence to support it. Do you think the review gives enough evidence to support the writer's opinion of the performance? Explain your answer.

_____

_____

_____

_____

_____

_____

_____

© UPI Photo/Ezio Petersen/Landov

It's hard to blame him. Director Daniel Sullivan has chosen actors who seem to come from different planets. On the one hand, you have actors who speak Shakespeare's words in an
30 easygoing way. On the other hand, you have actors who are performing Tragedy with a capital *T*.

Emmon Walker plays Mark Antony as fierce—but impossible to understand. Jack Willis plays Casca as a gossip. William Sadler plays Caesar as if he were a gangster. And Kelly AuCoin gives Octavius Caesar the feel of a pop singer.

The overall effect is confusing. It's like a concert with opera, jazz, light rock and musical comedy playing all at once. The characters rarely connect emotionally. For example, there is little sense of the changing relationships among those who kill Caesar.
40 When Cassius and Brutus fight and make up, it looks as if scenes from different films have been mixed together. Everyone acts intense. But no one is in character.

The setting is a ruined ancient city. Plaster falls, and bombs explode loudly. Added things like metal detectors and modern IDs distract viewers, however.

Mr. Sullivan does keep things moving. In the second half of the show, blood flows constantly. The deaths of Brutus and Cassius are shown in disgusting detail. But since viewers don't feel connected to the characters, it's hard to care.
50 Brutus dies with convincing boldness. But his loud dying noises make his final words to Caesar's ghost difficult to hear.

A Big-Name Brutus in a Caldron of Chaos

INFORMATIONAL TEXT FOCUS: EVALUATING AN ARGUMENT

DIRECTIONS: Circle the answer to each multiple-choice question.

1. What **argument** does the reviewer make about this production of *Julius Caesar*?

   A. It has some good points but overall it is poorly done.

   B. There is nothing good about it.

   C. It is a great production.

2. What is one standard the reviewer uses to judge the actors?

   A. fame

   B. success

   C. clear speaking

DIRECTIONS: As a reader, you must **evaluate** a reviewer's argument, judge the evidence, and decide whether or not you agree. On the lines below, summarize Ben Brantley's overall opinion of the production. Be sure to clearly state what his **intent** in writing this review was.

_____

_____

_____

_____

_____

Word Box

assassinating

interaction

intense

VOCABULARY REVIEW

DIRECTIONS: Fill in the blanks with the correct words from the Word Box.

1. The man was charged with _____ the famous leader.

2. According to this reviewer, the _____ between the characters was not good.

Collection 8

VOCABULARY REVIEW

DIRECTIONS: Write the letter of each definition from the second column next to the correct vocabulary word in the first column.

Vocabulary Words	Definitions
1. ____ intense	**a.** most important
2. ____ highlight	**b.** performed with great energy
3. ____ assassinating	**c.** make a subject or idea stand out so people will pay attention
4. ____ criteria	**d.** murdering an important person by a secret attack
5. ____ predominant	**e.** more noticable than others
6. ____ principal	**f.** rules or standards for making a judgment

Skills Review

Collection 8

LANGUAGE COACH: PREFIXES

DIRECTIONS: A **prefix** is a word part added to the beginning of a word in order to change its meaning. Look at the chart below. Either a word, a word with a prefix, or the meaning of the word with the prefix is missing. Fill in the missing boxes. Use a dictionary if needed. The first row has been completed for you.

Word	Word with prefix	Definition of word with prefix
settled	unsettled	"worried"
predictable		"impossible to predict"
	insecure	
school		"a school for children too young to attend kindergarten"
fit		"not fit"
	disrespect	

WRITING ACTIVITY

DIRECTIONS: In this collection, you **evaluated** a review of a theater production. Now, it is your turn to write a review! Think about a book, play, movie, or song that you are familiar with, then write a review of it. Remember, a strong, critical review gives both an opinion and some evidence that supports that opinion. As part of your review, you must state what your criteria, or standards, for quality are. For example, what qualities are usually present in books that you like? What do you think is an example of strong acting? Also be sure to include enough evidence to support your opinion. Write your one or two paragraph review on a separate piece of paper.

The Hero's Story

Literary and Academic Vocabulary for Collection 9

LITERARY VOCABULARY

myths (MIHTHS) *n.:* traditional stories based on a certain culture that are religious in nature.
Myths show the traditions and values of the society that tells the story.

legend (LEH JUHND) *n.:* a story about amazing deeds based on real events or people.
The legend of King Arthur and the Knights of the Round Table is one of my favorite stories.

hero (HEE ROH) *n.:* in myths and legends, a hero is usually a person that is the child of a god who faces an incredibly difficult task, and who usually has superhuman strength.
In the Greek myth, Theseus is a famous hero who kills a monster.

chivalry (SHIH VUHL REE) *n.:* the code of behavior that knights followed.
King Arthur's knights were expected to practice chivalry.

ACADEMIC VOCABULARY

recurring (RIH KUR IHNG) *v.* used as *adj.:* coming up again; being repeated.
The hero's journey is a recurring theme in literature.

exhibit (EHG ZIHB IHT) *v.:* show; display; indicate.
Joyce was reluctant at first to exhibit her feelings for Adam.

retain (RIH TAYN) *v.:* continue to have or hold.
Although the basketball team was winning going into halftime, they could not retain the lead in the second half.

recount (RIH KOWNT) *v.:* tell or give an account of.
The ability to recount a story accurately can be an important skill.

Theseus

Based on the myth, as retold by Edith Hamilton

LITERARY FOCUS: MYTHS AND HEROES

Myths are traditional stories told over time about gods and heroes. However, myths were more than just fun stories. In ancient Greece, myths were an important part of the Greek religion and they told about the values of the people.

The **heroes** in the Greek myths are humans who sometimes have special powers. In a typical hero myth, a young man is sent on a journey to find something important. As he travels, he usually finds qualities such as knowledge or self-control. These hero stories show qualities that the ancient Greeks valued and taught to their children.

READING FOCUS: SUMMARIZING

When you **summarize** a story, you briefly retell it in your own words. Your retelling should be short and should only include the most important points and events from a story. Summarizing helps you see which parts of the story are the most important.

As you read "Theseus," use a chart like the one below to keep track of the most important events that occur in the myth.

Event 1: Theseus finds his father's sword.
Event 2:
Event 3:

SKILLS FOCUS

Literary Skills
Understand heroic characters and external conflicts in epics and myths.

Reading Skills
Summarize.

VOCABULARY

Look for these words as you read the following selection.

banquet (BAN KWEHT) *n.*: a formal meal for many people.

maidens (MAY DEHNZ) *n.*: young women who are not married.

Labyrinth (LAB RIHNTH) *n.*: a maze.

THESEUS

Based on the myth, as retold by Edith Hamilton

INTO THE MYTH

Most people believe that the myth of Theseus is completely made up. In the story, Theseus brings several kingdoms together to form Athens. Athens was a city-state in Greece. It was the first place in the world to have a democracy for free males. According to the myth, Theseus created the first people's democracy where people governed themselves.

Theseus was a great Athenian hero. He was the son of the Athenian king, Aegeus. He spent his youth in his mother's home in southern Greece. Aegeus returned to Athens before the child was born. But first he hid a sword and a pair of shoes and covered them with a big stone. He told his wife that when the boy—if it was a boy—was strong enough to move the stone and get the objects, she could send him to Athens. The child was a boy, and he grew up to be very strong. When his mother took him to the stone he lifted it easily. She told him that it was time

10   for him to find his father in Athens, and his grandfather gave him a ship. **A**

Theseus refused to travel by water. That would be too safe and easy. He wanted to become a hero. The journey to Athens by land was long and dangerous. The road was full of thieves and murderers, but Theseus killed them all.

All of Greece praised the young man who had cleared the land of these criminals. He reached Athens as a hero, and the King invited him to a banquet. The King didn't know that Theseus was his son. In fact, he was afraid that the young man

20   might want to be king. So he invited him with the idea of poisoning him. But Theseus wanted his father to know who he was right away. He took out his sword. The King recognized it and threw the poison to the ground. **B**

A (**HERE'S HOW**)

Literary Focus

Since Theseus is a Greek **hero** in a **myth**, he has to go on a journey. I know that Theseus is traveling to Athens to find his father. I will read on to find out what happens on his journey.

B (**QUICK CHECK**)

How does the King recognize that Theseus is his son?

_____

_____

_____

"Theseus," adapted from *Mythology* by Edith Hamilton. Copyright © 1942 by Edith Hamilton; copyright renewed © 1969 by Dorian Fielding Reid and Doris Fielding Reid. Retold by Holt, Rinehart and Winston. Reproduced by permission of **Little, Brown and Company** and electronic format by permission of **Alice R. Abbott**.

Aegeus proclaimed that Theseus was his son and would someday be king. Theseus soon had a chance to impress the people of Athens. **A**

30 Years earlier, a terrible thing had happened to Athens. The only son of Minos, the powerful ruler of Crete, had died while visiting Athens. King Aegeus had done what no host should do: He had sent his guest on a dangerous mission to kill a bull. **B** Instead, the bull had killed the youth. Minos invaded Athens. He said that he would destroy it unless every nine years the people sent him seven maidens and seven youths. When they reached Crete they were given to the Minotaur to eat.

The Minotaur was a monster. It was half bull, half human. When the Minotaur was born, Minos did not kill him. Instead, he built the Labyrinth. It was impossible to escape from this maze. Once inside the twisting paths, one might never find the exit. This is where the young Athenians were taken and left to the

40 Minotaur. There was no way to escape. A few days after Theseus reached Athens, it was time for the next maidens and youths to go to Crete.

Theseus offered to be one of the victims. **C** He told his father that he would try to kill the Minotaur. He promised that if he succeeded, he would have the black sail on his ship changed to a white one, so that Aegeus could know as soon as possible that his son was safe. **D**

When the young victims arrived in Crete, Minos' daughter Ariadne fell in love with Theseus. She sent for him and told him

50 she would help him escape if he would take her to Athens and

marry her. Of course he said yes. She gave him a ball of thread.
He was to tie one end to the inside of the door and unwind it as
he went on. Now he was certain that he could find his way out,
and he walked boldly into the maze. He found the Minotaur
asleep and pinned him to the ground. With his fists—his only
weapon—he killed the monster. **E**

Then Theseus used the ball of thread to lead everyone out.
They found Ariadne, and they all rushed to the ship.

On the way back to Athens, they stopped at the island of
60   Naxos. It's not clear what happened next. One story says that
Theseus left Ariadne. The other story says she was seasick, so he
put her ashore to recover and returned to work on the ship. Then
a huge wind carried him far out to sea. When he returned, he
found that Ariadne had died, and he was heartbroken. **F**

Whatever happened at Naxos, Theseus forgot to raise the
white sail when the ship got close to Athens. King Aegeus saw
the black sail and believed his son was dead. He threw himself into the sea and drowned. After that, the sea was called the
Aegean Sea.

70   So Theseus became King of Athens. He was wise and just.
He told the people that he did not wish to rule over them. He
wanted a people's government where all would be equal. He gave
up his royal power and organized a democracy. The only job he
kept for himself was army commander. Athens became the
happiest and richest city on earth. It was the one place in the
world where the people ruled themselves.

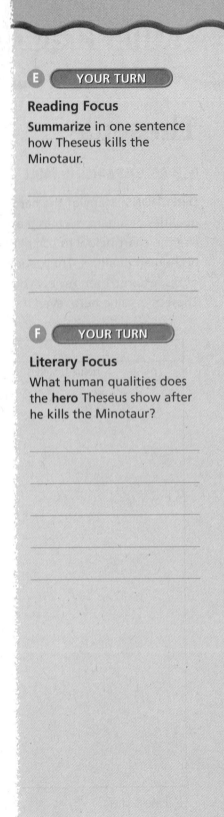

E   YOUR TURN

Reading Focus

Summarize in one sentence
how Theseus kills the
Minotaur.

_____

_____

_____

F   YOUR TURN

Literary Focus

What human qualities does
the **hero** Theseus show after
he kills the Minotaur?

_____

_____

_____

_____

Theseus   **309**

Skills Practice

Theseus

DIRECTIONS: Many of the **heroes** in Greek **myths** are humans. Theseus has qualities of a hero, such as bravery, but he also has many human qualities. Use the chart below to compare and contrast Theseus's heroic qualities and his human qualities. Think about the mistakes Theseus makes and the results of his actions. Then review your chart. Use your examples to decide whether Theseus is still a hero, even though he has human problems.

Is Theseus a Hero?	
Heroic Qualities	Human Qualities

Is Theseus a hero?

Applying Your Skills

Theseus

LITERARY FOCUS: MYTHS AND HEROES

DIRECTIONS: Review the **myth** and think about the qualities of a **hero** that
Theseus shows. Use these qualities to answer the following question:

1. What does this myth tell you about the values of the ancient Greeks?

_____

_____

_____

_____

_____

_____

READING FOCUS: SUMMARIZING

DIRECTIONS: Review the chart you were told to make on the Preparing
to Read page. Use your examples to write a short **summary** of the myth in
your own words. Compare your summary with a partner's. Did you cover the
same points?

Summary: _____

_____

_____

_____

_____

Word Box

banquet

maidens

Labyrinth

VOCABULARY REVIEW

DIRECTIONS: Fill in the blanks with the correct words from the Word Box.
Not all words will be used.

1. _____ are unmarried women.

2. Theseus needed help to get out of the confusing

_____.

The Sword in the Stone

By Sir Thomas Malory, as retold by Keith Baines

LITERARY FOCUS: ARTHURIAN LEGEND

A **legend** is a story that describes some extraordinary act or deed. Legends are told and retold across many generations and often involve magical, fantastic characteristics.

The **Arthurian legends** are medieval stories about King Arthur and his brave knights of the Round Table. King Arthur is probably based on a fifth or sixth-century Celtic warlord who lived in Wales and defeated invaders from Germany. In the stories, King Arthur is a great warrior and the leader of his people.

READING FOCUS: UNDERSTANDING SEQUENCE OF EVENTS

The order in which things happen in a story is called the **sequence of events**. Most often, a story is told in **chronological order**. Events that happened first are told first, and so on. Sometimes there will be a **flashback**, which is when the present action is stopped for a moment and an earlier event is recounted.

As you read, you may want to keep track of the sequence of events on a chart like the one below.

Page	What Happened?
1	Churchgoers walked into a churchyard and found a sword stuck in a stone.
2	

VOCABULARY

Look for these words and their context as you read the selection.

confronted (KUHN FRUHNT EHD) *v.:* faced.

inscribed (IHN SKYRBD) *v.:* marked or written on a surface; engraved.

tumultuous (TOO MUHL CHU UHS) *adj.:* wild and noisy.

realm (REHLM) *n.:* kingdom.

THE SWORD IN THE STONE

from *Le Morte d' Arthur*, by Sir Thomas Malory, as retold by Keith Baines

> ### INTO THE LEGEND
> "The Sword in the Stone" tells the story of Arthur, son of Igraine and King Uther of England. Many men wanted Uther's throne, and so any heir would be seen as a dangerous rival. The story goes that a wise man named Merlin took Arthur from Uther, fearing for the child's safety. Arthur was raised by Sir Ector and his wife alongside their own son, Kay. As the story begins, a contest is being set up to decide the next king of Britain.

The archbishop held his service in the city's greatest church (St. Paul's), and when matins[1] were done, the congregation filed out to the yard. **(A)** They were confronted by a marble block into which had been thrust a beautiful sword. The block was four feet square, and the sword passed through a steel anvil[2] which had been struck in the stone and which projected a foot from it. The anvil had been inscribed with letters of gold:

WHOSO PULLETH OUTE THIS SWERD OF THIS
STONE AND ANVYLD IS RIGHTWYS KYNGE
BORNE OF ALL BRYTAYGNE **(B) (C)**

10

The congregation was awed by this miraculous sight, but the archbishop forbade anyone to touch the sword before Mass had been heard. After Mass, many of the nobles tried to pull the sword out of the stone, but none was able to, so a watch of ten knights was set over the sword, and a tournament[3] proclaimed

---

(A) (**HERE'S HOW**)

Language Coach

I know that the prefix *arch–* means "supreme" or "most." So I think that the *archbishop* must be the highest-ranking bishop.

(B) (**HERE'S HOW**)

Vocabulary

I have seen the word *inscribed* before. I think it means that these words are carved, or engraved, on the stone in which the sword is stuck.

(C) (**QUICK CHECK**)

What does the inscription say in modern English?

_____

_____

_____

---

1. Here, **matins** (MAT UHNZ) are morning prayers.
2. An **anvil** is an iron or steel block on which metal objects are hammered into shape.
3. A **tournament** is a sport in which two knights compete on horseback, trying to unseat each other with long pole-like weapons called lances.

for New Year's Day, to provide men of noble blood with the opportunity of proving their right to the succession. **A**

IN OTHER WORDS A group of churchgoers walked into their churchyard and discovered a beautiful sword stuck in a stone. It was written on the stone that whoever could remove the sword would be the next king of Britain. When no one was able to pull the sword out, the congregation decided to hold a tournament to determine the next king.

Sir Ector, who had been living on an estate near London, rode to the tournament with Arthur and his own son Sir Kay,
20 who had been recently knighted. When they arrived at the tournament, Sir Kay found to his annoyance that his sword was missing from its sheath, so he begged Arthur to ride back and fetch it from their lodging. **B**

Arthur found the door of the lodging locked and bolted, the landlord and his wife having left for the tournament. In order not to disappoint his brother, he rode on to St. Paul's, determined to get for him the sword which was lodged in the stone. The yard was empty, the guard also having slipped off to see the tourna-ment, so Arthur strode up to the sword and, without troubling to
30 read the inscription, tugged it free. He then rode straight back to Sir Kay and presented him with it. **C**

Sir Kay recognized the sword and, taking it to Sir Ector, said, "Father, the succession falls to me, for I have here the sword that was lodged in the stone." **D** But Sir Ector insisted that they should all ride to the churchyard, and once there, bound Sir Kay by oath[4] to tell how he had come by the sword. Sir Kay then
40 admitted that Arthur had given it to him. Sir Ector turned to Arthur and said, "Was the sword not guarded?"

"It was not," Arthur replied.

© David Crausby/Alamy

---

4. An **oath** is a vow to another person.

"Would you please thrust it into the stone again?" said Sir Ector. Arthur did so, and first Sir Ector and then Sir Kay tried to remove it, but both were unable to. Then Arthur, for the second time, pulled it out. Sir Ector and Sir Kay both knelt before him. **E**

"Why," said Arthur, "do you both kneel before me?"

50   "My lord," Sir Ector replied, "there is only one man living who can draw the sword from the stone, and he is the true-born king of Britain." Sir Ector then told Arthur the story of his birth and upbringing.

"My dear father," said Arthur, "for so I shall always think of you—if, as you say, I am to be king, please know that any request you have to make is already granted."

IN OTHER WORDS Sir Ector and his son Sir Kay traveled to London for the tournament. When Sir Kay noticed that he had forgotten his sword, he sent his adopted brother Arthur to get it. Arthur was unable to obtain Kay's sword, so he ran to the churchyard and removed the beautiful sword without reading the writing on the stone. When he returned to Ector and Kay, they acknowledged him as the rightful king of Britain.

Sir Ector asked that Sir Kay should be made royal seneschal,[5] and Arthur declared that while they both lived it should be so. **F** Then the three of them visited the archbishop and told him what

60   had taken place.

All those dukes and barons with ambitions to rule were present at the tournament on New Year's Day. But when all of them had failed, and Arthur alone had succeeded in drawing the sword from the stone, they protested against one so young, and of ignoble blood, succeeding to the throne. **G**

The secret of Arthur's birth was known to only a few of the nobles surviving from the days of King Uther. The archbishop urged them to make Arthur's cause their own; but their support

---

5.   The **royal seneschal** (SEHN UH SHUHL) was a person in charge of the king's household. This was a powerful and respected job.

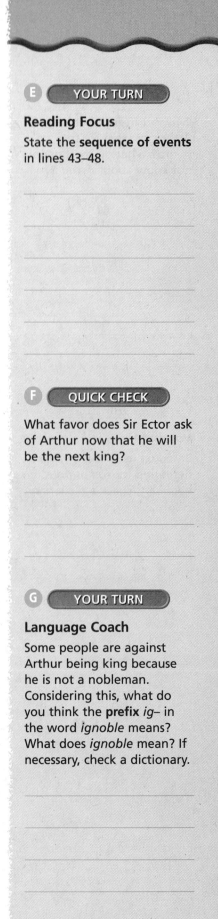

E   **YOUR TURN**

Reading Focus
State the **sequence of events** in lines 43–48.

_____

_____

_____

_____

_____

_____

F   **QUICK CHECK**

What favor does Sir Ector ask of Arthur now that he will be the next king?

_____

_____

_____

G   **YOUR TURN**

Language Coach
Some people are against Arthur being king because he is not a nobleman. Considering this, what do you think the **prefix** _ig–_ in the word _ignoble_ means? What does _ignoble_ mean? If necessary, check a dictionary.

_____

_____

_____

_____

_____

Why is it fitting that only Arthur can remove the sword? What do most people not know about Arthur?

_____

_____

_____

_____

_____

B **YOUR TURN**

Vocabulary

Based on its context, write a definition for *tumultuous*. If necessary, check a dictionary.

_____

_____

proved ineffective. The tournament was repeated at Candlemas[6] and at Easter, with the same outcome as before. A

Finally, at Pentecost,[7] when once more Arthur alone had been able to remove the sword, the commoners arose with a tumultuous cry and demanded that Arthur should at once be made king. B The nobles, knowing in their hearts that the commoners were right, all knelt before Arthur and begged forgiveness for having delayed his succession for so long. Arthur forgave them and then, offering his sword at the high altar, was dubbed[8] first knight of the realm. The coronation took place a few days later, when Arthur swore to rule justly, and the nobles swore him their allegiance.

IN OTHER WORDS Ector, Kay, and Arthur told the archbishop what happened. He believed that Arthur should be king but many British noblemen did not. Few people knew that Arthur was actually the son of King Uther, and therefore, the heir to the throne. Arthur continued to prove that he could remove the sword from the stone, but nobody else could do so. Eventually, Arthur was officially made king.

---

6. **Candlemas** is a Christian festival that honors the purification of the Virgin Mary after the birth of Jesus. It falls on February 2.
7. **Pentecost** is a Christian festival celebrated on the seventh Sunday after Easter, commemorating the descent of the Holy Spirit upon the Apostles.
8. Here, **dubbed** means "made a knight by tapping his shoulder with a sword."

© The Everett Collection

Applying Your Skills

The Sword in the Stone

LITERARY FOCUS: ARTHURIAN LEGEND

DIRECTIONS: Decide whether the following statements about **legends** and "The Sword in the Stone" are true or false. Write "T" for true or "F" for false on the blank lines.

1. Arthur pulled the sword out of the stone because he always wanted to be a king. _____

2. Legends often involve extraordinary deeds and magical characters.

   _____

3. The legend of Arthur is probably not based on a real person. _____

READING FOCUS: UNDERSTANDING SEQUENCE OF EVENTS

DIRECTIONS: Circle the answer below that recounts the events of "The Sword in the Stone" in the correct **sequence**.

1. Arthur pulls the sword out of the stone; he uses it to slay the evil dragon; he rescues the prince from the tower.

2. A group of church people discover the sword in the stone; the guard leaves the sword unguarded momentarily; the archbishop of St. Paul's finishes the morning prayers.

3. Sir Kay discovers the sword stuck in the stone; Sir Ector pulls the sword out; Arthur is made the new archbishop.

4. A group of church people discover the sword in the stone; they decide to hold a tournament to determine the next king of Britain; Arthur pulls the sword out of the stone and unknowingly becomes the next king.

VOCABULARY REVIEW

DIRECTIONS: Write "Yes" after each sentence if the boldfaced vocabulary word is being used correctly. Write "No" if it is not being used correctly.

1. The message **inscribed** on the stone gave instructions for determining the next king. _____

2. Sir Ector accused Sir Kay of being **tumultuous** when he claimed that he had removed the sword. _____

3. After Arthur repeatedly removed the sword from the stone, his fame spread throughout the **realm** of Britain. _____

Birth of a Legend

Based on the online article by Stephen Lyons

INFORMATIONAL TEXT FOCUS: GENERATING RESEARCH QUESTIONS

When you read an article, you may want to do research to learn more about the topic on which the article focuses. The first step in researching a topic is to come up with a **research question**. Your research question is the question that you will answer with your research. You will want to find correct information in several different sources. Use the tips below to help.

Tip 1   Think of a specific question you have about a topic. This will help you focus your research. Asking *What causes train accidents?* is too broad. Instead, you could ask *What causes accidents at commuter train crossings?* Remember that your research question will help guide you in finding accurate information.

Tip 2   Use the *5W-How?* question strategy to ask *Who? What? When? Where? Why?* and *How?* As you read, make an organizer like the one below to write down questions about your topic. This will give you different ideas to explore.

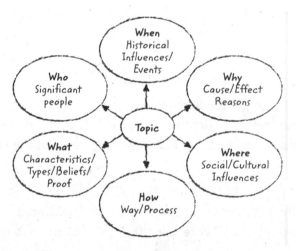

Tip 3   Write more than one research question. Then choose the question that interests you the most. Choose a question that you think you will be able to answer given the resources available to you.

VOCABULARY

creature (KREE CHUHR) *n.:* an animal.

legend (LEH JUHND) *n.:* a traditional story that many people know.

SKILLS FOCUS

Informational Text Skills
Generate relevant, interesting, and researchable questions.

BIRTH OF A LEGEND

Based on the online article by Stephen Lyons

> ### INTO THE ONLINE ARTICLE
> Loch Ness (LOCK NESS) is a large, deep lake in Scotland. *Loch* is the Scottish word for "lake." It is a very beautiful place. It also holds a mystery. Some people believe in a "Loch Ness Monster." They think the Monster lives in the lake. The following article tells of how the mystery of the Loch Ness Monster began and continues to interest people. Read on to decide for yourself if the Monster really exists.

Since ancient times, people have believed that some kind of creature lived in Loch Ness in Scotland. But the modern legend of Loch Ness began in 1933. That's when a new road opened and let people see the lake from the northern side for the first time. One April afternoon, a couple was driving along this road. Suddenly, they saw "an enormous animal rolling and plunging on the surface." **A** A local newspaper editor used the word "monster" to describe it. **B**

10   Public interest increased after another couple reported seeing one of the creatures crossing the road. By October 1933, several London newspapers had sent reporters to Scotland. Radio broadcasts brought listeners the latest news from the lake.

In December, the London Daily Mail hired an actor and hunter named Marmaduke Wetherell to track down the beast. After a few days, Wetherell reported finding large footprints. He made models of the footprints and sent them to the Natural History Museum in London.

In early January, museum experts announced that the footprints were made by a hippopotamus foot. It wasn't clear 20   whether or not Wetherell knew about the trick. Either way, this trick kept people from taking the Loch Ness Monster seriously. For the next 30 years, most scientists ignored reports

A **HERE'S HOW**

Vocabulary

I am not sure what *plunging* means. I know a big animal is in the water, so maybe the animal is moving quickly. I looked up *plunging*, and it means "jumping or diving quickly." This is close to my definition.

B **HERE'S HOW**

Reading Focus

The writer begins this selection by talking about when the Loch Ness Monster was first seen. I think the writer's **research question** could have been "What is the history of sightings of the Loch Ness Monster?"

From "Birth of a Legend" by Stephen Lyons adapted from *NOVA Online,* 2000. Copyright © 2000 by **WGBH Educational Foundation.** Retold by Holt, Rinehart and Winston. Reproduced by permission of the publisher.

Birth of a Legend   319

Language Coach

Some words have different **connotations**, or meanings that make the reader think of something beyond the actual meaning of the word. For example, *fakes* are things that are not real. Here, though, *fakes* also has a connotation of something not even worth paying attention to.

 YOUR TURN

Vocabulary

Underline the word or phrase that helps you understand the meaning of the word *humps*.

_____

_____

_____

 YOUR TURN

Reading Focus

What are some **research questions** you could ask that have to do with these eyewitness accounts?

_____

_____

_____

_____

_____

_____

_____

of strange animals in the lake. Many sightings were fakes, they said. **A** The rest were boats, floating logs, otters, ducks, or swimming deer.

They Did See Something

Nevertheless, people have reported seeing the Loch Ness Monster more than 4,000 times. Most people described a large creature with humps sticking up above the surface of the water. **B** Others reported seeing a long neck or flippers. What

30 was most amazing was that many serious people said they saw the monster. They included priests, scientists, teachers, and even a Nobel Prize winner.

Eyewitness Accounts

There is no evidence that the Loch Ness Monster exists. But there are lots of stories. Read what two people from Scotland said.

It happened in June 1965. A friend and I were fishing in Loch Ness. I saw something break the surface of the water, and then it disappeared.

But I kept watching. I saw a large, black object. It rose in

40 the water like a whale. It went back down, then appeared again.

So my friend Willie Frazer came up and joined me. We realized that it was drifting toward us. It came to within 250, 300 yards.

I'm not trying to get anyone to believe me. If I hadn't seen it I wouldn't believe it either. But I saw it, and nothing can take that away.

—Ian Cameron used to work for the Northern Police Force. He lives with his wife in Inverness, Scotland, by the lake.

I'm driving by the lake and looking out the window. I saw

50 this boiling in the water. I thought, "No, it can't be anything," and I kept going. Then I looked again, and I saw three black humps. But what is it? **C**

© Vo Trung Dung/Corbis Sygma

© John Frost Newspapers

D YOUR TURN

Vocabulary

Sane means "of sound mind." Why does Richard White say that he is *sane*?

_____

_____

_____

I didn't want to lose sight of this thing. So I pulled over, grabbed my camera, and took pictures.

Two other people were there. They saw it too. There was a lady in her fifties. And her husband said, "Ach, it's an eel!" And I said, "There's no eels that big!" And he said, "Ach, it's otters!" And I said, "You don't get otters swimming out like that!"

I saw what I saw. It wasn't just my imagination. I'm a sane

60 guy. **D** I sell pet food! What use to me is the Loch Ness Monster? Unless I can invent a food called, I don't know, Monster Munchies perhaps?

—Richard White lives in the village of Muir of Ord, north of Inverness. He runs a business selling pet food.

Skills Practice

Birth of a Legend

USE A *5W-HOW?* CONCEPT MAP

DIRECTIONS: A *5W-How* concept map helps you come up with **research questions** to ask about a topic. Think of a topic that you would like to learn more about. It could have to do with something you have read or seen on the news recently. Write the topic in the middle of the chart. Then, write *5W-How?* questions in the rest of the ovals: *Who, What, When, Where, Why,* and *How.* In each oval, write down one question that you could ask about your topic. Use these questions to help you think of a research question that you could ask about your topic.

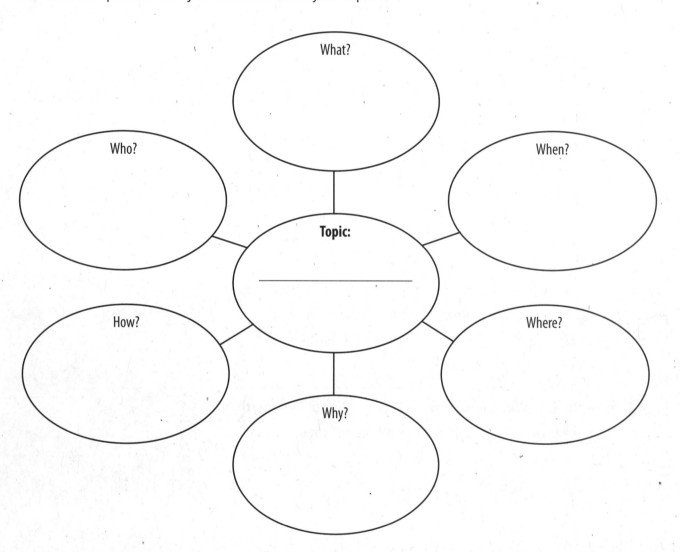

Birth of a Legend

INFORMATIONAL TEXT FOCUS: GENERATING RESEARCH QUESTIONS

DIRECTIONS: Circle the best answer to each multiple-choice question.

1. Which of the following questions asks a specific **research question**?

   A. Why do people try to catch the Loch Ness Monster?

   B. How many people have claimed to see the Loch Ness Monster?

   C. Do most people in Scotland believe in sea monsters?

   D. Does the Loch Ness Monster exist?

2. What is the main problem with the above research question, "Do most people in Scotland believe in sea monsters?"

   A. The question could lead to many different sources.

   B. The question may offend some people.

   C. The question does not go beyond a simple "yes" or "no" answer.

   D. The question does not specify the Loch Ness Monster.

DIRECTIONS: Use the *5W-How?* chart you made on the Skills Practice page to come up with a specific **research question** that you could ask about the Loch Ness Monster. Remember that your research question should help you find information about the topic. Write your research question below.

_____

_____

_____

_____

VOCABULARY REVIEW

DIRECTIONS: Fill in the blanks with the correct words from the Word Box.

Word Box
creature
legend

1. A monster is a scary kind of _____.

2. The old story is a _____ about sea monsters.

Real Princess—A Portrait of Pocahontas

Based on the magazine article by Jessica Cohn

INFORMATIONAL TEXT FOCUS: GENERATING RESEARCH QUESTIONS

Once you have come up with some good **research questions**, your next step is to think about your main ideas, or most important points. Then, think about possible sources that you can use to research these points.

Tip 1 Review your *5W-How?* questions. Which questions do you already know the answers to?

Tip 2 Narrow your topic. As you read, create a topic organizer like the one below to see how the author supports his or her main idea.

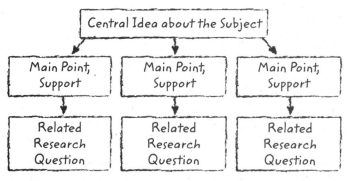

Tip 3 Think about the questions you have come up with. Ask yourself if the questions are answerable. Ask yourself if you know where you can begin your research to find answers.

VOCABULARY

colony (KAHL UH NEE) *n.:* an area ruled by another, far away country.

ceremony (SEHR UH MOH NEE) *n.:* a formal religious or public occasion.

ransom (RAN SUHM) *n.:* payment in exchange for freeing a prisoner.

INTO THE MAGAZINE ARTICLE

Pocahontas was a Native American woman born in the area that is now Virginia. She came to know many of the white settlers there. Some of what we know about Pocahontas's life is true. Other parts are made up. The story of Pocahontas is a perfect example of a story that is based on history but changes with each retelling. One of these retellings was the Disney movie version of her life, which was released in 1995.

Informational Skills
Generate relevant, interesting, and researchable questions.

REAL PRINCESS

A Portrait of Pocahontas

Based on the magazine article by Jessica Cohn

In 1616, Captain John Smith wrote that Pocahontas had saved the Jamestown colony from death and famine. Since then, Pocahontas's reputation has kept growing. **A**

The facts about this Native American princess are unclear, however. Even before Jamestown was settled, European paintings showed America as a welcoming Indian woman. It seems that Pocahontas's name was simply attached to that image. **B**

10   Pocahontas is famous. Many poems and books have been written about her. But nothing written about her came from the woman herself. **C**

Collection of the New York-Historical Society, USA / Bridgeman Art Library

A   **HERE'S HOW**

Vocabulary

I am not sure what *reputation* means. Since Pocahontas's *reputation* is still growing, I think it has to do with what people know or think about her. I looked up *reputation* in my dictionary, and it means "the beliefs people have about someone or something." My definition was very close.

B   **HERE'S HOW**

Reading Focus

I think the author's goal in this article is to **research** who Pocahontas really was.

C   **QUICK CHECK**

What is the author's main point about what we know about Pocahontas?

_____

_____

_____

YOUR TURN

Language Coach

The verb *execute* means "kill." What **related word** in this sentence is the noun form of *execute*? Use your understanding of the verb *execute* to write a definition for this noun.

_____

_____

_____

Legend Has It

Pocahontas was a daughter of Powhatan, chief of the Algonquian Indians in Virginia. Powhatan had many wives and children. So it may be a stretch to call Pocahontas a "princess." But the colonists viewed royalty by European standards. As a daughter of a chief, Pocahontas was a princess.

In 1607, Pocahontas first met the English colonists. It was soon after they arrived in Virginia. Then the Indian princess made history when she saved the life of Captain John Smith. At 20 least that's how the story goes.

Captain Smith's Role

According to Smith, he was captured by warriors in December 1607. They took him to Powhatan. The captain was welcomed with a feast. But then he was made to lie on a stone. Warriors stood over him with clubs.

Pocahontas rushed to him, he wrote years later. She took his "head in her arms and laid her owne upon his to save him from death."

The English understood the story as Smith's being rescued from savages. But Native American ceremonies often included 30 fake executions. So Pocahontas's action might have been part of a ceremony. It's also hard to know because Smith wrote three different stories about important women saving his life. Perhaps Smith was just making it all up.

It is known for sure, though, that Pocahontas started to visit Jamestown regularly.

White Man's World

Sometimes the young girl carried messages from her father. Or she and others traded fur and food. Smith described her as a pleasant and high-spirited 10-year-old.

Settlers noted a friendship between the girl and the captain. 40 Many fictional accounts, such as the 2005 film *The New World*, show a romance.

What's certain is that Smith returned to England in 1609. By then, relations between whites and the tribes were deteriorating. Sometime before 1613, the Jamestown settlers kidnapped Pocahontas and held her for ransom. 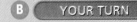 **B**

Playing the Pawn

The settlers wanted to exchange the princess for weapons, food, and English prisoners being held by Powhatan. Powhatan sent only part of what they asked for. He told the English settlers to treat his daughter well. **C**

50 Pocahontas was sent with some Englishmen to make a deal with Powhatan. But the group was attacked. In response, the English destroyed Indian villages. The situation was growing dangerous.

Pocahontas went to her father. She told him she was going to marry John Rolfe, an English tobacco farmer. The marriage would encourage good will. Some say she declared her love for Rolfe. But did she?

Rolfe wrote that the marriage was "for the good of the colony, the honor of our country, and the glory of God."

60 Chief Roy Crazy Horse says the marriage was "a condition of her release." We will never know. But in April 1614, Pocahontas became Rebecca Rolfe. **D**

© The Granger Collection, New York

B YOUR TURN

Vocabulary
Re-read this section. Based on the context, does *deteriorating* mean:
a) "getting better,"
b) "getting worse," or
c) "not changing?"

_____

_____

C QUICK CHECK

What is happening to Pocahontas now?

_____

_____

_____

_____

D YOUR TURN

Reading Focus
What **research question** could you ask to help you learn more about John Rolfe?

_____

_____

_____

_____

_____

Reading Focus

If I wanted to **research** Chief Roy Crazy Horse, I could look in different sources. I could read documents that recorded what he said. These sources would help me learn more about what he really thought about the story of Pocahontas.

Ætatis suæ 21. Aᵒ. 1616.

National Portrait Gallery, Smithsonian Institution, Washington, DC, USA/Art Resource, NY

Over the Sea

In 1616, a Jamestown leader took a group of Native Americans to England. They included the princess, her husband, and their young son. In London, she met King James I. She also saw John Smith. He claimed she called him "father." But Crazy Horse says she turned her back on him and called him a liar. **A**

In 1617, Pocahontas fell ill. She died in England at age 21 or 22.

70   "All must die," she supposedly said to her husband. But Pocahontas lives on, larger than anyone's life.

Applying Your Skills

Real Princess—A Portrait of Pocahontas

INFORMATIONAL TEXT FOCUS: GENERATING RESEARCH QUESTIONS

DIRECTIONS: Circle the best answer to each multiple-choice question

1. Which is the best **research question** to determine whether parts of the Pocahontas story are true?

   A. Why do people like romance stories?

   B. Was Captain Smith married?

   C. What did most Europeans believe about Native Americans during the lifetime of Pocahontas?

   D. How did the relationship between Native Americans and settlers change over time?

2. What is the main problem with the following research question: "Why did Pocahontas marry John Rolfe?"

   A. There are no records of Pocahontas's marriage.

   B. There may not be an answer to the question.

   C. The question is too general.

   D. The question is not important.

DIRECTIONS: Use the topic organizer you were told to make on the Preparing to Read page to write a sentence explaining the author's main idea, or most important point, about the subject.

_____

_____

_____

_____

VOCABULARY REVIEW

DIRECTIONS: Fill in the blanks with the correct words from the Word Box. Not all words will be used.

Word Box
colony
ceremony
ransom

1. The white men kidnapped Pocahontas for _____.

2. Jamestown was a _____ in Virginia where Europeans lived.

Skills Review

Collection 9

DIRECTIONS: Fill in the blanks with the correct words from the Word Box.
Not all words will be used.

Word Box

recurring

recount

creature

legend

colony

ceremony

ransom

banquet

maidens

labyrinth

confronted

tumultuous

1. The long journey on the crashing waves was _____.

2. The hero _____ the villain and the two began their battle.

3. Settlers created a _____ in the New World.

4. The _____ of King Arthur is famous and has been told for centuries.

5. The _____ was held in the great hall and the knights ate very well.

6. This mall is so confusing—it is like a _____!

Now, choose two words from the box that were not used in the above activity. Use each of those words in a complete sentence.

1. _____

_____

2. _____

_____

Skills Review

Collection 9

LANGUAGE COACH: SUFFIXES

DIRECTIONS: A **suffix** is a word part added to the end of a word in order to change its meaning. Look at the chart below. Either a word, a word with a suffix, or the meaning of the word with the suffix is missing. Fill in the missing boxes. Use a dictionary if needed. The first row has been completed.

Word	Word with suffix	Definition of word with suffix
vision	visible	"able to see"
	assistance	
fright		"full of fright"
help		
	complexity	

ORAL LANGUAGE ACTIVITY

DIRECTIONS: As you have learned, **myths** are stories that have been retold for hundreds of years. Myths incorporate traditions and qualities of the society that tells the stories. With a partner, make a list of the traditions and qualities that are important to you. Then, jot down some ideas for a myth of your own. Use these ideas to create and tell your own short myth. After you and your partner have told your myth, retell it to the rest of the class.

Reading for Life

© Todd Davidson/Illustration Works/Corbis

Literary and Academic Vocabulary for Collection 10

LITERARY VOCABULARY

consumer document *n.:* an informative text for consumers, such as a warranty, contract, or instructional manual.

My new computer came with a package filled with different consumer documents.

technical directions *n.:* directions for assembling and using electronic and mechanical devices and performing scientific procedures.

I had to refer to the technical directions that came with my new computer in order to hook it up properly.

ACADEMIC VOCABULARY

illustrate (IHL UH STRAYT) *v.:* show; demonstrate.

The author used a picture to illustrate how the task should be completed.

objective (UHB JEHK TIHV) *n.:* purpose; goal.

The objective of this article is to tell people about different types of stereo systems.

insert (IHN SUHRT) *v.:* add; include; put in.

Some technical directions will insert a photo to show how to perform a task.

format (FORH MAT) *n.:* design; arrangement.

Each document has a different format.

Following Technical Directions

INFORMATIONAL TEXT FOCUS: FOLLOWING TECHNICAL DIRECTIONS

Technical directions are instructions for using electronic, mechanical, and scientific products and procedures. You follow technical directions whenever you program ring tones and phone numbers into your cell phone. You also follow technical directions when you do an experiment in science class.

When you first look at technical directions, they can seem hard to understand. How will you be able to sort through all that information? Pay attention and follow each step carefully, that's how.

• Follow the **sequence**. Sequence is the order of instructions. When you follow technical directions, you have to follow the sequence and do each step in order. What type of sequence does the author choose?

• Look at the format. The format is the layout. How does the format help the author make his or her point? Does the author use graphics, headers, or different fonts to draw attention to certain parts of the document?

As you read, pay attention to the format of the document. Fill in a chart like the one below to describe what you find.

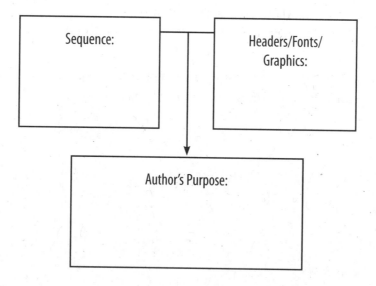

SKILLS FOCUS

Informational Text Skills
Follow multistep instructions in manuals and technical directions; identify and understand step-by-step sequence.

VOCABULARY

slot (SLAHT) *n.*: a long narrow opening that something can be put into.

installation (IHN STUH LAY SHUHN) *n.*: the process of making equipment or machinery ready to use.

INSTALLING A COMPUTER SOUND CARD *

*Instructions for PC users

INTO THE INSTRUCTION MANUAL
Installing a computer sound card can be difficult, even for someone who knows a lot about computers. These step-by-step instructions tell you how to change a computer to make it better. You follow technical directions like those found in a computer user's manual whenever you want to make changes to a piece of technology like a computer, cell phone, or television.

1. Turn off computer.

2. Touch something metal outside your computer. This gives off any static electricity. Then unplug your computer.

3. Open the computer case.

4. Find the slot you want on the computer's main circuit board. See the user's manual for instructions on the types of slots on the computer.

5a. If the slot is empty, unscrew the cover. Take the cover off and put the screw and the cover aside.

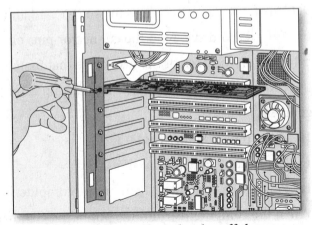

10   **5b.** If the slot has the old sound card, take off the screw and take the card out of the slot. Ⓐ Be firm but careful. Do not break

Ⓐ **HERE'S HOW**

Reading Focus

I notice that the number 5 appears twice in this **sequence** of **technical directions**. I think this means that there are two parts to step 5. They both begin with "if." If the slot is empty, I follow step 5a. If the slot has the old sound card, I go on to step 5b.

I do not know what *audio* in line 24 means. I can look for clues to help me. I know that the instructions are teaching me to put in a sound card, so maybe *audio* has to do with sound. I looked it up in my dictionary, and *audio* means "sound," so I was right. An *audio* cable must be a cable for passing sound from the computer to a set of speakers.

B **YOUR TURN**

Reading Focus

Why is it important to follow **technical directions** carefully?

_____

_____

_____

_____

_____

_____

_____

_____

_____

_____

_____

the card. You will see a cable attached to the sound card. The other end is attached to a CD or DVD-ROM drive. Take this cable off by pulling gently.

6. Put the new card into the slot. Push down until the connector is all the way in. Do not use too much force. If the card does not fit, take it out and try again.

7. Pull gently on the card to make sure it is in place. It should not move.

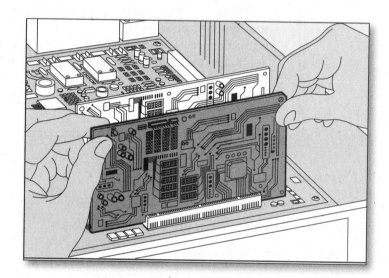

20 **8.** Find the screw and slot cover that you took off in step 5a. Put them back on. If the card comes with a cover, you will only need to put the screw back in. Be sure the slot is covered. Then tighten the screw to hold the new card in place.

9. Connect the audio cable to the sound card and to the CD or DVD-ROM drive. Find the connector pins on the sound card and on the back of the disk drive that match the plugs on the end of the audio cable. Line the pins up carefully and press gently. A

10. Close the computer case.

30 **11.** Connect the outside speakers.

12. Plug in the computer. Turn on the computer and monitor. When the computer is running, put in the CD that goes with the sound card. Complete the software driver installation by following the on-screen directions. B

Following Technical Directions

INFORMATIONAL TEXT FOCUS: FOLLOWING TECHNICAL DIRECTIONS

DIRECTIONS: Circle the best answer to each multiple-choice question.

1. What will happen if you skip step number two in the **technical directions**?

   A. The computer may be damaged.

   B. The computer will still be getting electricity.

   C. The computer case will stay closed.

2. Which format does the author use to draw your attention to certain parts of the text?

   A. pictures

   B. bold headers

   C. different fonts

DIRECTIONS: Review the chart you were told to fill in on the Preparing to Read page. Now use your examples to write a sentence explaining the author's main purpose in these technical directions.

_____

_____

_____

_____

VOCABULARY REVIEW

DIRECTIONS: Fill in the blanks with the correct words from the Word Box.

Word Box

slot

installation

1. The sound card fits into a _____ in the circuit board.

2. The _____ will make the new software work on the computer.

Reading Consumer Documents

INFORMATIONAL TEXT FOCUS: READING CONSUMER DOCUMENTS

You just bought a new stereo. Aside from the equipment, you find that the stereo comes with several **consumer documents**. It is important to read the **service contract**, **warranty**, **product information**, and **instruction manual**. These consumer documents will help you use and enjoy the products you buy.

The format of consumer documents has several **elements**, or basic parts. Here is a list of common consumer documents and the elements each has:

- **product information**—tells what the product is, and what it does

- **service contract**—a legal document spelling out the rights of who buys, makes, and sells the product

- **warranty**—a legal document saying what the maker will do if the product does not work the way the maker says it will

- **instruction manual**—instructions on how to use the product and how to troubleshoot, or fix, problems when they come up

- **technical directions**—directions for installing and using the product

Consumer documents may also explain the **features** of a product, or the things that make one kind of product different from other kinds.

VOCABULARY

claim (KLAYM) *n.:* demand for something.

clause (KLAWZ) *n.:* single part of a law or agreement.

void (VOYD) *v.:* legally cancel.

discretion (DIHS KREHSH UHN) *n.:* ability to make a choice.

INTO THE CONSUMER DOCUMENTS

The following consumer documents would be included with the purchase of any kind of electronic equipment. They include a warranty, an instructional manual for using the product and solving minor problems, and additional product information.

SKILLS FOCUS

Informational Text Skills
Read and understand consumer documents.

Aulsound Extended Service Contract

Read with a Purpose
Read the following selections to learn how to understand the paperwork that comes with the purchase of some electronic equipment.

ADMINISTRATOR
Aulsound Warranty Service Corporation
P.O. Box 840001 Century City, CA 90067
SERVICE CONTRACT AGREEMENT
Digital Multitrack Recorder DMR88

TERMS AND CONDITIONS

Details of coverage. This Service Contract provides coverage of any operating parts or labor required for the product listed above, for two years from date of original purchase. There will be no cost to the Purchaser for any authorized covered repair that is performed by one of our highly skilled service associates. **A**

Limitations. This Service Contract covers product failures occurring during normal use. It does not cover misuse or abuse of the product during delivery, installation, or setup adjustments. It does not cover damage that occurs while adjusting consumer controls, loss of data or programming support, unauthorized repair, customer-sponsored specification changes, cosmetic damage, or simple maintenance as recommended in the product owner's guide. It also does not cover repairs that are necessary because of improper installation or improper electrical connections. Consequential or incidental damages are not covered. Damage due to acts of God is not covered. **B**

Maintenance requirement. The Purchaser must maintain the product in accordance with the requirements or recommendations set forth by the manufacturer to keep this Service Contract in force. Evidence of proper maintenance and/or service, when required by the Administrator, must be submitted to validate a claim. **C**

Unauthorized-repair clause. IMPORTANT: Unauthorized repairs may void this Service Contract. The cost of these repairs will be the responsibility of the Purchaser.

Transfer of ownership. This Service Contract is transferable with ownership of the product. Transfer may be accomplished only if the Purchaser mails or delivers to the Administrator a twenty-five dollar [$25.00] transfer fee and registers the name and address of the new owner within fifteen [15] days of change of ownership.

Cancellation clause. This Service Contract may be canceled by the Purchaser at any time, for any reason. In event of cancellation, we will provide a pro-rated refund minus reasonable handling costs and any claims that may have been paid. Any cancellation requested by the Purchaser within thirty [30] days of the Service Contract application date will be 100 percent canceled by the Administrator.

Contract insurance. Your Service Contract is fully insured by Aulquiet Insurance Company, 80 Sampler Way, Los Angeles, CA 90017. Purchasers who do not receive payment within sixty [60] days of submitting a pre-authorized covered claim may submit the claim directly to Aulquiet Insurance Company, Contractual Liability Claims Department, at the above address.

Renewal clause. This Service Contract may be renewed at the discretion of the Administrator. The renewal premium will be based on the age of the covered product, current service costs, the covered product's repair history, and actuarial data.

A HERE'S HOW

Vocabulary
I am not sure what the word *authorized* means. I know the document is talking about a certain kind of repair, though. I looked *authorized* up, and it means "officially allowed."

B HERE'S HOW

Reading Focus
This **service contract** does not cover all kinds of repairs. It does not cover repairs that need to be made if the product is not used correctly. I know that if I drop or accidentally break the product, the company will not pay to fix it.

C HERE'S HOW

Language Coach
Some words have different **definitions** depending on if they are used as nouns or as verbs. When *claim* is a verb, it means "say strongly." Here, *claim* is used as a noun, so I know that it means "demand for something."

IN OTHER WORDS This service contract from Aulsound covers the product for two years from the date it was purchased, or bought. The purchaser will not have to pay for any repairs that the company approves. This only covers problems that happen from normal use of the product. The purchaser must maintain the product correctly. The purchaser must pay for other repairs that this company has not approved. The purchaser can transfer ownership of this product. The purchaser can cancel this contract. This contract is insured. It can be renewed by the company.

Reading Focus

I can use this **instruction manual** to help me solve problems. If my DMR88 does not turn on, the first thing I can do is make sure that the power cord is plugged in.

Language Coach

Some words have different **definitions** if used as nouns or as verbs. In this document, is *function* a noun that means "a basic task of an electronic object" or a verb that means "work in a certain way"?

Vocabulary

I am not sure what a *pitch* is. Because a problem occurs if the recordings play back at the wrong *pitch*, I think the problem has to do with sound. I looked *pitch* up, and it means "the degree of highness or lowness in a sound." I was right that the problem has to do with sound.

Reading Focus

Which section would you look to in this **instruction manual** for help if you were having trouble recording?

Troubleshooting Guide

If you encounter problems operating your Aulsound DMR88 or if the product does not work as expected, look up the problem in this table and follow the advice provided.

PROBLEM	ADVICE
The DMR88 does not turn on.	• Make sure that the power cord is plugged into an AC wall outlet. • Check the AC IN connector at the rear of DMR88. • Make sure that the DMR88 power switch is in the ON position. • If there is still no power, contact your Aulsound dealer.
No sound is coming from the connected music source.	• Make sure that the MONITOR LEVEL control is raised. • Make sure that the FLIP and MONITOR SELECT switches are set correctly.
The DMR88 does not record.	• Make sure that the disc's write-protect tab is set to UNPROTECT. • Make sure that the PLAY function is not on. • Press a REC SELECT button, and make sure that the track is ready to record. • Make sure that the signal you wish to record has been selected at the recording source for the appropriate track. Use the CUE LEVEL control to determine whether the signal is being sent to the track.
Level meters do not indicate signal levels.	• Make sure that the track you wish to record has been selected. • Press the REC button, and make sure that the DMR88 is in RECORD-PAUSE mode.
Recordings play back at the wrong pitch.	• Make sure that the PITCH function is not set at VARIABLE. • Make sure that the 1.2 PLAY function is turned off.

IN OTHER WORDS Use this document if you have problems making your Aulsound DMR88 work. You can look up the problem in this table. Follow the advice given. If the device does not turn on, check that it is plugged in and turned on. If you do not hear sound, check the volume levels. If it does not record, check that the correct buttons are pressed. If there is no signal, select the correct track and press the record button. If recordings do not play back correctly, change the pitch function and the play function.

FCC* Information (USA)

1. IMPORTANT NOTICE: DO NOT MODIFY THIS UNIT!
This unit, when installed as indicated in the instructions contained in this manual, meets FCC requirements. Modifications not expressly approved by Aulsound may void your authority, granted by the FCC, to use this product. **E**

2. IMPORTANT: When connecting this product to accessories and/or another product, the high-quality shielded cables supplied with this product MUST be used. Follow all installation instructions. Failure to follow instructions could void your FCC authorization to use this product in the United States.

3. NOTE: This product has been tested and found to comply with the requirements listed in FCC Regulations, Part 15 for Class "B" digital devices. Compliance with **F** these requirements provides a reasonable level of assurance that your use of this product in a residential environment will not result in harmful interference with other electronic devices. This equipment generates and uses radio frequencies and, if not installed and used according to the instructions found in the user's manual, may cause interference harmful to the operation of other electronic devices. Compliance with FCC regulations does not guarantee that interference will not occur in all installations. If this product is found to be the source of interference, which can be determined by turning the unit OFF and ON, try to eliminate the problem by using one of the following measures:

- Relocate either this product or the device that is being affected by the interference.
- Utilize other outlets that are on different branch (circuit breaker or fuse) circuits, or install AC line filter(s). In the case of radio or TV interference, relocate or reorient the antenna.
- If the antenna lead-in is a 300-ohm ribbon lead, change the lead-in to a coaxial type cable. **G**

If these corrective measures do not produce satisfactory results, contact the local retailer authorized to distribute this type of product. If you cannot locate the appropriate retailer, contact Aulsound Corporation of America, Electronic Service Division, 1000 Wilshire Blvd., Los Angeles, CA 90017.

*FCC: Federal Communications Commission, U.S. agency that regulates **H** communication by telegraph, telephone, radio, TV, cable TV, and satellite.

Read with a Purpose How do documents like these help you, as a consumer, get the most out of a product?

IN OTHER WORDS Do not change this unit. If connecting this product to another product, follow the instructions. This product has been tested to follow FCC rules. This product uses radio waves. If used correctly, this product should not stop other electronic products from working correctly. If it does, move the products away from each other, use different outlets, and change the antenna. If these steps do not work, contact the company store where you bought the product, or the company that makes the product.

E HERE'S HOW

Vocabulary

I do not know what *modify* means. I read the section that says not to make any *modifications*, but I still do not know what this means. I looked up *modify*, and it means, "change." So the notice tells me not to make any changes to the product that might go against FCC rules.

F YOUR TURN

Vocabulary

Re-read the first sentence of point 3. What is another word for *regulations*?

_____

G HERE'S HOW

Reading Focus

After reading this note, I know that this **product information** tells me what to do if this product causes other electronic devices to work incorrectly. It is important that I read this consumer document so that I know how to solve such a problem.

H YOUR TURN

Reading Focus

How do **consumer documents** like these help you get the most out of a product?

_____

_____

_____

Reading Consumer Documents

USE A CONCEPT MAP

DIRECTIONS: Choose one of the **consumer documents** you just read. Write the name of the document in the center circle. Fill in the outer circles with the main ideas, or most important points, from that document.

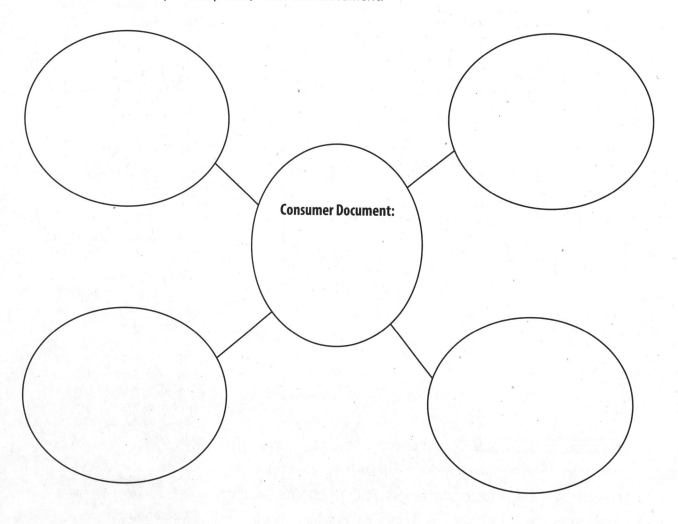

Consumer Document:

Applying Your Skills

Reading Consumer Documents

DIRECTIONS: Circle the best answer to each multiple-choice question about **consumer documents**.

1. A service contract usually describes all of the following **features** *except*—

   A. the time period in which parts will be replaced.

   B. FCC rules.

   C. the kinds of problems with the product that will be fixed.

   D. how to cancel the service contract.

2. The purpose of a troubleshooting guide, or **instructional manual,** is to—

   A. help consumers understand how to file a claim.

   B. give advice on how to use a device that is not working properly.

   C. make a service contract easier to understand.

   D. give information on how to contact an insurance company.

DIRECTIONS: Answer the following question with complete sentences.

3. Why are consumer documents like the ones you just read so important for a product to have? Explain your answer. _____

   _____

   _____

   _____

   _____

VOCABULARY REVIEW

DIRECTIONS: Fill in the blanks with the correct words from the Word Box. Not all words will be used.

Word Box

claim

clause

void

discretion

1. The document has a _____ that explains how to transfer ownership.

2. If we _____ the contract, we will no longer be legally held to follow it.

3. He has the _____ to make his own decision.

Skills Review

Collection 10

VOCABULARY REVIEW

DIRECTIONS: Write the letter of each definition in the second column next to the correct vocabulary or academic word in the first column.

Vocabulary Words

_____ 1. claim

_____ 2. clause

_____ 3. slot

_____ 4. insert

_____ 5. discretion

_____ 6. installation

_____ 7. format

_____ 8. void

Definitions

a. a long narrow opening that something can be put into.

b. legally cancel.

c. demand for something.

d. add; include; put in.

e. the process of making equipment or machinery ready to use.

f. single part of a law or agreement.

g. ability to make a choice.

h. design; arrangement.

Collection 10

LANGUAGE COACH: WORD DEFINITIONS

DIRECTIONS: A word's **definition** can change depending on whether it is used as a noun or a verb. The words below can be used as both nouns and verbs. Use a dictionary to look up the words and write a definition for each part of speech. Then, write separate sentences using each word as a noun and a verb.

1. contact

Definition as a noun: _____

_____

Sentence: _____

_____

Definition as a verb: _____

_____

Sentence: _____

_____

2. contest

Definition as a noun: _____

_____

Sentence: _____

_____

Definition as a verb: _____

_____

Sentence: _____

_____

WRITING ACTIVITY

DIRECTIONS: Choose a product that you are familiar with and know how to use. It could be a bike, a television set, a toaster, a DVD player, or something else. On a separate sheet of paper, write **technical directions** for this product, using only your own knowledge. Do not write more than one page. Your manual should include step-by-step instructions on how to use the basic features of the product. Feel free to add pictures to your written directions.

Index of Authors and Titles